NO-LOADS
Mutual Fund Profits
Using Technical Analysis

NO-LOADS

Mutual Fund Profits Using Technical Analysis

James E. Kearis

LIBERTY HALL
PRESS™

LIBERTY HALL PRESS books are published by LIBERTY HALL PRESS, a division of TAB BOOKS. Its trademark, consisting of the words "LIBERTY HALL PRESS" and the portrayal of Benjamin Franklin, is registered in the United States Patent and Trademark Office.

First Edition
Second Printing

©1989 by TAB BOOKS
Printed in the United States of America

Library of Congress Cataloging-in-Publication Data

Kearis, James E.
No-loads : mutual fund profits using technical analysis /
by James E. Kearis.
p.   cm.
Bibliography: p.
Includes index.
ISBN 0-8306-3036-8
1. Mutual funds. I. Title.
HG4530.K4 1989
332.63'27—dc19   89-2310
                                                  CIP

TAB BOOKS offers software for sale.
For information and a catalog, please contact:

TAB Software Department
Blue Ridge Summit, PA 17294-0850

Questions regarding the content of this book
should be addressed to:

Reader Inquiry Branch
TAB BOOKS
Blue Ridge Summit, PA 17294-0214

Contents

Introduction

MANY POTENTIAL INVESTORS BELIEVE THAT PLAYING THE STOCK MARKET IS, without exception, a risky, expensive, and complicated endeavor. This is utterly false. Investing in reputable no-load mutual funds is simple and very effective. With as little as $50 to invest, you can realize a return of 10 to 25 percent. Earning that money will be fun, too.

No-Loads: Mutual Fund Profits Using Technical Analysis will show you how to make money in no-loads (mutual funds with no "load" or commission involved) by following the advice of analysts and tracking your own funds. Everything you need to get started is in this book. No-load funds are explained, technical analysis is reduced to simple charts and graphs, and specific directions on how to apply what you learn are given.

BACKGROUND

This book is for the small investor. Small investors are as capable of investing wisely as large brokerage firms, but they can't function successfully without sound information and a good plan. Many small investors are confused by the tremendous barrage of advertisements, talk shows, newspaper and magazine articles—not to mention gossip at work—about hot stocks. With so much information available, bewilderment is the rule, not the exception.

No-Loads: Mutual Fund Profits Using Technical Analysis shows you how to track your investment using information gathered from a single source: an investment newsletter that you have chosen according to your needs. Your weekly burden is only about a half an hour. Your newsletter will arrive once or twice a month. Take an average of 15 minutes to read it, and count on another 15 minutes to jot down a few numbers from the Sunday paper. There you have it! For an easy, enjoyable 30 minutes per week, you are on your way to a successful investment program.

A no-load mutual fund is the best investment vehicle for you whether you are ultraconservative or a bit of a gambler. A money market fund is very safe because its main objective is preservation of the principal amount invested. At the other end of the spectrum, an aggressive growth fund incurs much more risk, but the rewards can be greater.

No matter what level of risk you feel comfortable with, there is a mutual fund for you. No-loads are better than loaded funds because no-load profits are generally as substantial as loaded fund profits—without the 3 to 8.5 percent commission. No-load profits are there for the taking.

While you read this book, ignore all other sources of information on the stock market, unless you are asked to do otherwise. You might find it difficult to focus on what follows in this book and ignore all the noise emanating from your television, radio, mailbox, and workplace; however, your concentration is necessary in order to realize the maximum reward. You will also be asked, at certain points, to obtain and study sample copies of newsletters and free information on no-load funds. By the time you finish this book, you should be ready to subscribe to a specific newsletter and send a check to a no-load mutual fund.

PURPOSE

No-Loads: Mutual Fund Profits Using Technical Analysis has three main goals: 1. to replace an avalanche of information and advice with a newsletter that will allow you to concentrate on the basics of good, sound investing; 2. to show you how profitable an investment a no-load fund can be; and 3. to give you just enough knowledge about technical analysis so that you will understand the basics of market forecasting. Understanding technical analysis will also bring confidence about how the market works.

You needn't be a mathematician to use technical analysis either. A knowledge of technical analysis is easy to come by when the math involved is treated in a conceptual way using simple graphs and doesn't require all sorts of number crunching. The humblest math rookie should be able to follow along. Technical analysis will bring into focus the fundamentals of the stock and bond markets, and will demonstrate the validity of what good technicians have to say about these markets in their newsletters.

SO WHAT EXACTLY IS TECHNICAL ANALYSIS?

Technical analysis, or TA, is the study of stock market numbers to show you how to be invested in the right place at the right time. Ever since stocks, bonds, and commodities have been bought and sold, there have been people around who use numbers to describe and predict price behavior. Technical analysis focuses on such factors as advance/decline lines, moving averages, normal yield curves, and market momentum. In contrast to this, fundamental analysis deals with the quality of a company's management, prospects for the economy due to political considerations, and psychological reasoning about investor and consumer sentiment. Though fundamental and technical analysis offer two different approaches to successful investing, neither type of analysis is of any use without the other.

Technical analysis is essential to investment planning. Just as you make plans before buying a car, going shopping, or taking a vacation, you will also need to make coherent plans for your investment dollars. All good planning is based on solid estimates of what the future holds in store. In order to design an investment plan, you need predictions about what the stock market will be doing in months to come. The best predictions come from people who base all or a significant amount of their investment advice on TA. Technical analysts provide clear-cut, consistent statements about what to expect from the stock market. Given that kind of information and advice, you can unequivocally decide what to do with your money, right now, based on what a TA professional says will happen.

Out of 100 newsletters, three of the top five are totally based on TA and the other two use TA as a significant element in their investment strategies. You don't have to become a TA expert to use a TA newsletter. The TA that a professional will do for you amounts to using some numbers and graphs to determine whether you should be in a stock or money market no-load fund at any given time. This is called "market timing," or "switching."

No-Load Mutual Fund Profits Using Technical Analysis will not try to sell you on the "numbers are god" approach, because they aren't. Without a firm fundamental basis in the real world, TA is just so much hogwash. Some newsletter writers talk about mysterious things like "300-year cycles," "Prussian helmets," or "shoulders and necklaces" they see in charts depicting stock market numbers. These people are from the same school that reads tea leaves and goat entrails to predict the future. TA of a much more solid variety is available. After you read this book, you will be able to distinguish good TA from bad TA.

WHAT YOU WILL BE DOING/
THE THREE-STEP PROCESS

Successful no-load fund investing is based on three simple steps: 1. choosing a good technical newsletter; 2. choosing good no-load funds to invest in; and then, 3. tracking your investments. Your aim is to be invested in a stock fund when the market is expected to do well and to be invested in a money fund when the market is about to do poorly. A good technician will guide you. Frequent fund switching is not advocated. You need only switch funds once every two years, or if you are an aggressive investor, two to six times a year.

Executing the first step of the three-step process is like choosing a good mechanic. If you don't feel confident in the work an auto mechanic does for you, you change mechanics. What if you knew of several mechanics who do good work at a reasonable price? You could then choose the one most pleasant, reliable, and convenient. Selecting a newsletter is a similar process and a very important part of your investment plan.

A list of 18 technical newsletters, impartially ranked by performance, is presented in this book so that you can choose a letter best suited to your needs. Confidence in a newsletter will help you follow its advice, refrain from going from one newsletter to another, and ensure that you keep the faith, instead of giving up investing altogether. Consistently following what your letter says will allow you to profit from the successes and knowledge the newsletter has achieved over the years.

The letters recommended to you have good track records of at least 3 years, according to an impartial third party who makes a business of ranking such newsletters. Subscription costs range from $49 to $250 per year—a nominal amount when you consider the proven success of these letter writers. For less money than you spend maintaining your car every year, you can subscribe to a good TA newsletter, and with the extra profits, you should be able to pay cash for a new car every 5 years.

Choosing a good no-load fund is the second step in the process. There are over 1000 no-load funds in the market and 80 percent of them are collected in fund groups, or "families of funds." You will be shown 12 fund groups, ranked by performance, from which you will select one or two. Once you select a group, choosing funds is easy. All you have to do is determine your risk level, determine the objective of your investment, and pick a fund that matches the risk/objective criteria. You will find that learning about no-loads, discovering what kind of investor you are, and focusing on a few good groups will allow you—once and for all—to pick specific funds that suit your investment needs. Nine out of 10 general-purpose stock funds in these 12 no-load groups averaged better than a 15 percent return on investment per year for the 10 years ending December 1987. Combined with a good letter and a few switches, even a conservative investor might realize a 20 percent annual gain.

The last step in the process is tracking your investments each week. You can decide how closely you follow your funds. For as little as 15 minutes each week, you can write down a few numbers from Sunday's paper, and if you wish, graph them. Or if you feel like doing more detailed tracking than the minimum essential amount, you can add on another 15 minutes, for a total of 30 minutes per week needed to stay on top of your investment performance.

PUTTING IT ALL TOGETHER

Finding out about technical analysis can help you make better investment decisions. Learning how is easy using this book. Each chapter begins with introductory paragraphs intended to give you a brief overview of what you will cover. Think of these introductions as roadmaps to help you plan your trip toward an understanding of the chapter.

The body of each chapter is your actual journey toward your destination of sound investments. You can dawdle, drive fast, stop and relax, or just cruise through the material at a comfortable speed. Try to get the most out of this information, as each chapter represents a leg of your trip, and succeeding chapters build on previous chapters.

The end of each chapter is like a slideshow of your trip. You will be given a summary of specific landmarks you should have noticed along the way. You need not immediately recognize every item to feel you've totally mastered the subject matter. However, you should be able to determine what you have absorbed and understood, and what you may need to review more carefully.

Some acronyms are used in the book to make things flow more smoothly. All acronyms are explained in the Appendix A. You will also find definitions of other terms like "three-step process" there as well. If you get stumped on anything, just refer to this appendix.

Here is a summary of the entire book so you can see what you are about to learn:

Chapter

1	Why no-loads are such a good investment
2	How to choose a good TA newsletter
3	How to choose good no-load funds
4	How to interpret simple graphs
5	How to track no-load funds
6	What trend-following is all about
7	How monetary factors affect the stock market
8	How volume factors affect the stock market
9	How price factors affect the stock market
10	The rudiments of stock market forecasting
11	Actual examples of predicting the future
12	What you have learned

Remember, when you have money to invest, there is no shortage of friendly, smiling faces to deal with: banks, insurance companies, brokerage houses, and financial planners to name a few. These investment advisors are only too glad to tell you how successfully they will handle your money. *You* must be able to determine how well your investments are doing in order to be a successful investor; otherwise, you may be unpleasantly surprised down the road. Absolutely do not take anyone else's word for how you are doing. Find out for yourself. How to manage and measure the success of your own investments are the key things you should learn.

Why No Loads Are the Best Investment

ADVERTISEMENTS TELLING YOU TO INVEST YOUR MONEY IN A PARTICULAR WAY hope to confuse you by making you ignore the basics. When you ignore basics, you have more of a tendency to take the bait. Some of the things you will see in this chapter will be old news to you, but there will also be a few surprises. The main surprise will be how easy it is to understand no-load funds and why they are such a good investment. We will focus your attention on the basics so you don't get hooked in by the ad people.

LOAD VERSUS NO-LOAD

Like any other investment vehicle, mutual funds have many frills attached to them. You can't go wrong if you keep it this simple:

> A mutual fund is thousands of people pooling their money and letting a few fund managers buy and sell stocks or certificates of deposit (CDs) for them.

Because of the Securities and Exchange Commission (SEC), fund managers cannot skip to the Bahamas with your cash. They also are required to invest in stocks (or bonds, CDs, and the like) according to investment goals stated in the fund's prospectus. You must be offered the prospectus before you buy shares in a fund. The SEC makes sure that everything is up-front and it has your security in mind. As long as you stick with reputable funds, you needn't worry about getting taken for a ride.

Before we go any further, here are a few questions I want to answer for you:

1. Why bother investing at all?
2. How much need I invest in a fund?
3. Since there is no free lunch, how much does it cost me?

The first two questions are easy to answer. The answer to the third question just takes a little more time.

In order to address the first question, think of yourself as the boss of your investment dollars. If those dollars go to work and earn only 5 percent a year for you, then you are allowing them to goof-off. With very little effort you can make those dollars earn an average of 15 percent per year. Let's see what happens to a $2000 Individual Retirement Account (IRA) over various time periods at 5 and 15 percent:

Table 1-1. Answer to Question #1.
(Using $2000 IRA)

	at 5%	at 15%	15% wins by
1 year hence	$2100	2300	200
2 years hence	2205	2645	440
5 years hence	2552	4023	1471
10 years hence	3258	8091	4833

If you don't work a little to make your money work, you are short-changing yourself.

Please make a mental note right now. IRA investments are used in some examples because taxation need not be considered for these types of investments. That is to say, when figuring out what kind of gain you can expect, your marginal income tax rate need not be considered. This is in line with our objective of focusing on the basics to eliminate confusion. It should be apparent that, whether you are in a very high or a very low tax bracket, if you maximize your gain before taxes, then you maximize your gain after taxes.

Now for the second question. One fund will require you to invest as little as $50 to open an account and another will want $25000. So there is quite a range on your ante in this game. An initial investment has absolutely no bearing on how well a fund has done, is doing, or will do. Most funds require $1000 to $3000 for an initial investment in a non-IRA account and appreciably less for an IRA account. There are excellent funds which require a $50 minimum and there are also horrible funds in this category. After that initial investment, you can send in $0.00, $50.00, $100.00, or $1142.02 as you please and when you please.

You can also opt to withdraw money whenever you wish. Unlike individual stocks (counterparts for a stock no-load fund) and unlike individual CDs (counterparts for a money market no-load fund), you can cash in whenever you want. Most fund groups allow phone redemptions. Since you and the other shareholders in a no-load fund (not the managers or the custodial bank) own the fund, you can access your money whenever you wish. Either phone-switch between a money fund and a stock fund, or write a check from your money market fund. You will get absolutely no hassle, there will be no early redemption or bookkeeping fees, and, best of all, there will be no 4½ to 8½ percent commission. In fact, the commission for no-load redemptions is 0 percent, so the cost to you is $0 and 60 seconds to make a toll-free phone call.

This trip is now becoming interesting. For, say $500, you can get into a good fund. You can also redeem some money and have it sent to your home with just a toll-free phone call. You can make 15 percent per year instead of 5 percent. The SEC is your watchdog and a very good one at that.

Now for the last question. A *load* (synonym for "commission") is what you pay to a mutual fund when you buy it to cover that fund's cost of operation and to give that fund a profit. Our investment universe will consist of only one type of fund—no-load mutual funds (NLFs). Just because you pay a charge up-front to get into a loaded fund, does not mean that loaded funds are better than NLFs. In fact, loaded funds are worse. Here's why: *NLFs perform at least as well (and possibly better) than fully-loaded mutual funds.* You can take that statement straight to the bank! The people who made that statement and the many people who have established its veracity have hung it out for anyone to contradict. Nobody has been able to prove it false. It follows that there is no sense in paying a 4.5 to 8.5 percent load for a fund which will in all likelihood perform no better, and possibly worse than, an NLF which has 0 percent load.

This is not to say that an NLF doesn't cost you anything. Instead of charging you 4.5 to 8.5 percent up-front, an NLF charges you ½ to 2 percent per year to cover its expenses and make a profit. This is called a "management fee." Loaded funds have similar management fees. The load you pay to buy into a loaded fund means that you start 4.5 to 8.5 percent in the hole and you don't have a better fund to show for it. That is why loaded funds are worse than NLFs.

Management fees vary from fund to fund because there are different types of funds. Funds which require very little buying and selling of stocks or CDs fall at the ½-percent end of the management-fee spectrum. Funds which require a lot of trading will fall nearer the 2-percent end. Whether a fund is fully loaded or an NLF, you still have to pay that yearly management fee.

You will know what the management fee is before you get into the funds we will be discussing. A fund may have 70 stocks in its portfolio and, a couple years later, not one of the original stocks will be there because the fund sold each one to buy something else. This is a 50-percent turnover and usually indicates a pretty conservative (or safe) fund. Another fund may have 70 stocks in its portfolio and, within 6 months, none of the original stocks will be there. In other words, two times each year (on the average), this fund will turn over its whole portfolio. This is a 200-percent turnover and usually corresponds to a very speculative (or volatile, or, perhaps, unsafe) fund.

Every few years, on the average, you will switch out of a stock-oriented NLF into one which buys and sells CDs. That ½-percent per-year management fee can mount up, but you are getting 15-percent instead of 5-percent return annually, so you can afford that extra ½-percent management fee. Good funds are very good at sending you statements so you can keep track of things. All you need do is buy a new pair of shoes and save the shoebox so you have a place to put those statements.

That concludes my answers to those three questions you had. But there are still other reasons NLFs are such good investments. One of these reasons is *diversification*. Studies have shown that ownership in at least 15 stocks covering a broad range of industry groups (utilities, autos, hotel chains, electronics manufacturers, and so on) is required for proper diversification. NLFs typically own many more stocks than this. Nondiversification will, 99 times out of 100, lead to disaster. You would have to sweat blood to choose 15 good stocks—let alone 70 good ones! You couldn't do nearly as good a job of stock selection as the fund managers of a healthy fund. It's beginning to look like, for ½ to 2 percent per year, NLFs are a very good deal, indeed.

One last thought before we discuss types of NLFs. When you buy a new car, you pay 15 percent of the cost of that vehicle to the automaker for its advertisements. When you buy fancy bluejeans, you are paying more like 30 percent for the manufacturer's advertisement costs. NLFs do little, if any, advertising. This is one big reason you pay 0 percent to get an account with an NLF. This is also one of the biggest reasons you pay 4½ to 8½ percent to buy into a loaded fund.

NO-LOADS FOR EVERY SEASON

Remember, we will be ignoring all those flourishes which will only confuse you. In other sources you will see information on why NLFs are so great, what kinds of NLFs there are, and how to select good NLFs. Ignore that stuff and concentrate on what follows in this book. People who speak or write about NLFs in that manner are out to paint a complex picture for you, so that you will buy their advice. What those advertisements tell you is no more profound than what you get from these pages. Those ads will lead you astray—that won't happen here. This book contains everything you will need to become a better, more independent investor. If you hear something that appears to contradict what is said here, then take neither my word nor their word for it. Call toll-free one or two of the 12 NLF groups listed in Appendix B, and listen to what they have to say. Then you can make up your own mind.

Basically, there are six types of NLFs:

―――――――――――――――Table 1-2. Types of No-Load Funds ―――――――

Type of Fund	*Investment Objectives*
Money Market	preserve your investment and get some interest income
Fixed Income	preserve your investment and get some interest and dividend income
Income	get interest and dividend income and a little growth
Balanced	get more growth but still go for interest and dividend income
Growth	growth over the long term is the primary consideration but you still get interest and dividends along the way
Aggressive	growth for the sake of growth

Let's clarify some of the terminology used above. You will see many other names given to types of funds. For example, the aggressive type might also be referred to as Capital Appreciation, Option Income, or Sector. The intent of the list shown here is to classify NLFs by objective. That way we can say "Money Market NLF" instead of "NLF which has as its objective the preservation of the money you invest while giving you some interest income."

There are three types of gain (or income) you can achieve in any investment: interest, dividends, and growth. Interest income is generated for you by a money market NLF in the same way that a bank generates interest for you. The basic difference is that you get more interest income from an NLF on the average and over the long haul. Money market NLFs buy and sell CDs and other short-term types of interest-bearing paper. These types of funds are the safest funds, and you get a monthly statement from them to boot. Stock funds can have some interest income, too, but that is just incidental unless you are in a fixed-income or income fund.

Dividend income is taken out of profits a company makes and is distinct from interest income. On a regular basis, dividends are set aside to pay shareholders their dividend payments. Some people buy stock in companies almost purely for the dividends they receive. A good example of this is people buying stock in utility companies. These stockholders would get very mad if dividends fell or weren't paid at all.

Growth is a "paper" increase in the stock of a company. If IBM sells for $140 today and $145 tomorrow, there would be a "paper" gain of $5 per share in IBM stock. If you had 100 shares today, tomorrow you would be $500 richer—on paper. You would still have to sell the stock and pay commissions to a broker before you realized any profit. For stocks or for NLFs, the price per share is called the *net asset value* (NAV). This term will crop up quite often throughout the rest of our discussions.

In exactly the same way as stocks, you achieve gain in NLFs in three main ways:

1. Interest Income   ("8% per year")
2. Dividends   ("paid $2 per share")
3. Growth   ("NAV went from $10 to $12")

The safest way to make your money grow is with interest income. The more speculative way to make your money grow is through growth-type funds (which simply invest in dozens of growth-type stocks). In an aggressive fund, you can just as well observe the NAV of your fund go from $10 to $8 as you can observe it go up to $12.

RISK

Gambling of any type is unacceptable to some people. Religious issues aside, some people can't sleep at night unless their money is safe in the corner bank (to which a South American country is in hock). Anyone who has insurance is a gambler. You bet $300 per year that you will die and the life insurance company bets $50,000 you won't die. When you fly from St. Louis to Detroit you are taking a risk 100 times less than driving there. So when someone tells you that investing in NLFs is gambling, they are, in the strictest sense, correct. But what so many are really saying is "If you put your money with me, it isn't gambling," which is, of course, untrue. In the investment ocean, there are many sharks. Don't be a fish.

Fig. 1-1. Which horse to bet on?

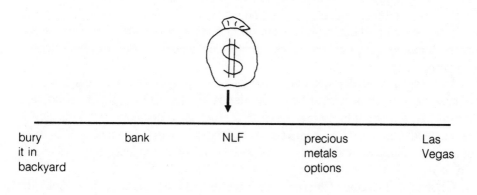

| bury it in backyard | bank | NLF | precious metals options | Las Vegas |

If you had to put all your money on one horse, which one would you put it on? Now, let's examine the risk of this bet more closely:

Fig. 1-2. Zoom in on NLF area

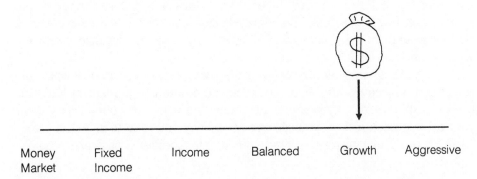

| Money
Market | Fixed
Income | Income | Balanced | Growth | Aggressive |

Figure 1-2 means that you can sleep at night if you have some of your money in a growth NLF.

So you have found your risk niche for your IRA. What? You didn't know that this investment would be for your IRA? I suggest you find your overall risk niche first and then determine what purpose the investment will serve.

Fig. 1-3. It's an IRA investment!

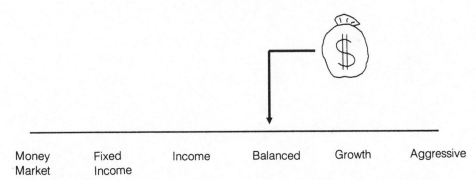

| Money
Market | Fixed
Income | Income | Balanced | Growth | Aggressive |

You have now learned the first lesson of investing: Before you place your bets, make sure you know how much or how little of a gambler you are. You must also consider the purpose of the investment you are making. If you have read this much of the book, chances are you are not the type to bury your money in the backyard (a move that always loses because of inflation). Savings accounts are probably not your cup of tea, either. However, I doubt that you are a candidate for Gamblers' Anonymous.

SUMMARY

Buying into a fully loaded mutual fund should, by now, be the furthest thing from your mind. You are an NLF buff! You can enter and exit NLFs cheaply and easily. You will do better in an NLF than you will in a bank savings account. The SEC will protect you. There are many types of funds for you to choose from according to your risk level. Your risk level depends on what your investment objective is. You would make a less risky investment with IRA money than you would with "mad" money.

You, yourself, must determine what kind of risk taker you are and what your investment objectives are. Why pay someone 4½ to 8½ percent or $500 up-front to make decisions you are smart enough to make for yourself? By being your own decision maker, you can use the money you save to invest in a good NLF, or to fly to Jamaica and send your ex-stockbroker a postcard.

2

Picking the Best Newsletter

THE SINGLE MOST IMPORTANT INVESTMENT DECISION YOU WILL EVER MAKE IS choosing a newsletter to follow. Since investing wisely is going to be one of your regular activities from now on, the newsletter you marry-up with will be yours for the long haul. This means that you want a newsletter that will make you richer, not poorer. A good newsletter can give you an important intangible benefit, as well. If you like to read it and find it interesting, you will enjoy your investing more. This is an important benefit because it will keep you enthusiastic enough to stay on top of things.

There were about 1000 newsletters out there before the Crash of October 19, 1987. Some of those newsletters have by now vanished. There are about 70 newsletters that provide advice about NLFs. Out of those 70 letters, 18 are tracked by a man named Mark Hulbert. Mark Hulbert's letter concerns the performance of other newsletters. You will use *The Hulbert Financial Digest* to help you select a newsletter.

THE CRASH OF '87

The Dow Jones Industrial Average (DJIA) is an average of 30 stocks out of about 2000 stocks which are listed on the New York Stock Exchange (NYSE). These 30 stocks are popularly taken to represent what is going on in the stock market. Ignoring the fact that there are many markets for stocks other than the NYSE, the DJIA does symbolize to many people how things are going in the whole investment world.

During 1987, the Dow reached its highest level ever, 2722.42 points, on August 25th. About 2 months later, on October 19th, the DJIA closed the day at 1738.74 points for a decline of 36 percent from its August high. Like the funny Count Dracula on Saturday morning TV says "That's pretty scary, isn't it?". It sure is! Once again, let me put a few questions in your mind:

1. Why did the crash happen?
2. What did it mean to the average investor?
3. Which newsletters avoided the crash?

There are many reasons why the Dow fell so precipitously. No one knows exactly how the various factors interacted to cause this fall, nor does anyone know how much of the blame should be assigned to any one of the factors. But most would agree that the main factors contributing to the crash were:

1. programmed trading
2. futures-related trading
3. institutional participation
4. highly over-valued stocks
5. rampant nervousness
6. bad monetary conditions

Let's look at causes 4 through 6 first.

Remember the dividend and interest components of gain I told you about in the last chapter? Say a stock sells for $100 and is expected to earn $10 in dividends and interest in the coming year. An indication of the value of this stock is its price-earnings ratio (or P-E value). For this stock, the price-earnings ratio would be $100/$10 = 10 (or 10-to-1). This is a reasonable P-E value. In general, P-E values for stocks were very high (above 20-to-1), well before the crash. Because of this (and for some other reasons), investors both small and large were becoming very edgy. Monetary conditions as reflected by, for example, higher interest rates, had become quite unfavorable. In other words, causes 4 through 6 already boded ill for the market. There probably would have been a nice "correction" (this is when the market takes a significant, though not necessarily disastrous, dive) of a couple hundred points in October; but what happened was an absolute massacre! Why? Because of causes 1 through 3.

The first three factors above are closely related. Institutions (insurance companies, pension plans, and the like) account for about 70 percent of the business on the NYSE. As the saying goes, when they cough, the rest of the investment world comes down with pneumonia. Well, the institutions came down with pneumonia and the rest of the investment world almost expired. Institutions do a lot of programmed trading with computers which are set to automatically trigger buying and selling of stocks and futures. Futures are like insurance—a pure numbers game, but perfectly legal. An institution, say, owns 100 stocks because it believes those stocks will go up in value and make some money for them. Institutions know they are not infallible, so to hedge their bets, they buy those things called futures which protect them just in case the market goes down. When you have 70 percent of the market acting computer-fast and in a panic, you get a 600-point massacre instead of a 200-point correction.

The probability that a crash of such magnitude can happen again has been reduced because of actions taken by the SEC and by exchanges themselves. An upward/downward limit of 100 Dow points has been suggested. At this point trading would stop to put a damper on stock and futures market actions for a while. Programmed trading would be halted. Futures traders would be required to put more cash on the line to back their bets (right now they only need 10 percent of what they bet, but 20 percent is suggested). Don't worry about future crashes. If you do, you might as well bury your money in the backyard and ignore the significant gains you can make in good NLFs.

In answer to the second question, the average investor got zonked just like the big investor. So it goes. If the average investor had been in a good NLF, following the advice of a good newsletter and making 20 percent per year for the 10 years ending December 1986, then the crash of 1987 wouldn't have hurt as much. The average mutual fund gained 1.4 percent during 1987 so performance for funds was, on balance, flat for that year. The 20 percent yearly gain for 10 years becomes an 18 percent yearly average when 1987 is thrown in as the 11th year. Beginning in 1988, investors should be in funds to partake in the long-term gains available in the stock market. The worst thing these people could do would be to get scared and stay out of the market.

In answer to the last question, who cares? That's right! Who cares? Indeed, there were a few heroes who bailed their subscribers out in time and a few of these people can be rightly proud. But there were also those who advised their subscribers to be out of the market for a very long time before the crash. The latter group of newsletters did not permit their fans to partake in a lot of the gain given by the lately departed bull market before the crash. As a result, many of these letters fared no better in the last few years than did many of those letters which had their subscribers fully invested during the crash. You see what I mean by "who cares"? The long-term record of a newsletter is much more important to you than whether or not a letter had its subscribers invested at the time of the crash.

There remains only one burning question we have to deal with: How can you find a letter with which you can live? We will answer this question, as usual, by keeping our eyes on the basics involved. Any more than the basics will just confuse the issue. Just because there is more detail to get into, doesn't mean that, if we did get into it, we would be doing a better job. In fact, we would be doing a worse job because we would be expending more effort and obtaining no better result.

YIKES! IT'S HULBERT!

It used to be that when you bought a car, the salesperson would say "This baby gets 50 miles per gallon!" It didn't matter much whether that salesperson was selling you an El Dorado or a Pinto. As soon as he or she discovered that you were hot on fuel economy, you would get the sales pitch.

Nowadays what you hear car salespeople say is: "The EPA (Environmental Protection Agency) doesn't know what the heck it is talking about!" The Federal Government imposed fuel economy standards on cars sold in the U.S. and directed the EPA to determine those miles-per-gallon figures and make them available to the public. The reason wasn't consumer protection, it was the oil embargo which made us more conservation-minded.

It is true that you will not get exactly the fuel economy listed on a new car sticker; but it is also true that a salesperson will have a rough time telling you "50 miles per gallon" when the sticker reads "20 miles per gallon." Since the EPA has made it possible for you to watch salespeople squirm, you should be very happy with that particular agency. If fuel economy is important to you, you have an unbiased source which gives you solid information on which to base a decision.

Mark Hulbert has appointed himself the EPA of the newsletter industry—much to the dismay of hundreds of newsletter writers. His monthly publication, Hulbert's Financial Digest (see Appendix C), arouses fright and anger in newsletterdom just like the EPA does in the auto world. The Hulbert Financial Digest is a very valuable newsletter because it is a solid and unbiased source of information on which you can base your decision to purchase the services of a newsletter.

There is a case when an automaker will praise the EPA. You guessed it! When the EPA says that the automaker has a tremendous fuel economy rating for one of its cars. The same goes for letter writers and Mark Hulbert. They will damn him if his ratings might ruin their advertisements, but they will praise him if they receive an "attaboy" from him. Sometimes in a newsletter ad, you will see Mark Hulbert quoted out of context with the implication that the newsletter has been blessed by his *Digest*. Don't let a newsletter drop Hulbert's name and fool you into believing it is the greatest.

Hulbert's *Financial Digest* has been in business for 8 years and that business has been stating in print the actual gain of newsletters which Mark Hulbert's subscribers ask to be tracked. Hulbert's *Digest* has been sued at least twice and hasn't lost a case. Mark Hulbert has a standing offer to any newsletter writer that goes something like this: "If how I rank you seems unfair, we can go to a third impartial party and, if that party says I am tracking you inaccurately, I will print a retraction and track you like that party suggests." No one has taken him up on that yet.

Newsletter gains reported in Hulbert's *Financial Digest* can be improved by getting into one or two good NLFs. This does not invalidate gains reported by the *Digest*. Gains are still valid because, when the *Digest* calculates gain, it uses all the funds suggested in a letter's portfolio. If the *Digest* gives a newsletter, say, 10 percent per year, it is possible to make 15 or even 20 percent per year by choosing one or two good funds instead of all the many funds recommended by the newsletter. If the EPA sticker says "30 miles per gallon," you can get 35 miles per gallon if you drive the car properly and under the right conditions. If Mark Hulbert says "10 percent per year," you can probably do significantly better just by being more selective about the NLFs you choose. (There will be more about NLF selection in the next chapter.)

To do an accurate and impartial job of rating newsletters is very difficult. Mark Hulbert does his job extremely well. He won't track a letter unless that letter gives clear-cut advice. This is one reason to look at the *Digest* when choosing a newsletter. If the letter doesn't give you clear advice on what and when to buy or sell, then the way is left open for interpretation on your part. For you, being an NLF buff, the ability to choose what is best to buy or sell will come with a little practice and experience. The timing of the buying or selling is the most difficult task but it is very important. That is where your newsletter will come into play.

Frequent switching in and out of the market leads to under-par performance. A little switching can improve performance, but it is quite difficult for any letter to beat the buy-and-hold approach over the long run. There are several letters from which you can obtain trial issues and which have good long-term track records, according to Hulbert's *Digest*. As you will see below, there are factors other than long-term gain which should determine your choice of a newsletter. Here is a quote from the October 29, 1987 issue of the *Hulbert Financial Digest*:

> The HFD acts on the premise that following the lead of the best performers will increase the odds of investment success.

He adds that, even taking the crash into account, long-term performance is one of the most important things to look at when selecting a newsletter for purchase.

There are 18 letters (or sections thereof) which the *Hulbert Financial Digest* tracks that have something to do with NLF investing. (Information on all these letters is given in Appendix C.) As long as a newsletter comes close to beating the market, it should be a candidate for your investment plans. A good letter will give you the direction you need to stick to a good investment strategy. Investing without a newsletter is exactly like trying to find your way out of a huge wilderness area without a compass in a snow storm. A good letter will also beat just parking your money in some money market fund. What more could you ask?

THE BEST TECHNICIANS

Once you read through this section, you will know how to go about choosing a newsletter. Since this is the most important investment decision you will ever make (except for the recurring decisions whether to follow a particular piece of advice from that letter), please pay special attention to what follows. So far you haven't seen much TA in this book. This section is where hard numbers will come into play. Any math presented here is only meant to explain what the numbers mean. You needn't follow along with a calculator because this book is not going to degenerate into a math textbook. A personal computer will crunch numbers for you. The final decision about which letter to choose will be made by you. That decision is a personal, gut-level decision, but it will be based on the information presented to you in this section.

Addresses and phone numbers of the 18 newsletters listed in Table 2-1 appear in Appendix C. Four attributes of a newsletter will cause you to buy it: cost, gain, clarity, and readability. Before you read the discussion of how these four attributes affect your decision to purchase a newsletter, make a mental note about the philosophy of this book. One of the lessons you take away from this book should be: Don't trust any numbers unless you understand what they mean. In keeping with that philosophy, the meaning of the numbers in Table 1 should now be discussed.

Table 2-1 is derived from data in various issues of the *Hulbert Financial Digest*. Costs are direct quotes from the *1988 Newsletter Directory*. Short-term gains are calculated from the First Quarter, 1988 issue. Long-term gains are based on a point system using data from the February, 1988 issue. Rankings of the 18 newsletters are based on a math process called *Technique for Order Preference by Similarity to Ideal Solution* (TOPSIS). TOPSIS will also be used to rank NLF groups. Don't worry about what you fear this math acronym, TOPSIS, might hold in store for you. TOPSIS is a widely used method for ranking alternatives (in this case, different newsletters). The method itself will stay comfortably hidden from view—you won't have to bother with its details. The methodology of TOPSIS will be explained a little later on.

Costs range from $49 to $250 per year but you can usually get a reduction in these figures when you actually purchase a newsletter. Reductions can be due to subscriptions taken out for more than 1 year or due to a special offer made

──────────── Table 2-1. Newsletter Numbers ────────────

Newsletter Name	Cost $/Yr	Gain (Performance) Short-Term	Long-Term	Rank
Fund Exchange	99	5.8%	1	15
Growth Fund Guide	85	6.8%	3	6
Investech Mutual Fund Advisor	150	32.1%	3	5
Kinsman's Low-Risk Growth Letter	175	5.4%	1	18
Lynn Elgert Report	190	5.5%	3	14
Margo's Market Monitor	125	36.8%	4	3
Mutual Fund Forecaster	49	8.9%	5	2
Mutual Fund Investing	99	15.0%	1	10
Mutual Fund Strategist	149	29.8%	4	4
No-Load Fund-X	95	16.8%	1	7
No Load Fund Investor	82	7.4%	1	11
Peter Dag Investment Letter	250	8.1%	2	17
Professional Tape Reader	250	12.3%	2	16
Stockmarket Cycles	198	19.4%	1	12
Switch Fund Advisory	140	10.1%	3	9
Telephone Switch Newsletter	117	17.4%	8	1
Weber's Fund Advisor	135	14.5%	1	13
Wellington's Worry-Free Investing	99	12.2%	2	8

by the letter to attract new customers. If you feel that all you can afford is the $49 newsletter, then by all means, choose that one. It holds second rank out of the 18 letters anyway, so it is definitely one of the best. If this is the case, your decision to marry a newsletter is based on the sole attribute of cost. In fact, the *Mutual Fund Forecaster* even had an offer of a 5-year subscription which brought the cost down to $36 per year.

Hopefully, you won't have to base your decision solely on cost. Shop around and sample several of those 18 letters mentioned in Table 2-1. If you change your mind after subscribing, don't worry. Most letters offer a prorated rebate if you cancel your subscription. In addition, many of the letters offer free samples. You can also go through the Select Information Exchange (see p. 186 in Appendix C) and get samples of up to 20 newsletters for about $20. Some letters let you deduct that $20 from the subscription cost.

Short-term gains are calculated using gains from 1986–87 in the *Digest*. You need to see how one gain calculation is made so you can feel at ease with the numbers in Table 2-1. *Margo's Market Monitor* gained 9.5 percent from January 1, 1986 through December 31, 1986 and gained 71 percent from January 1, 1987 through December 31, 1987. The phenomenal 1987 gain will be hard to repeat for any letter. These two percentages are multiplied and the square root is taken to give the 36.8 percent gain listed in the Table. (The actual calculation is to take the square root of 1.8725 = [1.095][1.71] and you get 1.368, or 36.8 percent.) Your main concern here is that, had you done what the *Monitor* told you to do for those 2 years, you would have averaged 36.8 percent per year. Don't rush out and buy the letter with the highest short-term gain. Sample it if you wish, but don't base your final choice on just one number—no matter how appealing that number may be.

Long-term gain is derived from data in several tables in the February, 1988 *Digest* issue. Each of the 18 letters in Table 2-1 is given 1 point for appearing in the table itself. A newsletter is awarded an additional point for each time it appears in Mark Hulbert's "Top Ten" for the years 1984 through 1987. Since there are 4 years here, this means a letter can gain up to 4 points. Two points are awarded each time a letter appears in the Top Ten for 1980 through 1983. A total of 8 points can be gained in this way. So there is a maximum possible score of 13 for the long-term column in Table 2-1. Since the *Digest* has been tracking letters for 8 years, newsletters with an 8-year track record should be rewarded for good performance over the long haul. Letters that have come on strong in the last few years should also get credit for that performance.

The *Mutual Fund Strategist* appeared in the Top Ten for 1985, 1986, and 1987, and so receives three points. Every letter gets at least one point so the *Strategist* has a total of 4 points. (It was not tracked by Mark Hulbert before 1985.) The long-term point system does not penalize a letter which has no 8-year track record with the *Digest* because such a letter can still get 5 out of 13 possible points. The *Telephone Switch Newsletter* appeared in the Top Ten for 1981 to 1982 (2 + 2 = 4 points) and for 1984 through 1986 (1 + 1 + 1 = 3 points), and so gets 8 points total (remember, 1 point is given to each of the 18 letters). Half of the 8 points awarded to the *Telephone Switch Newsletter* come from long-term performance, a very important consideration.

TOPSIS takes the cost, short-term gain, and long-term gain, to determine the ranks in the last column of Table 2-1. The lowest number in this column, a rank of 1, belongs to the *Telephone Switch Newsletter*. This means that, based on the other three quantities in the table, Richard Fabian's newsletter was deemed best. The rank of *Investech* is 5, so this letter is fifth out of the 18 letters shown in the table. You shouldn't necessarily purchase a higher-ranking newsletter and ignore lower-ranking letters. All that has been considered so far in ranking the letters are cost and gain. You still need to look at clarity and readability. Before you consider those two important attributes, you should first understand how TOPSIS ranks alternatives.

TOPSIS first makes numbers comparable to each other. It is an old math saying that you "can't add apples and oranges," so dollars are stripped from costs and percents are stripped from gains. There are still inequities to overcome, due to the fact that, for instance, one newsletter costs $250 and gained 8.1 percent over the short-term. It is true that units aren't in the picture anymore, but how can "250" and "8.1" be sensibly compared? So TOPSIS transforms numbers to the same scale after stripping the units from them. The scale used makes the smallest possible number 0.00 and the largest possible number 1.00. Now TOPSIS has all those numbers in the cost and gain columns of Table 2-1 right where it wants them. The ideal solution is figured out and newsletters are ranked by how close they come to that solution. The closer to the ideal, the higher the ranking that a newsletter receives.

The ideal solution for Table 2-1 is a newsletter which costs $49 per year, has a short-term gain of 36.8 percent per year, and has a long-term score of 8 points. You could gaze at the table all day long and not find one newsletter that achieved an ideal of minimum cost, maximum short-term gain, and best long-term performance. Actually, you would find three letters, each of which fit the bill for just one of those ideal values of cost, short-term gain, and long-term performance. What TOPSIS does for you is combine the initially unwieldly costs (in dollars), short-term gain (in percent), and long-term performance (no units), and then ranks each newsletter on how close it comes to meeting the ideal of $49 per year, 36.8 percent over the last 2 years, and 8 out of 13 possible points for the long haul.

Now for clarity and readability. All letters in the table have good clarity rankings from Mark Hulbert. The *Digest* would not (in fact, could not) track a letter unless its advice was clear-cut. Mark Hulbert ranks clarity of advice by using the letter "A" for the clearest advice and "D" for marginally clear advice. All letters in the table are ranked "A" or "B" except one which is ranked "C." Clarity is one of those intangible and important aspects you need to judge for yourself. Don't subscribe to a newsletter until you have test-driven it. Make sure that you can readily follow the advice given there. Clarity is important because you need to know which investments to make and when to make them.

Readability is considered separately from clarity for two reasons: 1). clarity of advice is important in its own right; and 2). you need to enjoy reading your newsletter, or you will quit doing so and then ignore your investment plan. The term "enjoyability" could have been used as well as "readability." Out of all four attributes needed to win your subscription dollars, readability is the most intangible. You might get samples of all 18 letters and find that the only one you care to read is the one ranked 18. If that is the case, then the best letter for you is *Kinsman's Low-Risk Growth Letter*. This Kinsman example is very important. Robert Kinsman got the lowest short-term gain, one point for long-term gain, and his letter is not among the cheapest. But with all that apparently going against this letter, it has one of the two lowest (that is, "safest") risk ratings of the letters given by Hulbert's Financial Digest. (The lowest risk rating belongs to the *Peter Dag Investment Letter*.)

In spite of a letter's low ranking in Table 2-1, you might still wind up subscribing to it for readability alone. That does not refute the validity or usefulness of the numbers, especially the rankings, in this table. You don't jump on the least expensive letter and ignore all else, or blindly choose the letter with the biggest short-term gain, or the best long-term gain. Take these three attributes into consideration by using the ranking number as a good summary of the numbers in the first three columns. Then sample several newsletters, and only after you feel comfortable about clarity and readability, choose one.

One last note about letter selection. A hotline can be a very valuable feature of a newsletter. Don't buy a letter which charges an additional fee for its hotline services. You *will* have to pay for the phone call at about 50 cents to a dollar a throw, but it will be worth it if you need reassurance between issues. You might have just received a copy of your letter and your letter comes out once each month. That same day on the radio, you hear that the market bounced up 100 points. Since you won't be getting the next copy of your letter for another month, it would be nice to place a phone call and hear a recording of what your letter writer has to say about what happened in the market. Out of the 18 letters listed in the table, five don't have hotlines. These include *Margo's Market Monitor, No-Load Fund-X, No Load Fund Investor, Peter Dag Investment Letter*, and *Worry-Free Investing*. If you are interested in these letters, but want to have the hotline feature, call them to see if they have installed a hotline since the publication of this book.

HOW TO USE YOUR NEWSLETTER

When you receive your newsletter, immediately punch holes in it. Then store it in its own binder with previous issues. After that, you may read it. Invariably, newsletters refer to their past issues so it works out better to bind a new issue right away and then read it. After you've read your letter and gleaned all its knowledge, it is neatly bound and ready for you if you need it again at some future time.

Be sure to read your letter as soon as it comes. This is a good habit to get into and will help you maintain momentum in your investing. The market might be going either quite well or quite poorly (in which case you would be in a money market NLF), and you think that there is no reason to pay attention to your letter's advice when the situation is so clear-cut. That is false. When things look bleakest, your letter could well recommend buying into a good growth NLF.

You will see a lot of garbage on TV, hear it on the radio, and read it in the newspapers. "Garbage" is not being used as a synonym for advertising here. Garbage refers to all those conflicting conjectures and prognostications about what will happen to the DJIA, gold, the U.S. economy, our trade deficit with

Japan, mutual funds, insider traders, and many other things. This stuff is called garbage (some of it is pretty good, actually) because it must be emphasized that the only advice which you follow is that advice from your well-chosen newsletter.

Use your letter to avoid flip-flopping in your investment decisions. Don't listen to friends, relatives, hairdressers or bartenders. Don't become unglued just because your investments have turned sour. As long as your letter says to stick with it, then stick with it. Since you will choose a very good newsletter to begin with, this shouldn't be a problem, in spite of other temptations. Remember that the only way you can achieve the long-term consistency that your letter has attained is by following its advice with a passion.

SUMMARY

Though scary, the Crash of '87 will do its damage to those who stay out of the market after 1987. The people who really got hurt are those who stayed out of the market for 10 years preceding the crash. If these people had been in some good NLFs for those 10 years and followed the advice of a good newsletter, they would have gone from averaging 20 percent per year to averaging only 18 percent per year. Only? What is wrong with making 18 percent per year over a long period of time? You will hear people who want to manage your money use the Crash to coax you into being their client. You might hear them say that they can also do 15 to 20 percent per year for you. TA is stronger than BS. Make those people produce a hardcopy of their long-term track record, verified by an impartial third party.

Maybe this year will be a good year to be in a money market NLF. Who is to say? Your trusty newsletter will tell you what to do. Before you begin the next chapter, call or send for some sample copies of newsletters listed in Appendix C. If you order the samples now, by the time they begin arriving, you will have finished this book. At that point you will be able to analytically devour each one and pick out the best one to subscribe to. One important quality of a newsletter is that you have confidence in it. Another quality, just as important, is that you enjoy reading it. In any case, without a good friendly newsletter, you might as well put your money in a bank.

3

How to Choose
Good No-Load Funds

THE ONLY WAY YOU WILL BE BEWILDERED IN CHOOSING AN NLF OUT OF
hundreds available is if you pay attention to friends or if you pay attention to
advertisements given by stock brokers, bankers, or financial planners. In this
chapter you will see how to get readily available, free-to-cheap information which
you can use to select NLFs. You will also see how to use that information.
Hundreds of NLFs will be clobbered off that initial list of over 1000 by first choosing
a good NLF group. After that task is accomplished, you match your risk level
with a fund in that group. This fund is the NLF you open your account with.

~ You can't learn to swim unless you get your feet wet, so even if you have
a minimal amount of cash, the best way to start investing in NLFs is to dive
right in. You will be told how to do this and what to expect. All it takes is a toll-
free phone call to your NLF group, a request for information on particular funds,
and then a check to the fund of your choice. A good incentive you saw in Chapter
1 was to compare how your particular NLF is doing with what 5 percent in a
bank would have done to your money. This drives home the point that you are
investing wisely, especially if you dream a little and pretend your initial contribution
was $50,000 instead of $2,000.

WHITTLING DOWN THE FIELD
Here are five requirements for an NLF group to be a good group:

1. Good money market NLF in the group

2. Toll-free switching privileges
3. Enough switches to suit your needs
4. Clearcut, prompt, courteous service
5. Sufficient variety of good funds

All 12 NLF groups in Appendix B have a good money market NLF in them. This makes it convenient to switch and makes doing other business with a group easier. Think of the money NLF in your group as you would your neighborhood bank. It is safe, it sends you monthly statements, and it allows you to write checks. Some conservative investors prefer to put all their money in money NLFs. These investors may never switch any of their money into a stock NLF. Other conservative investors put half their money in a money NLF and put the other half in an income or balanced NLF. It is very convenient to switch money when you have a good money NLF in your group. All you do is place a toll-free call and say "please switch $1,500 from my money NLF to the XYZ balanced fund."

The 12 groups offer from two switches to unlimited switches per year. No fee is charged to switch unless a certain number of free switches is exceeded. Unless you trade actively in aggressive or sector NLFs, you should need, at most, two switches per year. Check with NLF groups you are interested in for the most recent switching information. Data in Appendix B is as up-to-date as possible. Even if you don't plan on switching, the privilege is good to have.

You will find the service in all 12 groups clear-cut, prompt, and courteous. It is a good idea to make a list of questions before you call, so you don't forget to ask an important question. After a few months of NLF investing and a couple of calls to the NLF group of your choice, you will feel good about the service you receive. Usually you only need call the group infrequently, maybe six times a year, in order to have just a few specific questions answered.

Don't select an NLF group that doesn't provide a range of NLFs to match your needs. If you have a full range of investment needs (that is, if you have a lot of different risk/objective levels), then you must choose an NLF group which has good money market, fixed-income, income, balanced, growth, and aggressive funds in it. If you are strictly a conservative investor, then such a group would still do, but you could just as well select a group which has only money market, fixed-income, income, and balanced funds in it. The best way to start is to select a group with a broad range of NLFs in it so you can experiment to find your risk/investment niche. If you are certain to only invest in balanced NLFs, then you only need a money fund and a balanced fund in your group.

There are other reasons to consider joining a broader based group. As you grow in your investment expertise, you might find a need for more types of funds than you originally thought you might need. Perhaps a high-rolling friend will ask you for investment advice. If you joined a broad-based group to begin with, you can speak from experience and tell that friend about your NLF group that not only contains your balanced fund but also contains growth and aggressive funds.

This is not to say that you can only use one NLF group. You can use many. The primary concern here is to get you started.

All the NLF groups in Table 3-1 are good groups, judging from the five requirements just discussed. They vary in the number of NLFs, but all contain enough funds from which to choose. Data for the two tables in this chapter come from the *Handbook for No-Load Fund Investors* (1988 Edition). This is an excellent reference book which comes out about May or June of each year and cost $38 last year. Sheldon Jacobs, who publishes the *No-Load Fund Investor* newsletter, also puts out the *Handbook*. Mr. Jacobs does a superb job handling the most thankless task in TA—gathering and putting into a useful format a wealth of accurate and timely data. Half of the *Handbook* gives a good explanation of NLFs and the other half gives the data. It would be money well spent for you to get the 1989 version (see Appendix C for details). If $38 is not to your liking, free information can be obtained from the Investment Company Institute. (See Appendix B for details on this source.) You can also call (toll-free) the fund groups themselves and ask for information on particular NLFs listed along with fund group information in Appendix B. Appendix B gives you NLF type so you don't ask for information on a balanced fund when you want an aggressive growth fund.

─────────────── Table 3-1. NLF Groups to Consider ───────────────

	—Percent Gain—			*No. of*	
	10 Yr	*5 Yr*	*Risk*	*NLFs*	*Rank*
Dreyfus	14.6	12.9	0.77	4	3
Fidelity	13.6	12.3	1.00	7	7
Financial Prgs	13.9	11.7	1.06	3	12
Founders	15.1	12.8	.91	5	5
Neuberger-Berman	17.7	12.8	.95	3	4
T. Rowe Price	14.5	11.2	1.02	7	8
SAFECO	14.2	10.7	.94	3	9
Scudder	15.4	12.3	1.07	5	10
Stein,Rowe&Farnham	15.6	13.1	1.08	8	6
TwentiethCent	24.5	18.2	1.36	5	2
Value Line	15.4	11.8	1.06	5	10
Vanguard	15.4	11.5	.82	15	1

Any of the 12 NLF groups listed make fine starter groups. The first two columns in the table give average percent gain over the last 10 years and last 5 years (ending December 31, 1987). The third column measures risk. Risks for individual funds can be as low as 0.25 or as high as 2.00. The standard for average risk is a value of 1.00. The risk column shows the average risk for each group, taken over all NLFs in that group which are income, balanced, growth, and aggressive growth. For the averaging of risks in an NLF group, money and fixed-income NLFs were excluded because these types of funds generally have the lowest risks and Table 3-1 is meant to give an indication of how risky a group is in general. None of the groups in this table are risky at all, though individual NLFs you can get into in these groups can be very risky. (Don't worry, very risky funds are easy to avoid.)

The fourth column (No. of NLFs) shows how many NLFs are available in each fund group. Only income, balanced, growth, and aggressive growth funds are counted. The number does not include special purpose NLFs like sector funds or international funds. Some of the NLFs included in the count are closed to new customers because the fund managers felt that money was entering the fund too quickly to be invested wisely. This could mean getting shut out of a good thing, but with so many good NLFs around, you needn't worry about a fund closing.

Closing of an NLF happens infrequently. The intent of the fourth column is to convey how likely you are to find NLFs of interest in a particular group. Fidelity is the biggest fund group of all, but it is not an NLF group. Since the NLFs in Fidelity constitute a subgroup of their own, by the definition of a good NLF group, Fidelity was given a score of 7 in the number of NLFs column. Stein, Roe & Farnham received a score of 8 but has far fewer funds overall than does Fidelity. Don't hop in a group just because it has a lot of funds; the great majority of those funds might not be NLFs. More on this later.

Now it is time to get oriented. The five requirements for a good NLF group ensure that you will get into a group you can live with. All NLF groups in Table 3-1 fulfill these five requirements. The table shows the longer-term average yearly percent gain (10 years) and the shorter-term gain (5 years) for 12 NLF groups. None of these groups is very risky, although individual NLFs in any group can have a high-risk rating. Each group has at least an NLF subgroup (Fidelity) or is composed of only NLFs (Stein, Roe, & Farnham). But what does the last column indicate?

TOPSIS is again used to rank alternatives. In Chapter 2, newsletters were ranked and reasons were given why you wouldn't necessarily choose the letter ranked 1. The same goes for NLF group rankings. The best group as indicated by TOPSIS is Vanguard. TOPSIS took the two gain columns, the risk column, and the number of NLFs column into consideration and arrived at the rankings. Suppose you assembled 10 experts on NLF groups and showed them Table 3-1. These experts could look at it all day long and would wind up giving you 10 different opinions on which group was best and for what reasons. In this case, TOPSIS is used to eliminate all the subjective noise you would get out of a panel of 10 experts. TOPSIS objectively ranks the 12 NLFs for you based on the data in the first four columns.

But you still have to make up your own mind. As in the newsletter application of TOPSIS, you might well pick one of the lower-ranked NLF groups. (Value

Line and Financial Programs are very good groups.) Salient features of each of the 12 groups are listed in Appendix B. These features are names and types of NLFs open to investment, minimum initial investment required (for non-IRA and IRA), telephone redemption privileges, and number of switches per year. Get the basic facts from Appendix B. Then, based on your risk/objective levels, choose two or three NLF groups and call them for information on the NLFs you are interested in. You will see examples of selecting specific NLFs a little later in this chapter.

You will be sent fund prospectuses in the mail. Look them over and see how you like them. Each will have past performance listed in a clear fashion dictated by a new SEC ruling. Even if you get 5 or 10 prospectuses and spend an initial 2 or 3 hours digesting them, the time will be well spent. You might only choose one or two NLFs to send money to, but after that initial two or three hour investment of your time, you will see how easy it is to pick an NLF you can be satisfied with.

Now for a word of warning: Beware of hidden fees charged by some so-called NLFs. It is OK to pay a 1 or 2 percent front-end or rear-end load if you are going into sector fund investing. Fidelity and Financial Programs are the two biggest sector fund groups and Vanguard also has some good sector funds. But if you expect to go the pure no-load route, make sure that there are no sales charges. The specific NLFs listed in Appendix B are truly NLFs. Hidden loads aren't really too well hidden anymore because of new SEC rules on mutual fund reporting. Read the prospectus. If you get the faintest mention of a load of any type, just call the group. They will have to honestly answer your question: ''Is your Bonanza fund a pure NLF or are there hidden loads or sales fees?''

Just because a fund group happens to have some loaded funds in it, doesn't mean you should avoid it. However, be careful to avoid loads and hidden fees. Some groups have 12b-1 fees which are moderate and offer no cause to avoid the group. Founders is such a group. It is a very good NLF group with outstanding service. The ¼ percent 12b-1 fee charged is a maximum-allowed percentage and will not be used unless warranted. Founders has been around a long time, has an excellent philosophy (it wants to stay a small group and give good, personalized service), and is ranked 5 out of the 12 NLF groups in Table 3-1.

This section is called ''Whittling Down the Field.'' Has that been accomplished? Out of over 80 NLF groups and 1034 NLFs, you now have a table of 12 NLF groups and, in Appendix B, about 82 NLFs to look at scattered across these groups. The cheapest way to get information is to call a few of those groups toll-free and have them send you prospectuses on specific NLFs. You must, by now, know whether you want to bury your money in the backyard or go to Las Vegas with it. Scan Table 3-1 and Appendix B and pick a few good NLF groups. Read the rest of this chapter, then call those groups and ask for prospectuses on some specific NLFs you like. After you've read the prospectuses, send one or two of the NLFs some money and do what your newsletter tells you to do.

A SPECIFIC EXAMPLE

You will become quite intimate with the Vanguard NLF group. This particular group was chosen because it is a large group, is full of good NLFs, has some sector funds, and has one of the best reputations of any NLF group. This is your chance to view an actual, and very good, NLF group before you put any of your money on the line. You are going to learn about what "good" is first so you can identify the bad.

Don't let the use of Vanguard as a specific, detailed example necessarily convince you that you are being led into Vanguard as the best out of all NLF groups. No matter how groups are ranked, Vanguard would have to be among the best. So would the other 11 groups in Table 3-1. As with newsletters, "best" is what is best for you and only you can make your mind up about that. Try to view this section in the following way: "Using Vanguard as an example, I will get the details on how to invest in specific NLFs. After learning that, I can go to any NLF group I wish and pick the NLF which is best for me."

Table 3-2 is only a partial list of over 40 funds (including money market and bond NLFs) contained in the Vanguard group. The last column (Min. $) gives the minimum initial investment required for a non-IRA account. Subsequent investments can be as small as $100. For IRA accounts the initial minimum is $500, and, subsequently, you must send in at least $50.

Vanguard contains all types of funds: Money Market (MM), Fixed Income (FI), Income (I), Balanced (B), Growth (G), and Aggressive (A). All these NLFs did much better in 1986 than they did in 1987. Of course, the 1987 gains include the crash. What is of interest is that, even though the average mutual fund lost about 20 percent during the period of the crash itself, over the whole year losses for all but two of the Vanguard NLFs did not exceed 10 percent. These two NLFs are sector funds and are not for conservative investors. In other words, if you were in a balanced NLF like Wellington, you would have made 2.3 percent for the year even though you lost 20 percent during the crash. That shows just how good a year 1987 was until October 19. The long-term view is what is important. During 1986, Wellington gained 18.3 percent and, in 1985, this balanced NLF gained 28.4 percent. Years like 1985 and 1986 tend to make up for years like 1987.

Another thing to note is that for 1987 Morgan, an aggressive growth NLF, gained 5 percent, while any of the three Vanguard money NLFs gained more. Morgan gained 5 percent with much more risk than did the money NLFs. The column to focus on is the 10-year column, though. Morgan gained 15.2 percent per year over the last 10-year period ending December 31, 1987. Vanguard Money Market Prime gained 10.1 percent per year. This means that buying and holding on to Morgan 10 years ago would have made $10,000 grow to $41,165. Doing the same in Money Market Prime would have resulted in $26,174. Morgan incurred more risk over that 10-year period but gained $14,991 more. If you can stomach the risk, you can make out more. If you can't handle the risk, making

$16,174 on top of your initial $10,000 in a money NLF over a 10-year period isn't bad either.

You would expect to see the percent yearly gain increase as you go from a money market NLF to an aggressive NLF. This doesn't happen in the table. The reason is two-fold. Aggressive NLFs should not be in your portfolio on a buy-and-hold basis. Some years are great for stocks and other years are lousy. A good newsletter will tell you when to be in stock NLFs and when to be in money market NLFs. If you had switched between Morgan and Money Market Prime (based on a switching strategy you will be shown later), you would have realized a 21.2-percent-per-year gain over the last 10 years instead of a 15.2 percent gain as indicated in the table. Using the 21.2 percent switch in Morgan in comparison to Buy/Hold in Money Market Prime, the 10-year score is Morgan: $68,395, and Money Market Prime: $26,174. Actively managing your money can pay off big.

The other reason aggressive funds seem to underperform the more conservative types of funds is that gains in the table are calculated on a calendar-year basis. This is to say that, for example, the 1987 gain is calculated by assuming that you were in the fund as of January 1, 1987, and that you remained in the fund through December 31, 1987. The 5-year gains are for calendar years 1983-87 and the 10-year gains are for calendar years 1978–87. Chances are very high that you would not have jumped into these funds exactly on January 1st and remained there for the entire year—not that you will be switching frequently between a stock and a money market NLF. You might enter a stock NLF on April 23, 1989 and exit to a money market NLF on August 11, 1991. Your newsletter will tell you what to do.

There is a very special fund in the Vanguard group. You cannot switch between this NLF and any other stock NLF in the Vanguard group. Vanguard Index 500 is an *index fund*. There are index funds in other groups as well. (Dreyfus has one, but the minimum initial investment is $1,000,000. If you have that kind of money, throw this book in a waste can and go fishing for the next 30 or 40 years.) An index fund buys into one of the market indices—usually the Standard and Poor's 500. The S & P 500 consists of 500 stocks and so tracks the overall stock market much more closely than does the DJIA. Looking at the yearly gain of Index 500 you can see almost an exact copy of what happened in the actual S & P 500 and, therefore, in the stock market at large. One good investment strategy a lot of people use is to plunk their wad down on some index fund and let it ride forever. This strategy is good because, over the last 70-odd years, the market as a whole has beat inflation by a factor of 3-to-1! When you think about it, that certainly is a good way to invest.

Vanguard refers to its "sector" funds as "special portfolio" funds. Sector funds invest in only one industry group and so are not diversified like, for example, a Wellington fund is. This means that sector funds are more volatile than growth funds. For this reason Vanguard's Special Portfolio funds are labeled "aggressive." If you enter a Special Portfolio fund, the switching rules are a little different than for the other Vanguard NLFs. The diagram below (Fig. 3-1) shows an initial investment in the Health fund, then an exit into MMP (Vanguard Money Market Prime). For the purpose of paying that 1-percent rear-end load, you are still considered to be in the Special Portfolio funds and so you don't pay the 1-percent rear-end load yet. Next, you go to the Energy fund and then to the Gold fund. All this switching around might well occur over a couple of years. Finally, you exit to the World International fund. Now you pay the 1-percent fee. Such a small fee is reasonable, considering all the buying and selling such volatile funds must do to stay well positioned in the market.

Fig. 3-1. Switching Vanguard Sector Funds

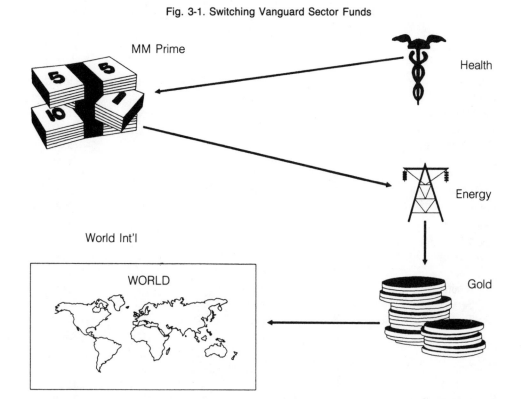

Vanguard is one of the best NLF groups around but there are others. Look at Stein, Roe & Farnham for example. This group has good funds of every type, though it has no sector funds. Lack of sector funds is not a disadvantage, unless you want to get into sector fund investing. If that is so, you can do your more conservative investing with, say, T. Rowe Price and use the Financial Programs group for your sector investing. Sector fund investing is a whole different game and will be mentioned later on.

WHICH NO-LOAD IS BEST?

You are now at the point where you can select a specific NLF to match one of your risk/objective levels. Just select one of the NLF groups out of Table 3-1 and fix in your mind one of your specific risk/investment-objective levels. The Vanguard group will again be used in what follows to give a range of examples. You will need a good money market NLF and that fund will be Money Market Prime (MMP). Three of the Vanguard NLFs mentioned in Table 3-2 are closed to new accounts because they were so popular with investors that the managers couldn't invest all that new money as wisely as they would have liked. Explorer II and Windsor II are managed by the same people who manage the very popular and successful Explorer and Windsor NLFs.

———————— Table 3-2. Vanguard No-Load Fund Group ————————

Name	Type	Gain (%) 1987	5 Yr	10 Yr	Min $
Explorer	A	−6.9	0.0	13.8	closed
Explorer II	A	−4.3	—	—	3000
Morgan W.L.	A	5.0	12.0	15.2	1500
Naess & Thomas	A	−7.0	0.0	11.6	3000
High Yield Stock	I	−4.8	20.1	19.2	closed
STAR	B	1.6	—	—	500
Ginnie Mae	FI	2.7	11.4	—	3000
High Yield Bond	FI	2.6	12.7	—	3000
Invst Grade Bond	FI	0.2	11.2	9.6	3000
Index 500	B	4.7	15.8	14.7	1500
Special Portfolios					
Energy	A	6.1	—	—	1500
Gold	A	38.7	—	—	1500
Health	A	−0.5	—	—	1500
Services	A	−13.0	—	—	1500
Technology	A	−11.9	—	—	1500
Wellesly	I	−1.9	15.4	15.9	1500
Wellington	B	2.3	16.2	15.0	1500
Windsor	G	1.2	19.3	18.7	closed
Windsor II	G	−2.1	—	—	1500
World International	G	12.7	31.2	—	1500
World U.S.	G	−5.4	11.8	14.4	1500
Money Market Funds					
Federal	MM	6.2	7.8	—	1000
Insured	MM	5.9	—	—	1000
Prime	MM	6.4	8.1	10.1	1000

Look at the two scales in Fig. 3-2. Locate yourself on the bottom scale and follow a vertical line up to the top scale. On the top scale, you will find possibilities for NLFs in which you should feel comfortable investing. Doing your own investing can be fun, right? You bet! It is turning out to be very easy also.

MM	FI/I	B	G	A
Prime	Ginnie Mae	Star	Windsor II	Explorer II
	High Yld Bd	Indx Trust	World Intl	Morgan
	Invst Gr Bd	Wellington	World US	Naess/Thom
	Wellesly			VSP

Ebeneezer Scrooge ⟵————————— YOU! —————————⟶ Bret Maverick

Fig. 3-2. How to Choose a No-Load

So is this all there is to it? No. But you have come two-thirds of the way. So far you have chosen a good newsletter (or are in the process of doing so), and you have chosen a good NLF group (or are doing so). Only *you* can do those two things. You must be comfortable with your choices. The third thing you must do is determine your risk/objective levels. Once you have those three items out of the way, choosing an NLF is as simple as using the two scales above. If you hear any differently, don't believe it. Confusion is a tool sometimes used to sell you on investment advice. You are smart enough to do your own investing.

Again refer to Fig. 3-2. Suppose you fancy yourself a Bret Maverick. This leads you to 8 Vanguard NLFs:

1. Explorer II
2. Morgan
3. Naess & Thomas
4. Special Portfolio Energy
5. Special Portfolio Gold
6. Special Portfolio Health
7. Special Portfolio Services
8. Special Portfolio Technology

Now suppose you've been in Morgan for a while and couldn't take the heat. Just slip over to Windsor II and see how you like that fund. What we are doing here is performing an experiment with two of your most basic emotions: fear and greed. If you already know yourself well enough, you won't have to be subjected to this trauma. But you must be sure that you know yourself.

If you wind up feeling comfortable about living with Windsor II and you have some IRA money to invest, I suggest you put it in one of the three balanced NLFs in the above scale. It is always better to be more conservative with your retirement money than you are with dollars which you don't depend so much on down the road.

If you are an Ebeneezer Scrooge-type of investor or maybe just a person who values safety above all else, there is no problem with investing in MMP. Though, generally speaking, one can't predict a fund's gain by basing that prediction on past gains, with MMP you could look forward to an average of 10 percent per year. When people warn you about predicting a fund's performance based on its past performance, they have in mind funds like the Special Portfolio Gold fund which gained 49.7 percent in 1986 but lost 5.4 percent in 1985. Feel free to base your prediction of what a good money market NLF will do on its past performance.

Another nice thing about money market NLFs is that you can write checks from them (if they are not IRA accounts). All you need do is keep the $1000 minimum (which is gaining 10 percent per year) and write a check for a minimum of $250 (check with individual groups for details about individual amounts). You can even have your paycheck sent to a money market NLF. If you have $576 worth of bills to pay this week and there is at least $1576 in your account, just write a check for $576 to your credit union, then write the smaller checks from there. Neat, eh?

Two growth funds on the Vanguard scale need special mention: World International and World US. International funds did very well from 1985 through 1987 as the US dollar was falling. You need special advice from a newsletter to invest in these types of funds. Don't equate them to Windsor II. World International and World US are given the Growth (G) label, but they are not ordinary growth NLFs. This demonstrates one of the most sacred commandments for NLF investing: Do not invest in an NLF until you have read its statement of investment objectives in the prospectus. You must know what type of NLF you are investing in before you can match it up with one of your risk/investment-objective levels.

HOW SHOULD YOU START?

First, get a piece of paper and a pencil. Write down your risk level by giving it the label of one of the NLF types: money market, fixed-income, income, balanced, growth, aggressive. Now list your investment objectives. Your financial planning sheet might look something like this:

I am a growth-type person.
I have four investment objectives:
IRA

New car
Trip to Las Vegas
Rainy day money
(for non-IRA security)

Since you are growth-oriented, select a balanced-type NLF for your IRA. Use the same type of fund for your rainy day money. A growth fund will do just fine for your new car money. And, what the heck, use an aggressive fund for that Las Vegas trip! Be sure to check with your newsletter to see whether you should be in a stock or a money NLF.

Call your NLF group for the prospectuses of all the funds you are interested in. (See Appendix B for details.) You will know how big that initial pot of cash is that you have to invest. Your own common sense dictates the rest. Allocate that pot of cash as you see fit. For example, if it is April 1st and you only have $2,000 but you haven't invested last year's IRA yet, then you had best put the whole $2,000 into that balanced fund as soon as possible! On the other hand, if you are confident that you are meeting all four of the above objectives, then, depending on the type of person you are, you can put any extra money you might have into a trip to Atlantic City or into the rainy day account. You can even switch money from one account to another.

SUMMARY

What you need to do right now is contact the NLF group of your choice and ask them about information on the NLFs you are interested in. Then check your mailbox to see if any sample newsletters have arrived. By the time you receive all those prospectuses and sample newsletters, you should be finished with this book. Then you can write checks to those NLFs you've selected and start tracking your funds.

Take time to read those prospectuses. Don't be afraid to call your NLF group and have them answer questions. Remember that those 12 groups all give clear-cut, prompt, and courteous service. The mutual fund industry is quite competitive, so use that fact to your advantage and don't be shy. You will find NLF group service representatives are very friendly people and enjoy helping you with your questions. They won't give you advice on when to buy or sell or what to buy and sell, but they will help you decide which NLFs to obtain prospectuses for if you are having any difficulty.

These first three chapters have been the "getting started" phase of your investment adventure. In the next two chapters you will be shown how to do your part of your own TA, after that a few chapters on how the professionals will do TA for you. The last chapter ties the whole book neatly together into one useful package. By then you will have settled on which newsletter you will be subscribing to and which NLF group you will be doing business with.

4

Graphs are
Pictures of Facts

TA IS THE ANALYSIS OF THE STOCK MARKET USING NUMBERS TO GET AN understanding of what is going on so that you can make intelligent investments. *Fundamental analysis*, on the other hand, is the nonnumeric analysis of the stock market so that intelligent investment decisions can be made. TA and fundamental analysis work together to complete the stock market picture. One without the other is no good.

Throughout the rest of this book, fundamental notions will be discussed, then numbers will be attached to those notions and graphs drawn so that the fundamental meaning of a situation will be made clear. Once you understand graphing, you will be on your way to understanding TA and reaping the rewards which follow from a coherent investment strategy.

Go to a magazine right now and look at any one picture in it. Describe in a couple paragraphs what that picture is saying. Now imagine that the picture didn't exist and all you could rely on is your description of what that picture contained. No matter how well you wrote those paragraphs and no matter how simple that picture was, the words you wrote are probably a meager replacement for the picture. The same is true with numbers and graphs. People who have spent their lives studying mathematics and statistics and who have applied their knowledge about math and stat to real-world situations (including teaching), have a common knee-jerk reaction when confronted with data to analyze. When these math/stat professionals see a mass of numbers, they immediately graph them. The first step in any analysis is to graph the data.

Making graphs, smoothing data (that is, removing wild up-and-down motions from graphs), and developing buy and sell strategies were everyday chores for a technical analyst until computers came along. Now computers suck in unbelievable amounts of data and spit out analyses at an alarming rate. What hasn't changed are certain basic tools that anyone, even if he or she is only dabbling in TA, must understand. Even experienced TA-ers sometimes forget about basics they learned long ago and wind up getting burned. Graphs, their interpretation, and moving averages form the basis for 90 percent of the TA you will ever run across. Anyone can pick up on what is contained in this chapter. Once you pick up on it, you will be ready to do your own TA.

YOUR FIRST GRAPH

If you need practice making graphs, get some graph paper, pencil, and a pen. If you are a whiz at graphing, follow along anyway to review the concepts discussed. The following data will be graphed:

———— **Table 4-1. Temperature for Unknown City** ————

Day	Date	Temp. (Fahr)
1	9/ 3	42
2	9/ 4	51
3	9/ 5	63
4	9/ 6	60
5	9/ 7	57
6	9/ 8	62
7	9/ 9	49
8	9/10	41
9	9/11	53
10	9/12	52

A graph has an X-axis (horizontal axis) and a Y-axis (vertical axis). You will graph "Temp." over "Day," which means you choose Day as the X-axis variable and Temp. as the Y-axis variable. Now, look at the Y and X Axes graph in Fig. 4-1. This shows you how the axes are laid out and is the starting point for all graphing.

You will be marking the axes with "ticks" so that you can graph the data in Table 4-1. To decide where to tick, you need to know the minimum and maximum X and Y values. By looking at Table 4-1, you can see that, for the X-variable "Day," all values fall between 1 and 10, inclusive. For the Y-variable, "Temp.," all values are between 41 and 63, inclusive. The graph in Fig. 4-2 titled "Tick the X Axis" shows you how to tick values for day 1 through day 10 along the horizontal axis. Now, with pen, tick for Day on your own graph

Y is vertical

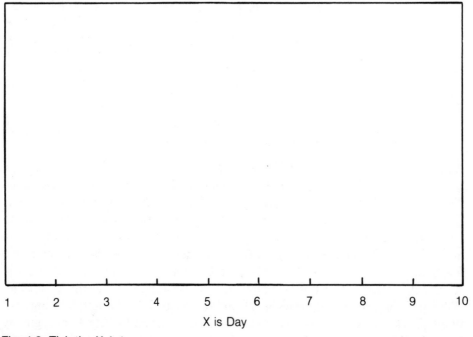

X is horizontal

Fig. 4-1. Y and X Axes.

paper. Use your pencil (not the pen) to tick for Temp. on your own graph paper, using Table 4-1, and then look at Fig. 4-3, titled "Tick the Y Axis". It is best not to put all numbers from 41 to 63 for Temp. because it will clutter the graph.

Y is Temperature

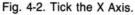

| 1 | 2 | 3 | 4 | 5 | 6 | 7 | 8 | 9 | 10 |

X is Day

Fig. 4-2. Tick the X Axis.

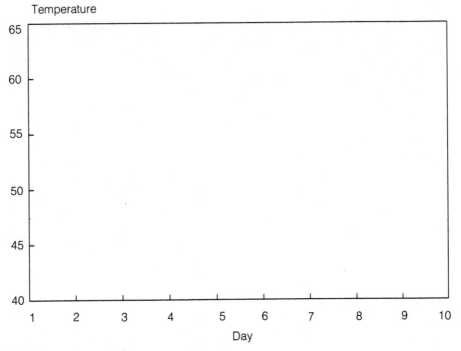

Fig. 4-3. Tick the Y Axis.

Now for the moment of truth: transfer the information contained in Table 4-1 to the sheet of graph paper. First, view Table 4-1 in a different way. You must pair-off numbers in the X-axis column, Day, with corresponding numbers in the Y-axis column, Temp., to get Table 4-2. These pairs are called "ordered pairs" because, by convention, the first member of the pair is to be graphed as the horizontal variable and the second member as the vertical variable.

——Table 4-2. Day, Temp Pairs——

Day	Temp.	Pair
1	42	(1,42)
2	51	(2,51)
3	63	(3,63)
4	60	(4,60)
5	57	(5,57)
6	62	(6,62)
7	49	(7,49)
8	41	(8,41)
9	53	(9,53)
10	52	(10,52)

Consider the pair (6,62). With pencil, locate 6 on the X-axis and lightly draw a vertical line parallel to and the same length as the Y-axis. Locate 62 on the Y-axis and lightly draw a horizontal line as long as the X-axis. Take a pen, and where these two lines intersect, draw a big fat period. Look at the graph called ''Plot the Pair (6,62)'' for guidance.

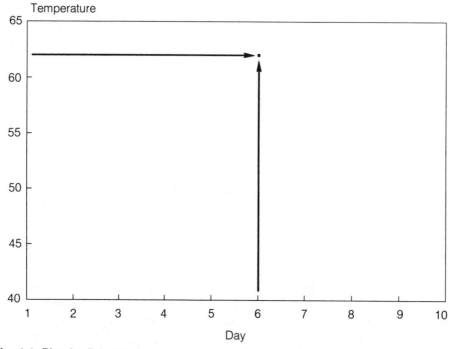

Fig. 4-4. Plot the Pair (6,62).

Follow this method for the other pairs in Table 4-2. Now erase the penciled lines and you are left with a graph of that mass of numbers in Table 4-1. This graph is a plot of all those points which are listed in Table 4-2. You have now accomplished what math and stat professionals do when they want to analyze data. You have replaced those numbers in Table 4-1 with a graph showing how the temperature varied up and down over a 10-day period in that Unknown City. Study Table 4-3 in conjunction with Tables 4-1 and 4-2 to get a feel for changing that ''raw'' temperature data to ordered pairs so you can readily graph those points.

The ''Plot All Pairs'' graph is your first graph. The numbers 0 and 11 have been added to the X-axis so you could see the points more clearly. If you understood how Tables 4-1 and 4-2 are combined to give Table 4-3, then, hopefully, you became a little disgusted looking at those numbers. Math and stat pros feel the same disgust when they look at tables of numbers. You now have

———Table 4-3. Combine Tables 1 and 2———

Day	Date	Temp. (Fahr)	Ordered Pairs
1	9/ 3	42	(1,42)
2	9/ 4	51	(2,51)
3	9/ 5	63	(3,63)
4	9/ 6	60	(4,60)
5	9/ 7	57	(5,57)
6	9/ 8	62	(6,62)
7	9/ 9	49	(7,49)
8	9/10	41	(8,41)
9	9/11	53	(9,53)
10	9/12	52	(10,52)

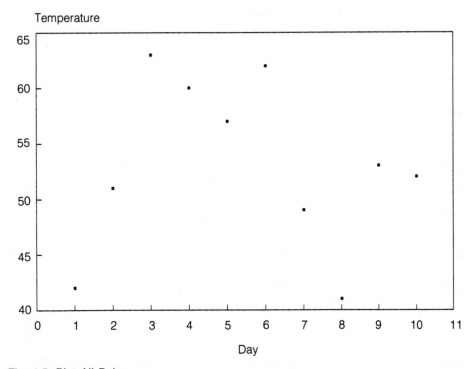

Fig. 4-5. Plot All Pairs.

something in common with professional mathematicians and statisticians. You would much rather look at a graph of some numbers than at a table full of those same numbers.

This brings up a point to make about the presentations in this book. You will look at numbers and discuss calculations on those numbers only enough to gain the basic insights needed. Remember, the basics are what are important. Once you understand these basics, the meaning of TA will come home to you and you will be able to see how TA will help you become a wiser investor. You are now ready to go on to the next section.

Hopefully you will do some graphing on your own. This will give you a better understanding of how to interpret them. There are a few additional things to note when making your own graphs. The first thing you should do when making a graph is to decide on the X and Y axes scaling. Just look down the table of numbers and find out what the biggest and smallest X and Y values are. Once you know this, you can graph any table of numbers.

You must anticipate the future when you graph. If you had wanted to graph temperatures over a 30-day period, you would have run into X and Y values outside the ranges of those given in Table 4-1. When ticking the axes for unknown situations like this, you need to allow room for growth. If, on a weather report, you hear that the record low temperature for September was 12 degrees Fahrenheit and the record high was 87 degrees Fahrenheit, then your ticking should look like the graph "Anticipate Axes Scaling."

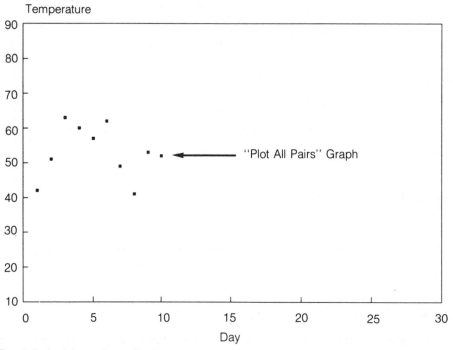

Fig. 4-6. Anticipate Axes Scaling.

If you decide to do your own graphing, you will soon find a type of graph paper you will feel at ease with. You won't be graphing scads of numbers all Saturday morning either. On a weekly basis, you only need graph a few points to keep up with things. This will add 10 or 15 minutes to your personal TA burden, but it will be fun and give you a better feel for what is going on. Data you might graph weekly are your NLFs (including a money market NLF), the S & P 500, and the Dow Jones Utility Average (DJUA). The DJUA is quite an important average and will be discussed later on.

Tracking your investments and some stock market averages by graphing them can be fun and rewarding. You make your own tables up from the Saturday or Sunday morning business section. You don't need to buy a computer. Your newsletter pro does all the fancy TA for you. Newsletters generally furnish you with ample graphs anyway. Doing your own graphing is the way you will gain fullest insight into what graphs mean. This will allow you to apply that deeper knowledge to what is going on in the stock market. Pride in how you track your investments and a better feeling for what you see in the papers and on TV will make the few extra minutes a week worthwhile.

GRAPHS SHOUT MEANING!

Look at Fig. 4-7, "Temp. vs. Day." This graph is like the one you just finished, but lines have been added connecting the dots and the dots have been dropped. In this manner, a clearer picture of the data is achieved. When you have many more than 10 points to graph, connecting the points with lines and erasing the points gives you a much clearer view of a situation. When you read your newsletter, you will come across graphs with dozens and even hundreds of points graphed. The line that connects the points will give you a feel for the flow of things—that's basically what you want to get out of any graph.

——— **Table 4-4. Bonanza NLF (1988)** ———

WK	Date	Friday Close
1	9/ 2	$42.00
2	9/ 9	51.00
3	9/16	63.00
4	9/23	60.00
5	9/30	57.00
6	10/ 7	62.00
7	10/14	49.00
8	10/21	41.00
9	10/28	53.00
10	11/ 4	52.00

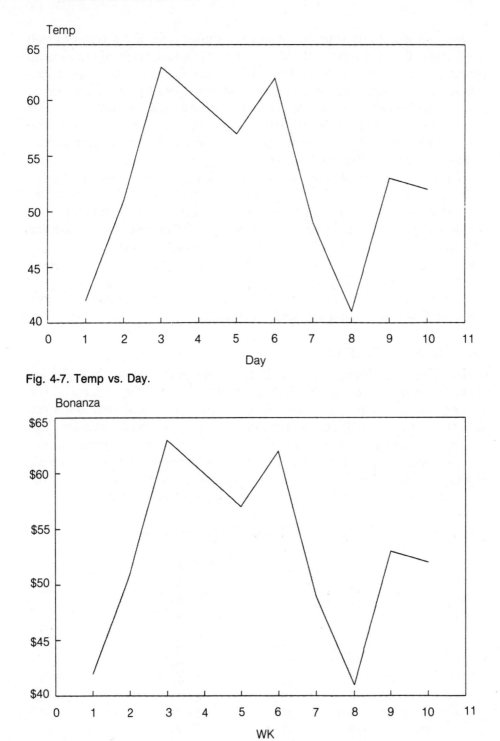

Fig. 4-7. Temp vs. Day.

Fig. 4-8. Bonanza vs. WK.

Figure 4-8, "Bonanza vs. WK," is a graph of the Bonanza NLF (Table 4-4). Graphically speaking, Figs. 4-7 and 4-8 are identical. Both graphs have the same shape and both graphs have the same scale on their axes. Their only difference is one graph uses "Day" and one uses "WK" (for "Week") for the X-axis, while the Y-axis is labeled with "Temperature" on one graph and "Bonanza" on the other graph. You could superimpose the first graph on the second and the up and down squiggles would coincide. This outlandishly simple observation leads to a very important point about graphical interpretation.

Don't rush to the conclusion that, if you can project what the temperature will be on Day 11 in Unknown City , you can buy or sell Bonanza today depending on whether the temperature will rise or fall. There is no fundamental relation between temperature and Bonanza, even though technically they are the same. On the one hand, we stick a thermometer out the window, and on the other, we take a number out of the Sunday paper. Suppose it is Day 11 and the temperature shot up to 85 degrees. Would you feel confident remortgaging your house and putting all that money into Bonanza just because the temperature shot up? Of course not. This example shows why there has to be a firm fundamental basis to TA, no matter how closely the numbers appear to be related.

You will be seeing two types of graphs: line graphs and scatterplots. Line graphs are graphs which look just like the Temperature and Bonanza graphs. Scatterplots are a different animal which we have to understand to know how forecasts are made. Recall that there are two types of technicians out there: trend-followers and projectors. Trend-followers use line graphs and projectors use scatterplots. Since 90 percent of the TA you will run across amounts to trend-following, you will concentrate on line graphs for now. The discussion of forecasting market behavior will start in Chapter 10.

Graphical interpretation will be simpler because the variable "weeks" is used for the X-axis variable on most of the line graphs in this book. No matter what is put on the Y-axis, "WK" will most always be on the X-axis. There is a good reason for this. Some people follow the market daily or hourly or monthly or quarterly. The best TA is generally done with weekly data. Good TA can be done using shorter or longer periods, but you are focusing on the basics so will only be concerned with weekly data.

Actual dates corresponding to weeks are given in Appendix D. Appendix D lists some data you can use for your own TA and corresponding dates are given along with numbers for the S & P 500, the DJUA and MMP. For example, Week 1 ended on Friday, January 2, 1981. That is the beginning of the 7½ years of data used in this book. Week 396 corresponds to Friday, July 29, 1988. That is the end of data for this book. Friday closing values of stock market Y-variables (which we will graph on the Y-axis) are what you see in graphs here. You will be seeing week-by-week graphs of the most recent 7½ years of stock market data.

Right now my PC will whack out four graphs for you. The PC does these four graphs (with a total of almost 2400 data points) in a matter of 10 minutes! This ignores the hundreds of hours spent learning computer languages and entering reams of data into that monster machine over the last 4 years, but one thing is quite certain, the PC makes very pretty graphs. And I like graphs.

There are reasons to show these four graphs to you:

1. the S & P 500 is a very important stock market index
2. MMP is a good proxy for overall interest rates
3. the S & P 500 and MMP are closely related

The relationship between the market and interest rates is an out-of-sync relationship. You have heard or will hear that ''falling interest rates foretell a rise in stock prices.'' This is to say that stocks go up when interest rates go down. It also says that stocks go down when interest rates go up. (Remember our discussion of the crash?) Now you will see this relationship first-hand.

Figure 4-9 is a graph of the S & P 500 for the last 7 years. You can see that there were times when it would have been good to be in a stock fund and times when it was bad. The whole point of TA is to be in the market at the right time, and to be out of the market and in an NLF like MMP at other times. Let's compare the graphs in Figs. 4-9 and 4-10.

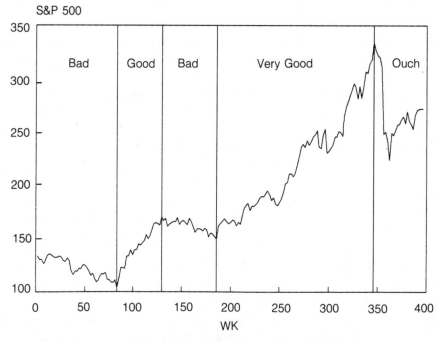

Fig. 4-9. Standard & Poors 500 Stocks (Jan 1981 thru Jul 1988).

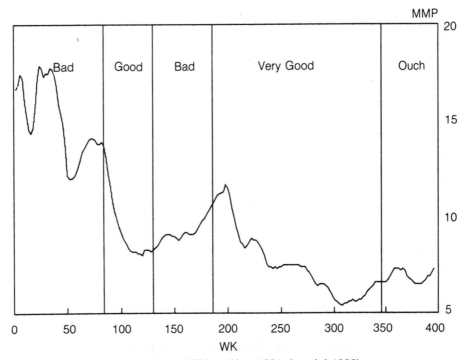

Fig. 4-10. Vanguard Money Market Prime (Jan 1981 thru Jul 1988).

The graph in Fig. 4-10 shows MMP for those same 7 years. If you had invested in MMP at the beginning, you would have made a good, steady rate of return on your capital. All money market funds make money no matter what the stock market is doing. The rub comes when you realize that it would be better to be making 20 percent over some period, switching between a money NLF and a stock NLF, than it would be to be making only 10 percent in a money market NLF over that same period. A good newsletter will tell you when to be in stock NLFs and when to be out of those funds and in a money market NLF.

Your eyes had to bounce back and forth between Figs. 4-9 and 4-10 to see when the S & P 500 was going up and MMP was going down and vice versa. It would be much nicer to have both these indicators on the same sheet of graph paper. This has been accomplished in the next graph. Anyone using this graph to explain how the market and interest rates move opposite one another would be avoided like the Plague.

There is a simple way to cure the ills apparent in Fig. 4-11. Use two different Y-axes! Look at Fig. 4-12. Much better! We can see that when the market goes up, interest rates go down and vice versa. To make this graph, first graph the S & P 500 using the left Y-axis. Then ignore that graph and graph MMP using the right Y-axis on the same sheet of graph paper. That's all there is to it.

There is pain involved in gathering data, and care involved in plotting even a few points. Now we have, in Fig. 4-12, a couple of curves with a lot of squiggles

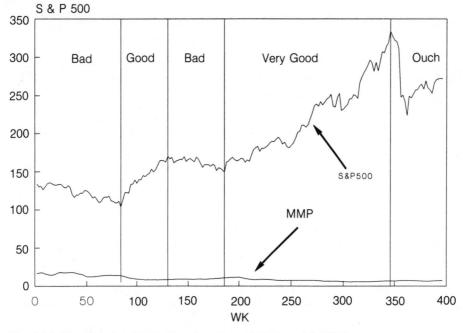

Fig. 4-11. The Graph with No Meaning (Jan 1981 thru Jul 1988).

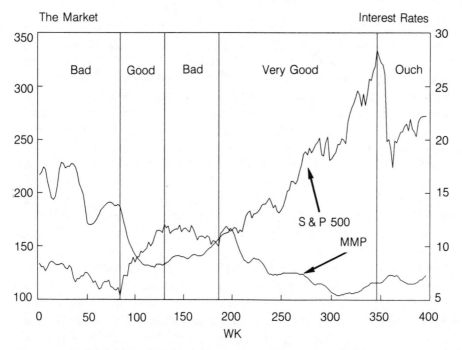

Fig. 4-12. The Market and Interest Rates (Jan 1981 thru Jul 1988).

that tell us interest rates don't move in tandem with the market. Hold on! We know a lot more! Interest rates appear to move exactly out of tandem with the market. This is an important fact we would have had trouble discerning from the data just by looking at two tables or looking at two separate graphs. Graphs give you ideas, destroy your pet notions and confirm your beliefs. Data tables just sit there and intimidate you.

The way that interest rates and the market move opposite one another is a very important example of how graphs shout meaning. As you progress, you will see many other examples. There is another way that graphs give you insight into the stock market. In this section raw data was graphed for the S & P 500 and MMP. Sometimes it is a good idea to "massage" that raw data a little, and come up with a different set of points to graph. You won't have to do any massaging yourself because a PC can do it for you. Follow the sample calculations so you can get the feel for what is about to occur. Remember that calculations will always take a backseat to graphs in this book.

MOVING AVERAGES

You might have noticed that graphs of real data contain a lot of bumps, squiggles, and ups and downs. For that 10 percent of technicians who use real math to forecast the stock market, this up-and-down variability is no problem. For the other 90 percent, variability is handled by "smoothing" the raw data. Smoothing is almost always accomplished by transforming raw numbers into a moving average (MAV from now on). When a graph of raw data and a MAV of that data are put on the same sheet of graph paper, a very useful interpretation can be given to the picture. This interpretation forms the basis of many good TA newsletters. But first you need to understand what a MAV is and what it does for you.

Suppose you started investing in MMP in July 1984. You recorded your monthly balance in a table like the one below for all 54 months ending December 1988.

──────── **Table 4-5. MMP Balance** ────────

(July 1984 to Dec. 1988)

Month	Date	Balance
1	July 1984	$2045
2	Aug 1984	1899
.	. .	.
.	. .	.
.	. .	.
53	Nov 1988	3780
54	Dec 1988	3864

This table should remind you of other tables you have encountered in this chapter. The first and second columns are read together as "the first month was July 1984, the second month was August 1984, . . . the 53rd month was Nov 1988, the 54th month was Dec 1988." (This makes for awfully dry reading, but soon you will ignore the table and examine the graph.) The first column in the table replaces the date in the second column with a number so we can graph the table. The month number is used as the X-axis variable. The X axis would be approximately 3 feet long if dates were used instead of the month number!

To start the graph in Fig. 4-13, "MMP Balance for 54 Months," you pair off, for example, Month 1 with the MMP Balance for July 1984 and get a point to plot (1,2045). Proceed like this for the other 53 points, and then make the graph. As you have come to expect, this graph fluctuates up and down. This graph is one part of a two-part standard used to compare your present performance with your past. You want to use this standard to change tactics when the situation calls for it. If you are doing very well in this MMP rainy day account but perhaps need more money in your Wellington new car account, the standard will tell you whether you have an excess of money to transfer from MMP to Wellington.

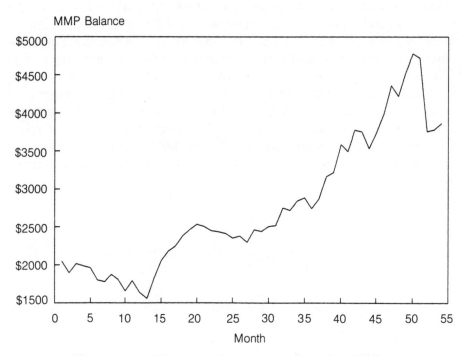

Fig. 4-13. MMP Balance for 54 Months (Jul 1984 thru December 1988).

A standard which makes sense is to compare your current MMP Balance with your average MMP Balance over the last year. The average of the most recent 12 months' balances indicates, in just one number, how you have been doing with your MMP investment. This average is the second part of the standard.

Going back over all 54 months, you can see that there are many periods of 12 consecutive months for which a yearly average can be calculated. The first such period starts with Month 1 and ends with Month 12. When you get your statement for Month 12, you have the first opportunity to compare an MMP Balance with an average yearly balance. The next time you will get a chance to do this is in Month 13. Then you will use Month 2 through Month 13 to compute an average balance for the most recent 12-month period. Keep doing this until you get the latest account statement (Month 54) and compare its balance with the average of Month 43, Month 44, and up to Month 54. Table 4-6 gives an idea of what the situation is now.

——————Table 4-6. MMP Balance and MAV——————

(June 1985 to Dec. 1988)

Month	Date	Balance	MAV
12	June 1985	$1637	$1855
13	July 1985	1558	1814
.	. .	.	.
.	. .	.	.
.	. .	.	.
53	Nov 1988	3780	4078
54	Dec 1988	3864	4086

Add the MAV curve to Fig. 4-13 to get the graph in Fig. 4-14. Graph the MAV by plotting pairs like (12,1855) and (13,1814). The MMP curve in this graph coincides with the MMP curve in Fig. 4-13, except that the first 11 months are chopped off. The 12-MAV (short for "12 month moving average") curve is a graph of the Month and MAV columns. The first 11 months were excluded because the 12-MAV couldn't be calculated for those first few months. To calculate a 12-month MAV, you need 12 months of data and this doesn't happen until June 1985. Later, when you get into MAVs using weeks as the unit of time, "12-MAV" will mean "12-week moving average".

When the actual MMP Balance lies above its 12-MAV, you know that you are doing better this month than you have been doing (on the average) over the past year. If the balance falls below the 12-MAV, you are doing worse than you have done over the last 12-month period. Now you have a gauge to tell you how you are doing with your MMP rainy day investment. You can dance or cry depending on whether your MMP Balance is above or below its 12-MAV. For example, at Month 27 your MMP balance fell below its 12-MAV. Maybe the fundamental reason for this is that you had an unexpected car repair. To make up for the plunge at Month 27, you begin to pump more money into MMP. By Month 33 you are doing fine again as indicated on the graph. Your MMP balance is now well above its 12-MAV.

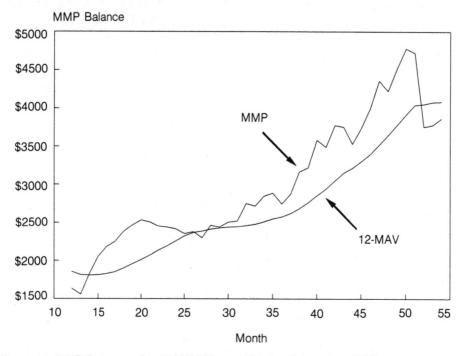

Fig. 4-14. MMP Balance with 12-MAV (June 1985 thru December 1988).

The same type of analysis is successfully applied to the stock market by trend-followers. Let's look at the 45-MAV of the S & P 500. (Throughout the rest of the book, units are weeks unless otherwise stated, so that "45-MAV" means the 45-*week* moving average.) For the same reason you feel like dancing when your MMP Balance is above its 12-MAV, you should feel like dancing when the S & P 500 is above its 45-MAV. This is a happy occasion because technicians have found that when an index like the S & P 500 is above a fairly long-term MAV of itself, the market is usually in an uptrend. Figure 4-15 depicts the S & P 500 and its 45-MAV for the last 6 years. There are 6 years instead of the 7 years of available data because the 45-MAV didn't exist for the first 44 weeks. This is all for MAVs right now. You will see them in more detail in Chapter 6.

S&P 500

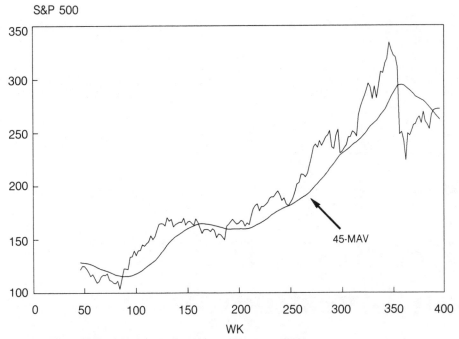

Fig. 4-15. S & P 500 and 45-MAV (Nov 1981 to Jul 1988).

SUMMARY

You've created (at least in your mind—which is just fine) your first graph. You are turned off by tables of numbers and have learned to appreciate the elegant beauty of a gyrating line. You have seen two important examples of the meaning contained in graphs. One example showed how the market and interest rates are related. This relationship was out-of-sync but it is still a very important relationship. Even though the market and interest rates move in opposite directions to one another, this very fact is used to tell you when to be in or out of the market. In Chapter 7, you will get into the fundamentals underlying this stock market versus interest rate relationship.

The MAV example about the MMP Balance showed how two graphs can be used in conjunction with one another to tell you how to feel about one of your investments. The fact that the curve of raw data is above one of its MAVs is interpreted as meaning that you are in a good investment environment. This observation forms the basis for 90 percent of the TA you will ever see. This type of TA is called "trend-following" and has proven to be as successful as the forecasting-type of TA, presented to you in Chapters 10 and 11.

I hope you have become comfortable with simple graphs and their interpretation. What you have learned in this chapter is all you need to know about graphs to understand basic TA. You should now be much less likely to run afoul of people who try to flimflam you with weird-looking curves. The more undulations there are, the bigger the chance that you are being sold a line.

5

Keeping a Handle on Investments

THERE ONCE WAS A PERSON WHO TOOK OUT A CD WITH A REPUTABLE BANK. THE interest rate on that CD varied month-to-month, depending on a government bond rate. Every month the bank quoted a yearly rate of return on that CD: 11.6 percent, 11.7 percent, 11.2 percent, and so on. Halfway through the 1-year term of the CD, the person found his balance had gone from $2000 to $2100. After 2 seconds with his hand calculator, he knew that he was having a "bank-job" pulled on him. The calculator showed a yearly gain of just over 10 percent. Even the downtown office couldn't explain the 1¼-percent discrepancy. ("Well, the computer did it, so it must be right.") At that point he saw the light and took an early withdrawal hit, plus a $35 "accounting fee" (in the fine print, of course), and sent the remnants of his $2100 to a money NLF.

The moral is that one must track one's own investments. Don't rely on what other people say about how well you are doing. For 15 minutes per week you can have a handle on your progress in a money market NLF and in stock NLFs. You simply record a few numbers on a couple of sheets of paper. This is the minimum amount of tracking you must do. For a few more minutes a week, if you wish, you can graph those numbers. Graphing is not necessary but, once you set up the graph paper, it takes very little time and you'll have fun gloating over your own graphs. Taking things one step further (again, only if you so desire), you can graph the S & P 500 and the DJUA. If you feel even more enthusiastic than this, you can reach for the ultimate in your personal TA and calculate and graph a few MAVs.

Even if you choose to do the minimal amount of required TA for yourself, read this whole chapter. You will see here, firsthand, how TA can help you to become a better investor. As always in this book, basics will be emphasized. You will see all you need to know about doing your own TA. Let your newsletter pro do the fancier calculations for you. Your minimum weekly input allows you to sit back (after that 15 minutes of record-keeping) and watch your money grow.

MONEY MARKET FUNDS

Here is a formal statement of the five levels of TA you can now do:

Level 1: Read your newsletter. Glance at a business section. Listen to radio and watch TV.

Level 2: Take a few numbers out of the Sunday paper and write them down in tables. (There are some templates for these tables at the end of this chapter.)

Level 3: Graph the tables in Level 2.

Level 4: Graph some MAVs.

Level 5: Graph the S & P 500 and DJUA.

You have been doing Level 1 (with the possible exception of reading a newsletter) for a while now or you wouldn't have bought this book. Just because you were warned earlier to ignore a lot of what is said on TV, radio, and other places, doesn't mean you should, for example, quit watching "Wall Street Week" on Friday evenings. You can pick up a lot from radio, TV, and other sources. The warning was intended to keep you from getting confused by sources other than this book. So Level 1 is a snap for you. The other four levels will require some work.

Level 2 is the very least you can do for yourself. It is necessary to keep you apprised of what is going on in the market and how well your investments are doing. Because tracking money NLFs is very easy, Levels 2 through 4 will be interpreted in terms of money NLFs first and then these levels will be interpreted for stock NLFs. Level 5 deserves a section all by itself. Make up your own brand of data sheets if you wish. Those sheets (templates) included at the end of this chapter will serve at least as a guide for the following discussions. To learn how to track your NLFs, begin with Level 2.

If you don't do Level 2, you won't be a good boss of your investment dollars. This level forms a solid basis for all higher levels of TA you can do. Glance at the two money NLF templates right now (pp. 67 & 68). In the business section of the Sunday paper, you will find quotes for taxable (as opposed to muni bond) money market funds. Choose the money NLF in your fund group to track. If you are in more than one NLF group, choose only one of the corresponding money market NLFs to track. Once you have made this choice, stick with it forever. You need to record from a single consistent source because, eventually, you will have hundreds of weekly quotes representing years of data. If you bounce from one money fund to another over those years, the picture you get will be slightly distorted because rates of return vary a little bit from fund to fund. If you don't feel like choosing a money NLF to track, use Vanguard MMP. Appendix D contains a table of values for this NLF for the year ending Friday, July 29, 1988.

In very good years for money market NLFs, you can expect as much as a 16- to 18-percent return on investment. Bad years will probably yield about 5½ to 6½ percent. You can pick a money market NLF by throwing darts and get about the same return from any one of them. Besides being a good investment, money NLFs are an excellent place to park your money when the stock market turns sour.

If you miss a week here and there, don't panic. Just put ''N/A'' for ''Not Available'' in the place you would have recorded the yearly percentage gain for the money fund that week. (Later, when you show your table off to a friend, you can say that your newspaper messed up for those N/A weeks.) Rates of return don't change much week to week for money NLFs. What you want to get out of writing that one number per week down is a feeling for how interest rates are doing so you can tell how the money in your money fund is doing.

You can't get the same feeling by tracking your monthly money NLF balance. Tracking this balance is useful for some purposes, but it can't be used to keep a handle on total return. This is because you don't just plunk $1000 in a money fund and let it ride. You keep adding or subtracting to or from the balance, and this wipes out any rate of return calculation which could be based on the balance. The same is true for stock NLFs. In fact, you might not have any money in a fund, but still want to keep an eye on it for future use.

Local papers, *Barron's* and other publications, pay the Donoghue organization (see *No Load Mutual Fund Guide* in Appendix E) a fee to use William Donoghue's figures for money market funds' rates of return. Don't use your fund's quotes. Not because your fund would pull a bank-job on you, but because Donoghue is *the source* for money market funds' rates of return. It is usually best to go to the same source everyone else is using.

Table 5-1 is a sample of what your money market NLF tracking might look like if you use the first template at the end of this chapter. Suppose you began tracking on Friday, November 6, 1987 and the most recent quote you wrote was for Friday, February 26, 1988. Friday dates are used because the money and stock markets all work on a basis of Friday closing values when you are tracking things weekly. Don't worry if Friday is a holiday and there is no business conducted on the exchanges. Record Friday's date anyway. Now you will see a good procedure to follow when using the templates provided in this chapter.

——————————— Table 5-1. 17-Week Sample Table ———————————
(*Vanguard MMP*)

WK#	Date	Gain (%)	WK#	Date	Gain (%)
1	11/06/87	7.3	27	/ /	.
2	11/13/87	7.3	28	/ /	.
3	11/20/87	7.3	29	/ /	.
4	11/27/87	7.3	30	/ /	.
...	...	...	...	...	...
17	2/26/88	6.7	43	/ /	.
18	3/ 4/88	.	44	/ /	.
...	...	...	...	...	...
25	/ /	.	51	/ /	.
26	/ /	.	52	/ /	.

Don't rush out and copy templates and transcribe data until you have finished this chapter. You will be picking up a few pointers on how to construct tables of data. These pointers will be handy to know when you go through the trouble of setting up your data tables initially. The roughest part is the initial part. After you have followed the procedure outlined here, you only need a few minutes each week to record a few numbers. The time-consuming part comes every 6 or 12 months when you need to make up new templates. So read this chapter first, then copy the templates you need as described in the following procedure.

The first step in using a template is to make only one copy of each type of template you need. (*Note*: Use the copy of the MAV template if you are going to track the 26-MAV of your money NLF.) When you have that one copy on your desk or table, fill in all 52-week Numbers and Dates (there will only be 26 for the MAV template). Then make a second copy of the template you just filled in on a photocopier. Besides saving you the trouble of writing all those week Numbers and Dates down again, this will set you up for one whole year (or 6 months). You have now finished the roughest part of Level 2.

Now go to your Sunday paper and fill in the "Gain" column for Week 1 on both copies of the template you will be using. Keep the two copies in different locations (possibly, one at home and one at work) so that if anything happens to one of them you still have the other one. This protects against jelly and coffee spills, losses, and so on. If your boss isn't looking, you can take some graph paper to your place of work and play with that copy. There is no worse disaster which can befall a technician than to lose the only copy of years of data which he or she has accumulated.

The starting date you choose to begin tracking your money NLF is very important. This will be a base date to which all your other tracking will be referenced. If Week 1 is November 6, 1987 for your money market NLF, then

Week 1 will carry the same date for your stock NLFs, the S & P 500, the DJUA, and whatever else you care to track. The purpose of this dating scheme is to avoid a huge mistake a certain technician once made. That technician mixed up his weeks once and spent several hours one Saturday straightening the mess out. The only exception to using your money fund Week 1 as the base for all your other tracking is if you use the tables in Appendix D. All tables in that appendix have Week 1 as August 7, 1987.

This idea about cross-referencing your data tables won't become clear until you can see a couple of tables in front of you. To learn about cross-referencing (it is a simple process meant to avoid mistakes) two tables will be used. One is Table 5-1 already given above. The other table is Table 5-2, which will be given a little later on. Right now all you need be concerned with is that the date you choose to give to Week 1 is the same in all of your data tables. This will save you a lot of grief down the road. The rest of this table-making business is quite straightforward.

At the very least, writing down weekly quotes for some money market NLF in a well-organized table will make you aware, on a regular basis, of how interest rates are trending. As you have seen, interest rates are an important indicator of what the stock market is doing. To know whether rates are going up or down, you need historical data so you can compare this week's value to what has happened in the past. You have that historical data at your fingertips in the money market table you keep updated. The cost to you is less than a minute a week to look the percent gain up in the Sunday paper and to write it down in your table.

Now for Level 3. If you choose to graph the data on that money fund you are tracking, the axes in Fig. 5-1 are suggested. The Y-axis scale is designed to accommodate all conceivable values that an NLF like MMP might take on over the 2-year period depicted on the X-axis. If the graph paper you use doesn't make the scales in Fig. 5-1 practical, then you can change the axes scaling to suit your requirements. The X-axis goes out to Week 110 to accommodate 2 years of data. You might decide to put more or less historical data on one graph. You can adjust that accordingly. The curve in the lower left corner of the graph is for MMP in Table 5-1 so that Week 1 is November 6, 1987. If you use the tables in Appendix D, Week 1 will have the date August 7, 1987.

For Level 4, you will be graphing MAVs. Figure 5-2 is a graph of MMP and its 26-MAV corresponding to Fig. 5-1. When calculating MAVs, use the second money NLF template to keep track of weekly sums. If you do this, then each week you only need add one number, subtract one number, and divide by 26. The time period "26 Weeks" is used because it gives a good idea of how interest rates are trending. Interpreting a MAV of interest rates is done in the opposite fashion of interpreting the S & P 500 and one of its MAVs. You dance when the raw data is below the MAV and cry when it is above the MAV for interest rates if you desire the stock market to go up. This is so because interest rates

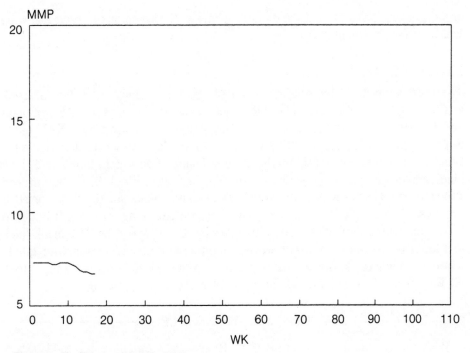

Fig. 5-1. To Track a Money NLF.

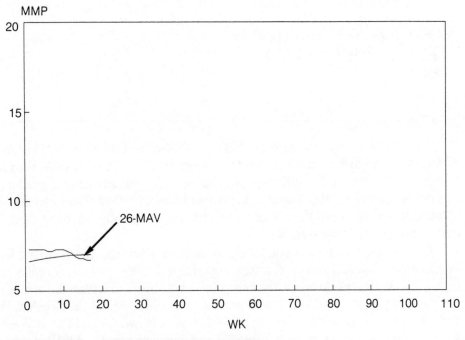

Fig. 5-2. MMP and 26-MAV (11/6/87 to 2/26/88).

are a contrary indicator of stock market behavior. (More detail on trend-following will be given in Chapter 6.)

STOCK FUNDS

The third template at the end of this chapter is for tracking stock NLFs. Look at the sample in Table 5-2. The difference between the money NLF template and the stock NLF template is that "Gain (%)" is replaced by "NAV ($)." Suppose that November 20, 1987 was the first Friday you wrote data down for Windsor. Since Week 1 is the earliest week in any of your data tables and since blank entries do you no good, you start Windsor off at Week 3. If you entered Weeks 1 and 2 in this table, you would have had no entries for the Windsor NLF for these 2 weeks. You'll discover that after you get going, you won't begin to track some fund until Week 105. In that case there would be 104 blank lines in a lot of blank tables. In other words, begin numbering Weeks in your tables when you begin tracking the NLF. Before you see the details for tracking a stock NLF, you need to understand the concept of cross-referencing.

──────────── **Table 5-2. Windsor NLF** ────────────

WK#	Date	NAV ($)	WK#	Date	NAV ($)
3	11/20/87	13.80	29	/ /	.
4	11/27/87	13.51	30	/ /	.
...	...	...	...	...	...
17	2/26/88	12.40	43	/ /	.
18	3/ 4/88	.	44	/ /	.
...	...	...	...	...	...
27	/ /	.	53	/ /	.
28	/ /	.	54	/ /	.

Should you want to compare the NAV of Windsor and the Gain of MMP for February 26, 1988 it is much easier to look for Week 17 in each table than it is to look for February 26, 1988 in each table. Besides this advantage, graphing is much less painful if the X-axis is in terms of weeks rather than in terms of actual dates. If you need the actual dates (and you frequently will need them), they appear in the tables anyway.

As an example, suppose you have just entered MMP and Windsor data for Week 44 (9/2/88). It is Sunday morning, September 4, 1988, and you are relaxing on the Labor Day weekend by reading your newsletter and jotting down a few numbers in your data tables. The urge hits to compare MMP this week with what it was doing 6 months ago. Since 6 months is 26 weeks and this is Week 44, you want to use Week 18 in Table 5-1 and compare it to the MMP number you just wrote down. After you do this comparison, you get another urge to see how Windsor has fared over the same 6-month period. All you need do now is flip to the Windsor data sheet, look for Week 18 and make a mental note of how that stock NLF did compared to this Friday's (Week 44's) closing value. This exercise should give you an idea of how much easier it is to cross-reference data tables using week numbers based on a common Week 1, instead of using the actual dates.

In the cross-referencing discussion so far, Tables 5-1 and 5-2 have been referred to but maybe you want to use a different date for your base week in all the tables you have. Tables 5-1 and 5-2 have the base week (which is always labeled Week 1) as November 6, 1987. For another example of base week numbering, suppose you use the MMP table in Appendix D. That has a base week of August 7, 1987. If you look at a calendar for 1987, November 6, 1987, becomes Week 14. The weeks labeled 17 in Tables 5-1 and 5-2 would then become Week 30. This is so because, just as you must add 13 to 1 to get 14, so you must add 13 to 17 to get 30. Once you get settled on a base week, the numbering scheme is easy.

The base week for all weekly graphs that go from Week 0 to Week 400 in this book is January 2, 1981. A list of all dates and week numbers is provided in Appendix D for Weeks 1 through 500. This information is provided for your convenience in case you want to go back and dig up more historical data. That way you needn't find a lot of calendars to figure out your numbering scheme.

Now that you are done figuring out your base week, it is time to get back to the details of tracking a stock NLF. For each stock NLF you track, the cost is 30 seconds per week because you already have the Sunday paper opened to the right part of the business section. (The first thing you did Sunday morning was to record the Gain percentage for your money market NLF.)

Each time you select a stock NLF to track, make one copy of the template, enter the proper weeks and dates on it, then copy that copy. Begin recording weekly values, keeping the two copies in separate locations. There is one twist to tracking a stock NLF you must be aware of or it can scare the wits out of you. That twist occurs when the fund goes "ex dividend." For example, Windsor went ex dividend in Week 7 in Table 5-2. That is the big reason there is a $1.40 difference between Week 3 and Week 17. Windsor did very well in this period. This NLF did not lose 10 percent, as you might first suspect when looking at Table 5-2. It gained 2 percent. Windsor had a distribution of almost $3. When tracking a stock NLF, you will need to keep track of ex dividend days and ex dividend amounts.

In the same manner that individual stocks distribute dividends and interest to their shareholders, so do stock NLFs. When an NLF takes money out of its NAV to pay this dividend and interest income, the event is called "going ex dividend." Depending on how often an NLF chooses to go ex, this occurs one to four times per year. For the week during which a fund goes ex, you will see a big "X" by your fund's acronym in the Sunday paper. Here is what you have to record in your table:

	WK#	Date	NAV ($)
	591	6/19/99	10.00
(Ex = $1.00) X	592	6/26/99	9.00

You should put an "X" next to the week number in your table to keep track of these very important and infrequent events. The fact that an NLF went from $10 per share to $9 per share in 1 week does not necessarily mean you lost $1 per share during that week.

The following table shows what happened. This will scare the uninitiated and confuse 90 percent of the rest of investors, so it is important to concentrate on it. Keep in mind that a good NLF will not perform any hocus-pocus on you. The fund is just distributing dividends and interest it has gained from the 70 or so stocks which are in its portfolio. In fact, you should think of the fund's portfolio as *your* portfolio. (How many friends do you have with 70 stocks in one of their portfolios?)

——————— **Table 5-3. Ex-Dividend Days** ———————

Date	NAV	What happened
6/19/99	10.00	Friday closing value of NLF
6/22/99	9.95	you lost 5 cents per share
6/23/99	9.95	you broke even
6/24/99	9.91	you lost 4 cents per share
6/25/99	9.94	you won 3 cents per share
6/26/99	9.00	you won 6 cents per share and were paid $1 in dividend and interest income

Now, look at Table 5-3. On Friday, June 26, 1999, your NLF gained 6 cents per share compared to its Thursday close. The NLF would have listed $10.00 = $9.94 + $.06 for its June 26 close if it had not gone ex dividend. Because it went ex dividend, it took the $1-per-share gained from its 70 stocks as interest and dividend income and put it in a special holding account. This account is for later distribution and for tax purposes. The fund closed at $9 = $10 − $1 per share instead of the $10 you would have expected.

Now to answer the question that is throbbing in your brain: What happens to my $1 per share distribution? Suppose you held 300 shares of this NLF. On Friday, June 19, your dollar balance in the fund would have been 300 shares times

$10 per share for a total of $3000. It is not true that on Friday, June 26, you wind up with 300 shares times $9 per share for a $2700 balance in the fund. You still have $3000. Here's why:

Your stock NLF reinvested that $300 = $3000 − $2700 for you by automatically buying you $300 worth of shares at $9 per share. This is an option widely used by NLF investors and is called "dividend reinvestment." You can choose the option of having your stock fund send you all or part of that $300 and reinvest the remainder in new shares. Many retired persons who have an account with an income NLF have the whole amount sent to them (or their credit union) to provide them with regular income.

Here is the arithmetic involved:

$$\$300 \div \$9 \text{ per share} = \ 33.333 \text{ new shares}$$
$$33.333 + 300 \text{ original shares} = \ 333.333 \text{ shares you own}$$
$$\text{after ex day}$$

So you went from 300 shares at $10 per share to 333.333 shares at $9 per share. Now watch this:

$$\text{June 19} \quad (300.000)(\$10) = \$3000$$
$$\text{June 26} \quad (333.333)(\$ 9) = \$3000$$

Many NLFs usually give the number of shares to three decimal places, so the above figures are realistic. Though each share decreased in value because the NLF went ex, you received more shares in the fund and still have the same dollar balance.

Because of ex days, the graph of your stock NLF will look something like Fig. 5-3. Just by looking at this graph, you can tell whether the fund went ex or took a big hit in a particular week. That is why you put the "X" to the left of the proper week number in your stock NLF's table. When you graph a stock NLF, it's helpful to place an "X" at the ex points on your graph also.

Because of ex days, MAVs should only be used for stock NLFs to smooth data and not to compare the fund's current performance with its past performance. The only way you can make such a comparison is to go through the trouble of computing the fund's total return. To perform this computation, you need the amount of the ex dividend payment and the NAV of the NLF on the day it went ex. You then plug those figures and a couple others into the following equation:

$$\frac{(\text{NAV \#???})[1 + (\text{amount of ex}) \div (\text{NAV on ex day})]}{\text{NAV \#???}}$$

The bottom "NAV #???" is the NAV of the week when you bought into the NLF. The top "NAV #???" is the NAV of the current week. The ex day will fall in between these two week numbers.

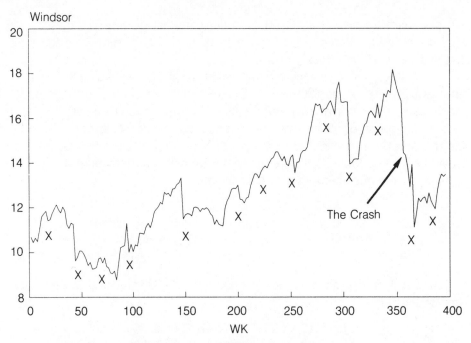

Fig. 5-3. Windsor with Ex-Dividends (Jan 1981 to Jul 1988).

Here is a sample calculation for a stock NLF over a 1-year period:

$$\frac{(\$10.00)[1 \ + \ (\$1.00) \div (\$9.00)]}{(\$8.95)}$$

$$[1.1173][1.1111] = 1.2415$$

Subtract 1 from this number, multiply by 100 percent, and you get a total return (or "gain") for your stock NLF of 24.15 percent for that particular time period. This result also says that, over that time period, you gained 11.73 percent from an increase in NAV and you gained 11.11 percent from dividends and interest income.

    Barron's puts out an issue every 3 months which contains an outstanding review of all stock NLFs. You can get this issue at a newsstand or get a subscription (see Appendix E). Another way to get these quarterly mutual fund issues is to go to a good library. Many libraries have hard copies or microfiches of *Barron's* going back several years. As of the writing of this book, the most recent issue of Barron's with the mutual fund review in it was dated August 8, 1988. On a weekly basis, *Barron's* has terrific NLF data, including ex dates and amounts. Barron's doesn't give the NAV on ex day, so you either get this out of a daily paper if you happen to catch it or from your stock NLF over the phone. In general, *Barron's* is an excellent source of data and articles on the stock and financial markets.

STOCK INDICES

Finally, let's go up to Level 5. If you already do Level 4 each week, it is not at all difficult or time-consuming to do Level 5, since it amounts to recording and graphing only two extra numbers. Data for the year beginning August 7, 1987 are given in Appendix D. These two stock market indices, the S & P 500 and the DJUA, are so important, it would be worth your while to track them. Use the same templates you use for stock NLFs.

The next two graphs (Figs. 5-4 and 5-5) present the S & P 500 and the DJUA over the last 7 years, along with one of their MAVs. For these graphs, Week 1 is January 2, 1981. The graphs in Figs. 5-6 and 5-7 show these indices with their MAVs but using only the 1 year of data in Appendix D. These two graphs will help you begin your own tracking of the S & P 500 and the DJUA. Note the room left at the right of the X-axis to show how this axis should be scaled for your own graphing.

When you see what TA professionals do in Chapters 6 through 11, you will get into the details of the graphs in Figs. 5-4 and 5-5. You should track these two stock indices only to get a good general idea of how the market is trending. Do not track them to develop your own switching strategy. Let your newsletter writer tell you when to be in or out of stock NLFs.

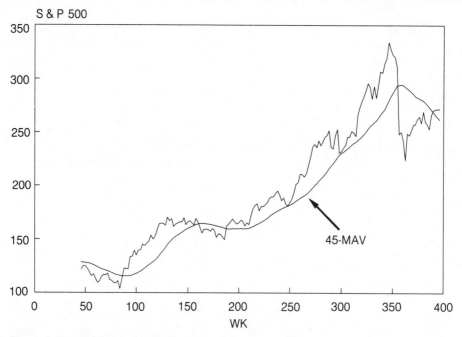

Fig. 5-4. S & P 500 and 45-MAV (Nov 1981 to Jul 1988).

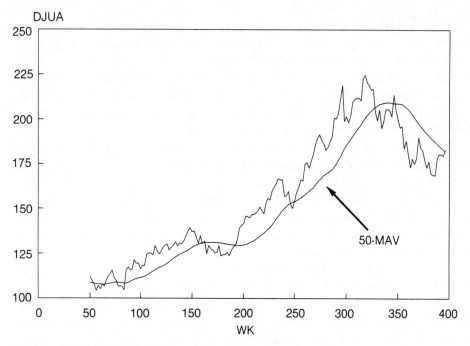

Fig. 5-5. DJUA and 50-MAV (Dec 1981 to Jul 1988).

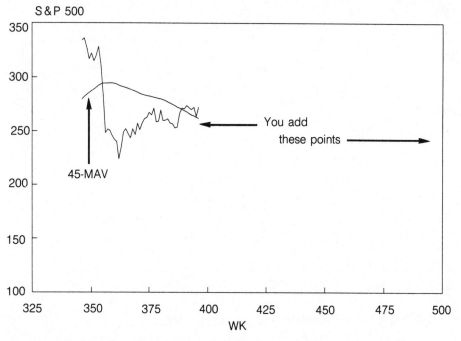

Fig. 5-6. Start Your Own S & P 500 (Aug 1987 to Jul 1990).

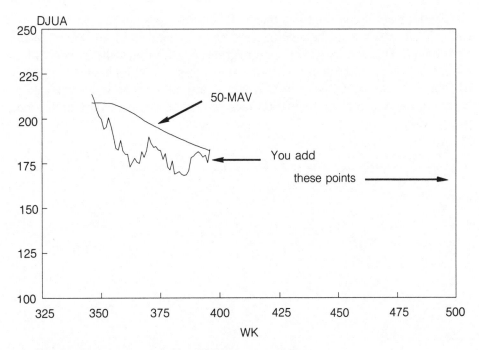

Fig. 5-7. Start Your Own DJUA (Aug 1987 to Jul 1990).

TIME, GAIN AND INFLATION

The length of the time period over which a stock NLF makes a particular gain is just as important as the magnitude of the gain itself. To understand this basic fact, ponder this question: Would you rather gain 20 percent over a 1-year period or over a 10-year period? Not much to ponder. Gain is really a rate, like miles per hour. Just as you wouldn't say "I was driving at 20 miles when I had to slam on my brakes," you wouldn't say "I made 20 percent while I was in that NLF." Synonyms for gain are total return, rate of return, and return on investment. Gain is meaningless unless the time period is stated.

For those of you who had trouble with the gain calculation at the end of the last section, here are the essential points. When the dust settled, the result of the sample gain calculation was that a stock NLF gained 24.15 percent in a 1-year period. There are two components to total return for any stock NLF: the gain due to an increase in NAV and the gain due to distributions (dividends and interest). For the 24.15 percent, NAV gain was 11.73 percent and distribution gain was 11.11 percent over that 1-year period. This leads to the following fact.

Averaged over the last 70 years, gains in NAVs and gains due to distributions have contributed about the same amount to overall gains in the stock market. The actual percentages are 53 percent for NAV gains and 47 percent for distributional gains. When the market is soaring, NAV gains predominate and distributions don't contribute as much. When the market is a bear, gains due to NAV increases lose their dominance and distributional gains come to the foreground. This is why growth and aggressive NLFs must be avoided when the market starts to go south. Growth and aggressive NLFs have a very small distributional component in their gain and so are not near as well cushioned as conservative NLFs when the market falls. To examine this in more detail, look at Fig. 5-8.

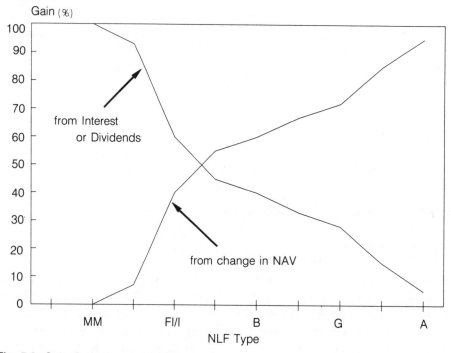

Fig. 5-8. Gain Components of NLFs.

As you proceed along the X-axis of the graph from left to right, you are traveling in the direction of increasingly aggressive NLFs. In this graph, MM stands for money NLF, FI/I stands for fixed-income/income NLF, B stands for balanced NLF, G stands for growth NLF, and A stands for aggressive NLF. Start with the risk-free money NLFs, hit the balanced NLFs in the middle, and wind up at the aggressive NLFs. Notice that money funds get all (100 percent) of their gain from distributions. In fact, all of a money NLF's gain comes from the interest part of its distributions. An aggressive fund has almost no distributions at all compared to other types of NLFs. Aggressive NLFs depend almost totally for their gains on increases in NAVs. When the market tumbles, NAVs fall like rocks—especially for aggressive NLFs. Those money funds just keep chugging along no matter what.

There is a rate of return you have grown to hate because it is almost always negative and totally unavoidable. It comes like a fox in the night and ravishes your gain just when your gain is flourishing. The name of this varmint is inflation. Another name used is the Consumer Price Index (CPI). But you can beat the CPI. As a matter of fact, that is a prime investment goal. You want to beat the CPI by a factor which is consonant with the risk you are willing to take. Values in Table 5-4 are derived from the 1988 issue of *The Handbook for No-Load Fund Investors*. For information on obtaining the *Handbook*, write to Sheldon Jacobs of the *No-Load Fund Investor* (see Appendix C for the address).

————— **Table 5-4. Beating the CPI** —————
(1978 to 1987)

NLF Type	Gain (%)	Factor
MM	9.97	1.56
FI/I	13.13	2.05
B	14.53	2.27
G	15.45	2.42
A	16.38	2.56
CPI	6.39	1.00
SPw	15.27	2.39
SPwo	10.02	1.57

To get a factor in this table, divide the gain of the NLF type your are interested in by the gain of the CPI. For the CPI itself, you get $1.00 = 6.39 \div 6.39$. The CPI is being used as the base because you dearly want to beat the CPI into submission—and then some. Table 5-4 covers the 10-year period from 1978–87.

The last two entries in Table 5-4 are titled "SPw" and "SPwo." These symbols mean, respectively, "S & P 500 with distributions reinvested" and "S & P 500 without distributions reinvested." Think of the SPw gain of 15.27 percent per year as what you would get if you had bought into an index fund and had all the distributions reinvested. The SPwo would be the yearly rate of return you would expect from an index fund if you had the fund send all your distributions to you instead of reinvesting them.

The "Beating the CPI" table is a really good table for doing your own financial planning. It says, for example, that if you went into the average money market NLF for 10 years starting in 1978 and stayed in that fund, you would have beat the CPI by 1.56, or more than 1½ times. That's pretty darn good for a safe way to invest. If you want more of a return but don't want to do too much to get it, put half your money in a money NLF and the other half in an index fund—you well might average out to beating the CPI by 1.98 times. This is almost twice the rate of inflation. You must remember though that Table 5-4 is only for planning purposes. There is no guarantee you will get the returns listed in that table.

If you do a little phone-switching based on what your newsletter tells you, you might be able to beat the CPI by factors of 2.50 to 4.00 over the long haul. If, for instance, inflation averages 6.39 percent over the next 10 years, you will need to average a gain of 25.56 percent per year to achieve a factor of 4.00. Good luck!

SUMMARY

Remember what happened to that person who took out a CD at the reputable bank? The important thing wasn't so much that he was being misled, but rather that he tracked his account so that he knew he was being misled. You will spend about 15 minutes a week on the average reading your newsletter. You must also spend the same amount of time each week tracking your investments. After you have been at it for a few weekends, there won't be anything to it. If you don't track your investments, you might well wind up getting burned.

One of the most frequently used ways to bamboozle investors is when advertising claims are made to the effect that stupendous gains (or maybe, just significantly better gains than you are now getting) can be made if you invest with the people who pay the advertisers. For switching between a good balanced NLF and its associated money NLF, you can expect over the long haul about 15- to 20-percent-per-year return on your investment. Most advertisements are careful to state that past returns are not indicative of future returns (probably because they break the law if they don't). They then go on to suggest that you can consistently make more than 20 percent per year. Watch out for those perfume-mouthed people. Even if they can prove that they made 100 percent last year, that doesn't mean that they won't lose 100 percent this year.

If someone asks you how your money market NLF is doing and either you can't answer at all or your answer is "Fine! I've got almost $5000 in there now," then you are not doing a good job of tracking. Your answer should be something like "I've been in it for a whole year and have realized a gain of 8.4 percent". Same goes for stock NLFs. For tracking purposes, it is not important how much money you have in an NLF, but it is quite important what the total return of that NLF is. A very important table in this chapter is Table 5-4. Use it for planning purposes and to compare how you are doing presently with what has gone on in the past.

Table 5-5. Money Fund Name is _____

WK#	Date	Gain (%)	WK#	Date	Gain (%)
	/ /	.		/ /	.
	/ /	.		/ /	.
	/ /	.		/ /	.
	/ /	.		/ /	.
	/ /	.		/ /	.
	/ /	.		/ /	.
	/ /	.		/ /	.
	/ /	.		/ /	.
	/ /	.		/ /	.
	/ /	.		/ /	.
	/ /	.		/ /	.
	/ /	.		/ /	.
	/ /	.		/ /	.
	/ /	.		/ /	.
	/ /	.		/ /	.
	/ /	.		/ /	.
	/ /	.		/ /	.
	/ /	.		/ /	.
	/ /	.		/ /	.
	/ /	.		/ /	.
	/ /	.		/ /	.
	/ /	.		/ /	.
	/ /	.		/ /	.
	/ /	.		/ /	.
	/ /	.		/ /	.

Table 5-6. Money Fund Name is _____

WK#	Date	Gain (%)	SUM	26-MAV
	/ /	.	.	.
	/ /	.	.	.
	/ /	.	.	.
	/ /	.	.	.
	/ /	.	.	.
	/ /	.	.	.
	/ /	.	.	.
	/ /	.	.	.
	/ /	.	.	.
	/ /	.	.	.
	/ /	.	.	.
	/ /	.	.	.
	/ /	.	.	.
	/ /	.	.	.
	/ /	.	.	.
	/ /	.	.	.
	/ /	.	.	.
	/ /	.	.	.
	/ /	.	.	.
	/ /	.	.	.
	/ /	.	.	.
	/ /	.	.	.
	/ /	.	.	.
	/ /	.	.	.
	/ /	.	.	.
	/ /	.	.	.

Table 5-7. Stock Fund or Index Name is _____

WK#	Date	Gain (%)	WK#	Date	Gain (%)
	/ /	.		/ /	.
	/ /	.		/ /	.
	/ /	.		/ /	.
	/ /	.		/ /	.
	/ /	.		/ /	.
	/ /	.		/ /	.
	/ /	.		/ /	.
	/ /	.		/ /	.
	/ /	.		/ /	.
	/ /	.		/ /	.
	/ /	.		/ /	.
	/ /	.		/ /	.
	/ /	.		/ /	.
	/ /	.		/ /	.
	/ /	.		/ /	.
	/ /	.		/ /	.
	/ /	.		/ /	.
	/ /	.		/ /	.
	/ /	.		/ /	.
	/ /	.		/ /	.
	/ /	.		/ /	.
	/ /	.		/ /	.
	/ /	.		/ /	.
	/ /	.		/ /	.
	/ /	.		/ /	.
	/ /	.		/ /	.

Table 5-8. Stock Fund or Index Name is _____

WK#	Date	Gain (%)	SUM	MAV
	/ /	.	.	.
	/ /	.	.	.
	/ /	.	.	.
	/ /	.	.	.
	/ /	.	.	.
	/ /	.	.	.
	/ /	.	.	.
	/ /	.	.	.
	/ /	.	.	.
	/ /	.	.	.
	/ /	.	.	.
	/ /	.	.	.
	/ /	.	.	.
	/ /	.	.	.
	/ /	.	.	.
	/ /	.	.	.
	/ /	.	.	.
	/ /	.	.	.
	/ /	.	.	.
	/ /	.	.	.
	/ /	.	.	.
	/ /	.	.	.
	/ /	.	.	.
	/ /	.	.	.
	/ /	.	.	.
	/ /	.	.	.

6

Market Timing
Using Trends

SIMPLE MAVs WERE INTRODUCED IN CHAPTER 4. THESE MAVs are "SIMPLE" because they are the easiest ones to understand. In fact, the term, *simple moving average*, is actually the name used by technicians to describe these kinds of MAVs. Many successful investment strategies are based on simple MAVs.

A trend is just a graph of some data along with a MAV of that data. A trend tells you whether or not the market or your NLF is strong. This strength depends on whether or not the actual data is above or below one of its MAVs. In this chapter you will explore trends.

Trends are one of the most basic concepts in TA. In order to get the most out of trend following you will need to delve a little more deeply into MAVs. You will look at what it means to weight MAVs and how this process of weighting is used by technicians for predicting market behavior. But our old friend, the simple MAV, is also a sound basis for some good TA. Trend following pays off. For example, the *Telephone Switch Newsletter* is a trend-following letter. When switching between a stock NLF and a money NLF using a good trend, it is possible to beat the Buy/Hold strategy by a significant amount.

There are many different trends you can follow, so the question arises: Which trend is best? Trends will be used to define switching strategies and those strategies will be evaluated to see which one gives the best gain over a certain time period. It is really very easy. The strategy will tell you when to buy into a stock NLF and when to sell that stock NLF and put your money in a money NLF. This is basically all there is to NLF switching: do what the trend tells you to do.

71

WEIGHTED MAVs

Weighting is the multiplication of actual data points by some numbers which fall between 0 and 1. The first set of numbers consists of real data on something like the S & P 500. The second set of numbers, "the weights," comes from a technician's imagination. The only restriction put on these weights is that they be greater than zero but less than one and that they add up to one. Data are weighted because weighting makes trends more sensitive to what is occurring in the more recent real data. Some examples will give you a feel for how weighted MAVs are calculated.

Recall the example in Chapter 4 in which a 12 month MAV of your MMP balance was graphed along with the actual balance. You might have wondered why a 6-month or an 18-month or even a 24-month MAV wasn't used. The reason is that the yearly average of MMP values seemed better than other averages from a fundamental point of view. Six months seemed just too short and the other two periods seemed too long. If the 12-month MAV didn't work for you in practice, you would have tried a different period. But, to begin with, 12 months seemed like a good period from which to gauge your current MMP balance. The 12-MAV acts as a gauge which warns you of critical points. Weighting a MAV can make a more sensitive gauge.

Why weight? Because, when looking back in time, it makes sense to give more consideration (weight) to more recent data. The simple MAV doesn't do this. If you calculate a simple weekly 45-MAV for the S & P 500, you are assigning just as much weight to an S & P 500 closing value from 45 weeks ago, as you are to this week's value. It can be reasoned fundamentally that more recent data has a greater effect on what will happen in the near future than data further in the past has. Of course, past data still does have some effect, so it is a good idea to use a lot of weeks (not just the most recent ones) when calculating a MAV.

————Table 6-1. Weight an S & P 500 5-MAV.————

WK	S & P 500	Weight	Weighted Data
351	314.86	0.10	31.49
352	320.16	.10	32.02
353	328.07	.20	65.61
354	311.07	.20	62.21
355	282.70	.40	113.08
Sum	1556.86	1.00	304.41

Example 1

Look at the situation in Table 6-1 (data are from Appendix D):

Please note that you needn't follow along with a calculator. Just get the feel for what is going on here. If the following arithmetic does not bedazzle you, then you can understand how a weighted MAV is calculated. Once you have a feel for that, you can ignore the arithmetic and concentrate on graphs of MAVs to visualize what is going on with the numbers. Remember that the flow of the graph is important and not the results of calculations. Here are the calculations for the "Weighted Data" column in Table 6-1:

$$\begin{array}{llll}
\text{WK 351 gives} & (314.86)(0.10) & = & 31.49 \\
\text{WK 352 gives} & (320.16)(0.10) & = & 32.02 \\
\text{WK 353 gives} & (328.07)(0.20) & = & 65.61 \\
\text{WK 354 gives} & (311.07)(0.20) & = & 62.21 \\
\text{WK 355 gives} & (282.70)(0.40) & = & 113.08
\end{array}$$

You have weighted with unequal weights and obtained a weighted 5-MAV for the S & P 500 of 304.41. The fifth data point (this is the one for Week 355 which is the most recent week in the calculations) carries 40 percent of the weight, the fourth and third data points carry 20 percent of the weight, and the first two data points carry 10 percent of the weight a piece. Remember that the idea is to put the heaviest weight on the most recent data. To calculate the weighted 5-MAV for Weeks 352 through 356, the same technique is applied to the five S & P 500 values for these weeks (see Table 6-2). Now apply the same calculation procedure used on Table 6-1 to this table and obtain the weighted 5-MAV for Week 356.

——— Table 6-2. Go On to the Next Five WK Period ———

WK	S & P 500	Weight	Weighted Data
352	320.16	0.10	32.02
353	328.07	.10	32.81
354	311.07	.20	62.21
355	282.70	.20	56.54
356	248.22	.40	99.29
Sum	1490.22	1.00	282.87

Example 2

Now you will look at Example 1 using a different set of weights. Notice that the sum of the weighted data in Table 6-3 is the simple 5-MAV. This happens because all five weights are equal. This is by far the most frequent use of MAVs in practice. Here you attach equal importance to all data points. All five weights are 0.20 or 20 percent.

——— **Table 6-3. Calculate a Simple 5-MAV** ———

WK	S & P 500	Weight	Weighted Data
351	314.86	0.20	62.97
352	320.16	.20	64.03
353	328.07	.20	65.61
354	311.07	.20	62.21
355	282.70	.20	56.54
Sum	1556.86	1.00	311.36

Example 3

For a last example, look at the S & P 500 and two of its MAVs. One MAV will be the old standby, the 45-MAV (it is a simple MAV). The other MAV will be a weighted 45-MAV using the weights given in Table 6-4. You already know how the simple 45-MAV is calculated. For the weighted MAV, you multiply the actual values of the S & P 500 by the 45 weights given in Table 6-4 before you add them all up. This gives a weighted 45-MAV for the S & P 500. Again, details of all calculations won't be provided because that would only cloud the issue.

Weeks in this table are numbered from 1 to 45. Just like in Example 1, the week at the bottom of the table and its weight (Week 45 with weight of 0.20) correspond to the most recent week of data. The weight at the top of the table (for Week 1 we have 0.01 for a weight) corresponds to the data point furthest in the past—in this case, about 10 months ago.

——— **Table 6-4. Weight a 45-MAV** ———

WK	Weight	WK	Weight
1	0.01	41	.10
2	.01	42	.10
...	...	43	.10
39	.01	44	.10
40	.01	45	.20

Suppose you want to apply these weights to Weeks 320 through 364 of the S & P 500 to give a weighted 45-MAV for Week 364. Begin by multiplying the S & P 500 data point furthest in the past (Week 320) by the topmost weight in the table:

$$\text{Week 320 gives } (279.70)(0.01) = 2.797$$

The same weight (0.01 or 1 percent) is used for the first 40 weeks. For the next four weeks, use the weight 0.10 and, for the last or most recent week (Week 45 in the table), use 0.20. Week 364 in the data will get this weight of 20 percent, Weeks 360 through 363 will each get 10 percent of the weight. All the weights add up to 1.00 (or 100 percent):

40 weights at 1 percent is 40 percent

4 weights at 10 percent is 40 percent

1 weight at 20 percent is 20 percent

The easy way to do this calculation would have been to add up the first 40 S & P 500 values first and take 40 percent of that sum. Then add up the next four S & P 500 values and take 40 percent of that sum. Then take 20 percent of the most recent S & P 500 value. Add those three numbers up and you get the same result you would if you did all 45 calculations independently of one another.

Enough messy arithmetic! Technicians use computers to do those calculations. The gist of a situation is not a lot of numbers in a table and laborious calculations on those numbers. What is important is the underlying meaning of those numbers and calculations. To get at this meaning you make those numbers vanish by picturing them in a graph. From those weighted 5-MAV calculations, you got the basic idea of how to arrive at a weighted MAV. The same method of calculating applies to a 45-MAV or a 4500-MAV, to the DJUA, your monthly money NLF balance, or any other real data you want to weight. The set of weights is not sacred. No one has a magic set of weights which gives the best buy or sell signals for the stock market.

My PC didn't feel taxed at all when it did the calculations for Fig. 6-1, but my brain would have been bored, my right index finger would be sore from entering all those numbers, and I most certainly would have made mistakes punching thousands of numbers into my hand calculator.

Whenever the S & P 500 crosses over one of its 45-MAVs in Fig. 6-1, it either falls below or rises above that MAV. If it falls below a MAV, then a sell signal is generated. If the S & P 500 rises above a MAV, then a buy signal is generated. With a 45-week MAV of a stock market index, there is not much rising above or falling below going on. This means buy and sell signals are quite infrequent, which is the way it should be. If a shorter-length MAV is used, say a 5-MAV, or if 99 percent of the weight is put on the last data point of a MAV, then buying and selling is done much more frequently. This gets you caught in a "whipsaw." More often than not, selling your stock NLF when the market is going up and buying into your stock NLF when the market is caving in. Frequent buy or sell signals are, 99 times out of 100, very bad news.

The region indicated in Fig. 6-1 has been exploded to obtain Fig. 6-2. This graph demonstrates a couple of important points. The two 45-MAVs generate buy or sell signals at different weeks. This means you would buy or sell your

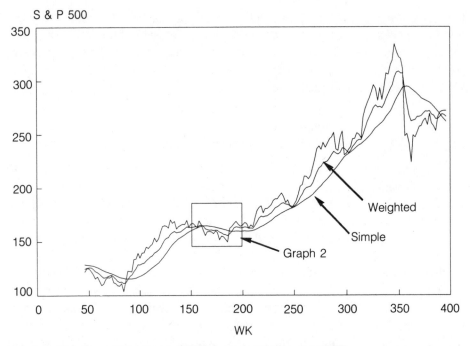

Fig. 6-1. Simple and Weighted 45-MAVs (Nov 1981 to Jul 1988).

stock NLF at different times, depending on which MAV you used. Also notice that the weighted MAV reacts more quickly than the simple MAV. A weighted MAV will generally give earlier buy or sell signals than a simple MAV of the same length. Weighted MAVs *are* more sensitive to market conditions than are simple MAVs but this doesn't make weighted MAVs superior to simple MAVs. Superiority can only be judged on a case by case basis. Besides, you should never base a Buy/Sell strategy on just one moving average! That is like buying a house because its basement doesn't leak—ignoring cost, school system, number of bedrooms, and so on.

The B's in any graph from now on will stand for "Buy into a stock NLF" and the S's will mean "Sell that stock NLF and buy into a money NLF."

Right now you need to get a preview of strategy evaluation, so look back at Fig. 6-2 for a moment. Just get a feel that each MAV does generate different times to buy and sell a stock NLF. (There will be more in a later section in this chapter about how to determine which MAV gives the best buy and sell signals.) To see how a switching strategy is evaluated, specific NLFs must be used. For purposes of explanation, the stock NLF used will be the Vanguard Windsor fund and the money NLF used will be Vanguard MMP. The simple 45-MAV in Fig. 6-1 says to be in Vanguard Windsor when the S & P 500 is above this MAV, and to be in Vanguard MMP when the S & P 500 falls below this MAV. Define a switching strategy in the same way for the weighed 45-MAV. Buy/Hold is the

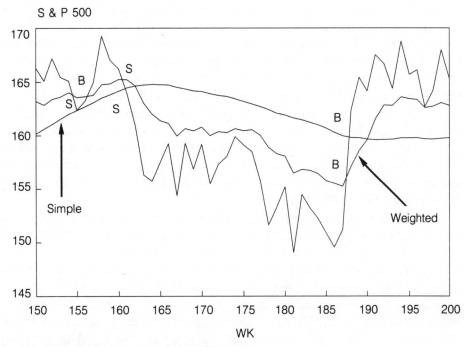

S & P 500

Fig. 6-2. MAV Explosion (Nov 1983 to Oct 1984).

strategy wherein you don't switch at all, you just buy shares in Windsor and stay in (or hold onto) Windsor for the whole time period of the two MAV strategies.

The Buy/Hold strategy is always the strategy to beat when switching because, if you can't do significantly better than Buy/Hold, you shouldn't bother switching. Your gain, averaged on a yearly basis, for the simple, weighted and Buy/Hold strategies are, respectively, 24.5 percent, 24.0 percent and 20.8 percent. Compare these with Buy/Hold in MMP, which yields an average of 8.7 percent per year. In this case, simple and weighted MAVs appear to perform almost equally well—or do they? The simple MAV calls for only four switches in the 352 week period involved, but the weighted MAV calls for 20 switches! For this reason, the simple MAV wins hands down over the weighted MAV.

How does one decide which weights to use? Professional weighters initially decide on weights by using gut-feeling. Some of these pros clothe their gut-feeling in something they call "exponential smoothing." What these weighters use is not, in a mathematical sense, exponential smoothing and some, not all, of these pros use the term because it is good show biz to throw jargon like that around. An "exponential smoothing constant" is selected (by gut feeling of course) between 0 and 1. For example, suppose 0.3 is selected. The 0.3 weight means that 30 percent of all the weight is given to the most recent data point and that a 1.0 − 0.3 = 0.7 weight, or 70 percent, is distributed equally over the rest of the data points. If this smoothing constant doesn't seem to work, then it is replaced by another constant. Exponential smoothing is fine, but it is only one of many ways to mathematically smooth a graph.

In other words, just as you would do, professional weighters try different sets of weights and select the one that appears to work best. When you hear someone state "... and the 200-day moving average says ...," don't accept it like the Sermon On the Mount. If you hear a reasonable sounding justification for a 39-week moving average like "it is used because it represents three-quarters of data," don't believe there is some mysterious significance to using three-quarters of data. Hopefully, the technician is using 39 Weeks of data to generate a buy or sell signal for you because, based on years of weekly data, he or she has found that the 39-MAV works better than the 1st through the 38th and the 40th through the 100th MAVs.

One last note. It is perfectly all right when a technician uses a MAV expressly for the purpose of smoothing data and not to generate buy or sell signals. Used this way, the right MAVs can give a good indication of when the market is strong or weak but buy and sell signals are given by other means at the technician's disposal. In other words, it's perfectly fine to use MAVs for explanatory purposes, even though they aren't used to actually generate buy or sell signals. For example, the DJUA and its 50-MAV is an extremely good indicator of market conditions. That is why, in Chapter 5, I suggested that you track the DJUA on a weekly basis. Don't use the DJUA/50-MAV combination as the sole basis for your buy or sell signals. Risking part of your investment capital on just one indicator is always dangerous. On the other hand, suppose you didn't use MAVs at all. How could you tell if the market is acting strongly or weakly? Without MAVs as a gauge, you would have no substantial, factual idea of what is going on.

TRENDS

So far in this book you have heard many times that, in order to understand 90 percent of what professional technicians do, all you need understand is the concept of trend-following. Pros use many methods along with trend-following. But following trends is by far the method used most often. To get a really sound idea of what technical newsletter writers do for you, all you need a feel for is how trend following works. The graph in Fig. 6-3 shows what a trend looks like. Look familiar? A trend is just a graph of the actual data along with one of its MAVs. You will now look at what trend-followers do, though of course, they all don't use the DJIA and its simple 39-MAV. From now on, unless weighting is specifically mentioned, understand that simple MAVs are the ones being discussed.

When the graph of a stock index lies above one of its MAVs, trend-followers say that the market is strong. When that index falls below its MAV, they say the market is weak. When the market is strong trend-followers tell you to be in a stock NLF. When the market is weak, you are told to exit to a money NLF.

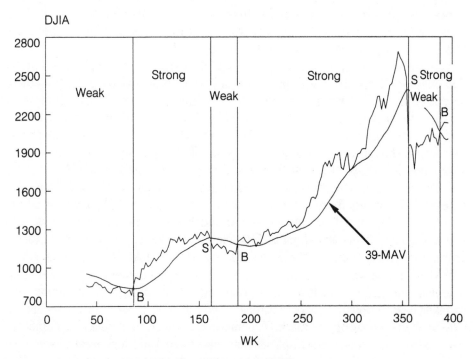

Fig. 6-3. The DJIA and 39-MAV (Oct 1981 to Jul 1988).

The trend in Fig. 6-3 tells you when to be in or out of a stock NLF, based on the relationship between the DJIA and its 39-MAV. In Chapter 5 you saw a graph of the S & P 500 and its 45-MAV. That graph defined another trend. The DJUA and its 50-MAV defines yet another trend. None of these three trends agree exactly on when to be in or out of the market. Seems like there are a lot of trends out there. That's right! You will get more details on trend evaluation in the next section but, for now, a little more discussion on trends is in order.

Absolutely no one has a magic trend which will always have you in a stock NLF at the right time and a money NLF at the right time. This is true for all TA methods (and fundamental methods), so a word of caution is in order here. In advertising hype, when you hear the phrase "proprietary method," a red flag of warning should flash in your mind. Cross that advice-giver off your list, unless he or she has a good, long-term track record which has been verified impartially by a reputable third party.

Some trend-followers will vehemently state that they do not predict the future. To these trend-followers, people who predict the future (also called "projectors") are nothing more than crystal ball gazers. Trend-followers who say that they are not projecting what will happen in the stock market are lying to you because they—just like projectors—must peek into the future so that they can advise you about what to do with your money right now. You can't bet on a horse after the race is finished, so you are forced to predict which horse will win. Same thing goes for predicting what the market will do; in this case, however, there are two horses: a good stock NLF and a money NLF.

There are four reasons that some trend-followers want to emphasize (falsely) that they don't predict the future. The first reason is that they don't want to be put on the spot having to project, for example, what the DJIA will close at on the last trading day of 1989. They, like all but one out of several hundred others attempting this feat, would probably be quite far off the mark. Why should they stake their reputation on such a game? Their way out when asked such a question is to say "I follow trends and don't make projections."

The second reason trend-followers don't want to be associated with projectors is, even if a very good projector was asked "What will the DJIA close at on the last trading day of 1989," he or she would have to qualify that guess with something like "2400 plus or minus 240 points." No one can predict future values of the stock market right on the nose without a considerable amount of dumb luck.

Many times you will hear a technician (or a fundamentalist) asked that question, and that person is forced to respond with a number. That number will be taken dead seriously by a lot of listeners and can spell disaster for the technician if he or she is too far off the mark. Technicians, because they deal with numbers, are expected to be much more specific than fundamentalists. Just because someone refuses to predict future stock market values, doesn't mean, in some sense, that person is more cautious than someone else who does project those numbers. Nosterdamus himself couldn't come close to predicting the closing value of the DJIA in 1989! (*He* was a fundamentalist.)

The third reason that some trend-followers divorce themselves from projectors is because these trend-followers don't know how to mathematically project what the market will do. They are afraid that, if they claim projection prowess, they will be asked how they do the projecting. Projection takes a lot of math sophistication, scads of data, computers, and constant expert attention. Most trend-followers are not sophisticated enough mathematically, or don't want to take the trouble, if they are sophisticated, to do all that projection requires. Why should they? In practice, trend-following works as well as projecting. The *Telephone Switch Newsletter* and *The Mutual Fund Strategist* are trend-following letters. *The Mutual Fund Forecaster* and *Investech* rely heavily on forecasting techniques. Those are four of the top TA letters going.

The last reason some trend-followers try to shoot down projectors is because they want to put that part of their competition in a bad light. Suffice it to say that, whether you take the advice of a good trend-follower or a good projector, you will get your money's worth out of that newsletter. Neither type of technician has a monopoly on success in calling shots in the stock market.

The point about trend-followers versus projectors is that they both necessarily predict the future. One does it in a relatively simple mathematical way and the other one gets fancy. Either type can do a good job for you. (Did you receive your sample newsletter copies yet?) So when a trend-follower states, with smoke coming out of his ears, that he is not a projector, just laugh it off. He means no harm and, besides, he might be able to make you some money.

The trend-following newsletters mentioned above are written by Richard Fabian and Charlie Hooper . I have never known Mr. Fabian or Mr. Hooper to put down projectors, but I have heard other trend-followers do this. Hopefully, the great trend-followers-versus-projectors battle has been put to rest. You needn't ever become involved in it again. Ignore it and choose the newsletter which is best for you.

Trend-followers speak of things like "confirmation," "resistance level," and "support level." Graphically, these three concepts are easy to understand. When one trend, say the DJUA and its simple 50-MAV, says to buy before another trend, say the S & P 500 and its simple 45-MAV, then you wait for the S & P 500 trend to give a buy signal confirming the DJUA buy signal. Confirmation is just following that sage advice about using more than one trend upon which to base your investment strategy. Figure 6-4 gives an example of this confirmation between the S & P 500 and the DJUA.

Figure 6-5 shows what resistance and support levels might be for the DJIA. These levels can be defined by taking a MAV, in this case the 39-MAV, then adding and subtracting a percentage (here 6 percent) to the MAV. This produces two more curves, one 6 percent above the MAV and the other one 6 percent below the MAV. Just like when weights are determined by a technician for use with a particular market index, the percentage here is obtained by gut-feeling, and a nice round number is used. Technicians wouldn't use a figure of 5.78 percent when describing to you how they define their resistance and support levels.

No matter what definition is used for resistance and support levels, the idea is that there is a tendency for the stock index in question to remain between the boundaries shown in Fig. 6-5 unless something wonderful or awful happens. If something awful happens, then the stock index will fall below its level of support. If something wonderful happens, then the stock index will rise above its level of resistance. These levels are not the endall of technical analysis. They, like the original MAV from which they are derived, are general gauges of market strength and must be taken with a grain of salt.

STRATEGY AND EVALUATION

Simply put, a strategy is a plan. Way back in the Introduction to this book, it was stated that, when it comes to investing, you need a plan. What a switching strategy boils down to in its most elemental form is giving you the answer to one question week-by-week: Should I be in a stock NLF this week or in a money NLF? By anyone's standard, a switching strategy is a plan, because such a

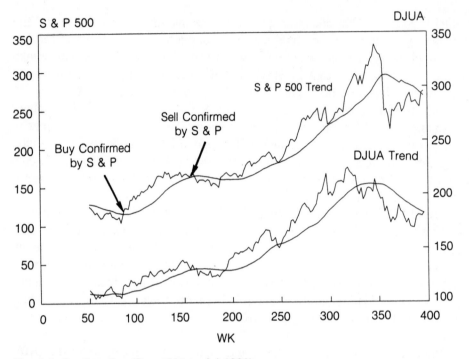

Fig. 6-4. Confirmation (Dec 1981 to Jul 1988).

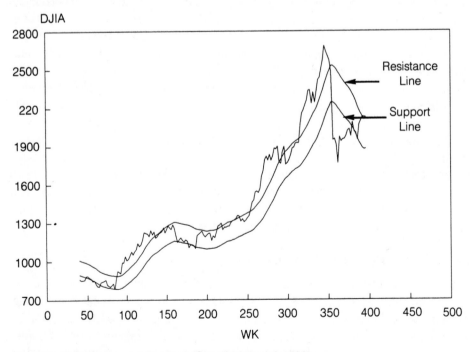

Fig. 6-5. Resistance and Support (Oct 1981 to Jul 1988).

strategy accomplishes what a plan accomplishes. A plan allows you to take action now based on what you think is most likely to happen in the future.

The act of using a switching strategy to be in stock NLFs at the right time is called "timing the market." Timing does not have to be right on the nose to be successful. You saw that this is true when you followed the example shown in Fig. 6-1. In that example, the 45-MAV of the S & P 500 defined a switching strategy which gained 24.5 percent per year compared to the Buy/Hold strategy which gained 20.8 percent per year for the 6-year period. The 45-MAV trend didn't have you in the Windsor NLF only when the fund was going up in value, nor did it have you out of the Windsor fund when that NLF was falling in value. Perfect market timing, like predicting what the DJIA will be at the end of 1989, is impossible to accomplish. The lesson of this example is that you don't have to be right on the money all of the time. It is only necessary to be right most of the time.

Besides the aspect of timing, there are two other parts which make up a good investment strategy. You have already seen how to choose a good NLF. Along with timing and NLF selection, you need to know how to allocate your money between several NLFs. This third aspect is called "making a portfolio of funds" and it will be covered in Chapter 12.

Timing is the trickiest part of investing, whether or not the investment vehicle is NLFs. Because market timing is the hardest part of investing, you will need the help of a professional. Some pros time the market by using "pure market timing." This means that they tell you either to have 100 percent of your money in stock NLFs or to have 100 percent of your money in money NLFs. Another way to time the market is by the *percent allocation method.*

If a letter writer advises you to be 80 percent in stock NLFs and 20 percent in money NLFs, then he or she is practicing the percent allocation method of market timing. Based upon TA practiced by this type of newsletter writer, he or she feels that it is a pretty good time to be heavily invested in the market, but that a 100-percent stock position is not warranted. If technical conditions improve, such a letter writer might in the future have you 100 percent (or "fully") invested. If conditions weaken instead, this type of newsletter writer might tell you to be 20 percent in stock NLFs and 80 percent in money NLFs. *Investech* practices this type of timing. Many other successful letters practice it too.

Whether a newsletter uses pure market timing or uses the percent allocation method, that newsletter is a timing newsletter. Because it is easier to understand what is going on with the pure market timing variety of NLF switching, that method will be used to explain how strategies are evaluated. Don't get the impression that pure market timing is better. Both types are equally successful. In fact, some newsletters practice both types of timing. Just be aware of the difference, and remember that the focus will be put on pure market timing in what follows so that you can get a firm grasp on how a strategy is evaluated.

You will now see how to evaluate and compare three investment strategies. To be able to compare any pair of strategies, two requirements must be met. First, the same stock and money NLFs must be used for each strategy. The two funds used in the following discussion are from the Vanguard group: Windsor and MMP. Second, the strategies must be compared over the same time period. The time period involved in the following discussion is December, 1981 through July, 1988. Three trends will be compared: the DJIA and its 39-MAV, the S&P 500 and its 45-MAV and the DJUA and its 50-MAV. Figures 6-6 through 6-8 show these trends with buy and sell points marked.

———— Table 6-5. DJIA/39-MAV Strategy ————

WK	Buy/Sell	WK	Buy/Sell
		161	Sell
69	Buy	188	Buy
70	Sell	206	Sell
71	Buy	207	Buy
73	Sell	355	Sell
86	Buy	388	Buy

Tables 6-5 through 6-7 show the switches dictated by these three strategies over the 346-week time period (about 6½ years). "Buy" means to switch into the Vanguard Windsor fund from MMP. "Sell" means to switch from Windsor into MMP.

————Table 6-6. S & P 500/———— 45-MAV Strategy

WK	Buy/Sell
87	Buy
161	Sell
188	Buy
355	Sell
389	Buy

Based on Tables 6-5 through 6-7, Table 6-8 gives the average yearly gains over those 346 weeks for the three trends in Figs. 6-6 through 6-8 and for the Buy/Hold strategy in Windsor and in MMP. This gives a total of five strategies. More frequent switching doesn't necessarily yield a significantly larger gain and, in fact, can decrease gain to the point where it is worse than buying and holding a good stock NLF. Table 6-8 is further verification of studies done by the *Hulbert Financial Digest.*

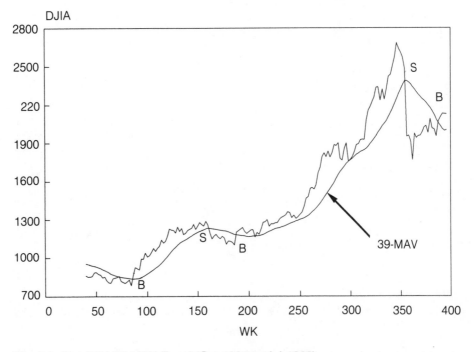

Fig. 6-6. The DJIA/39-MAV Trend (Oct 1981 to Jul 1988).

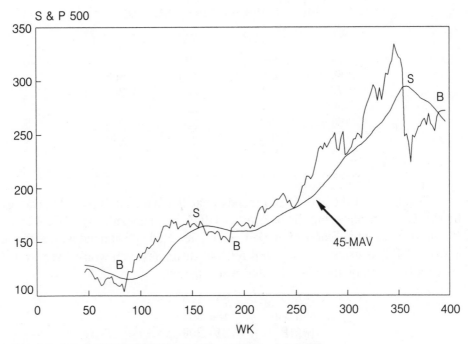

Fig. 6-7. S & P 500/45-MAV Trend (Nov 1981 to Jul 1988).

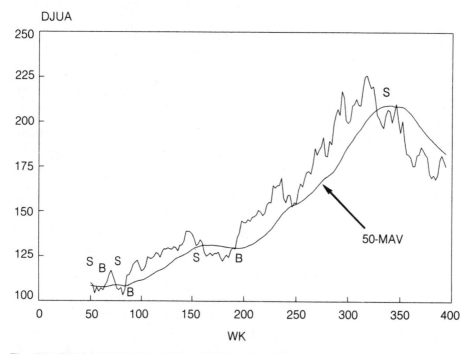

Fig. 6-8. DJUA/50-MAV Trend (Dec 1981 to Jul 1986).

──────── **Table 6-7. DJUA/50-MAV Strategy** ────────

WK	*Buy/Sell*	*WK*	*Buy/Sell*
54	Sell	194	Buy
65	Buy	246	Sell
77	Sell	249	Buy
86	Buy	328	Sell
160	Sell	346	Buy
161	Buy	348	Sell
163	Sell	396	Buy

The DJIA and the S & P 500 trends beat the Windsor Buy/Hold strategy by significant amounts, but the bellwether DJUA trend doesn't. The DJUA trend is still an excellent indicator of market conditions. Had you started with $10,000 in the S & P 500 strategy and both Buy/Hold strategies, you would have wound up with these amounts after the 346-week period:

S & P 500	$41,173
Windsor	$34,968
MMP	$17,209

———— **Table 6-8. Evaluation of Five Strategies** ————

Strategy	Number of Switches	Yearly Gain
DJIA	11	24.0%
S & P 500	5	23.7%
DJUA	14	20.3%
Windsor	0	20.7%
MMP	0	8.5%

Remember that gains given for the five strategies above are average yearly gains. Switching can beat Buy/Hold by a significant amount. Even though the S & P 500 beat Buy/Hold in Windsor by only 3 percent per year, you wind up with $6,205 more at the end of the 6-year period.

SUMMARY

Simple MAVs can define successful switching strategies, but so can weighted MAVs. Weighted MAVs place more emphasis on the more recent data points than do simple MAVs. Each type of MAV defines a trend. All a trend amounts to is the graph of actual values of some stock market data, along with a graph of some MAV of that same data. For every new MAV, a new trend is defined. Two different trends can give the same switching strategy if they choose the same points at which to get in and out of the market.

Any switching strategy can be evaluated by the gain it gives with respect to a specific stock NLF and a specific money NLF over a certain period of time. Two timing strategies can be compared only using the same NLFs and only over the same time period. When two switching strategies give about the same gain, choose the one that offers the fewest switches. Evaluating strategies is not a one-shot deal. Constant reevaluation is necessary to ensure that the best available strategy is being used. Of course, the best way to do your market timing is to use the advice of a newsletter pro, whether a trend-follower or a projector.

New strategies can be derived by either changing the length of a trend or by changing the weights of a trend. A strategy can also be a combination of two strategies. For example, take the S & P 500 45-MAV and the 50-MAV of the DJUA and use these two trends to confirm each other in a single strategy. Maybe the 50-MAV trend of the DJUA tells you to sell, but the trend of the S&P 500 and its 45-MAV tells you to hold on to your stock NLF. Just wait for the S&P 500 trend to confirm the DJUA trend before you take action. Like trends, resistance and support levels can be good gauges of market strength but, always remember, never base your switches on just one technical indicator.

7

How Money Affects
the Market

INDICES INCLUDE THE S & P 500, THE DJUA, THE 30-YEAR TREASURY BOND RATE, and so on. Technicians use indices and crunch years of data on them mathematically (as in calculating MAVs) to explain what the stock market is doing and to predict what it will be doing. Indices are the lifeblood of TA. You will look at the three broad categories of stock market indices in the next three chapters: monetary indices, volume indices, and price indices. When you are done, you will have a much better appreciation of what technicians do, and you will have a better understanding of how the stock market works. You will also be prepared to go off on your own and learn even more about the market. Everything you've learned so far about TA will come to bear in the next three chapters.

Indices will be presented in a uniform fashion. Fundamental considerations will be covered first. (What is the federal discount rate? How is it useful in explaining market behavior?) Next, technical aspects will be presented. (What is the technician's perspective of the federal discount rate? How does the federal discount rate correlate with market behavior?) Finally, a discussion of an index will be given, using graphs of recent data. You are going to see how the better pros will do TA for you.

One of the most important observations you will make is how intimately fundamental analysis and good TA are connected. You will get insight into how TA is accomplished by some of the best pros. You will wind up being able to understand the market itself and being able to evaluate, on your own, other methods you come across in magazines and newsletters, on TV, or just talking with friends. Many of the acronyms used in the following presentations do not appear in the Glossary (Appendix A) because these acronyms are meant only for temporary use in specific sections of these chapters. For example, FI stands for the "Pseudo Fosback Index." If an index is not discussed outside the section in which it is introduced, its acronym will not be in the Glossary.

PSEUDO FOSBACK INDEX

You have assets, some of which are liquid and some of which aren't. *Liquid* means that you can convert that particular asset to cash readily. For example, if you live in Michigan and have 100 returnable bottles at 10 cents apiece, you could convert them to $10 by going to the supermarket and cashing them in. Your car, even if you own it outright, isn't liquid. There is a process you go through to convert this asset to cash: find a buyer, settle on a price, go to the Secretary of State's office, sign papers, and put the cashier's check you receive in your account.

Stocks aren't liquid when compared to cash. (By "cash," I mean short-term, or "overnight," CDs.) Everyday, NLFs need cash on hand to pay for stock transactions or to redeem shares for their shareholders. Those two facts cause funds to keep a proportion of their assets in cash (or liquid), instead of investing those assets in stocks. When a shareholder says "send me $500," the fund can't send $500 worth of stock—it must send the money. This proportion of cash on hand is given in percentage form and is called the *liquid asset ratio* of a fund, because as opposed to stocks the fund owns for you, this percentage is the liquid portion of your fund. When averaged over all stock funds, this ratio is called the LAR. The more cash all these funds have on hand, the more cash they have to invest in the stock market. The rest of their money is already in the stock market.

When a fund has millions of dollars sitting on the sidelines in the form of liquid assets waiting to be called into action, the fund doesn't want to be getting 0 percent interest on that money. As a result, the fund invests this money in "short-term" interest-bearing certificates, most often in something called *commercial paper* (CP). The fund might put $10 million in CP at a 6.5-percent annual rate for 90 days and receive $162,500. The fund might also invest a few million dollars with a bank overnight at 5.5 percent on a yearly basis. This nets the fund about $440 for letting the bank use its money overnight.

CP gives lower yields than longer-term paper, like 30-year treasury bonds: but even low rates of return on millions of dollars tend to mount up appreciably. Short-term "paper" is used because the fund can't have its money tied up too long and still be able to buy stocks and redeem shares.

The proportion of cash NLFs have waiting to be invested in stocks has averaged out over the years to be seven-tenths of what the going CP interest rates are at any given time. The other component of cash on hand (assets held in cash for redemptions) has averaged about 3.2 percent of funds' assets over the years. On the other hand, the actual amount of cash that funds have on hand at a given time is the LAR itself. Funds can't predict exactly how much cash they need, so the LAR differs from what is actually required. Hopefully, for stock prices, the difference between the LAR and the cash funds need to carry on daily business is positive.

The pseudo Fosback Index is:

$$FI = LAR - [3.2 + (7/10)CP]$$

Where:

$$LAR = \text{liquid asset ratio}$$
$$CP = \text{commercial paper rate}$$
$$3.2 = \text{percent cash on hand}$$
$$\text{for redemptions}$$
$$7/10 = \text{historical fraction of CP}$$
$$\text{on hand for stock purchases}$$

For example, when the LAR is 10.2 percent and the CP rate is 8 percent, the FI is 1.4 percent because:

$$
\begin{aligned}
FI &= 10.2 - [3.2 + (0.70)(8.0)] \\
&= 10.2 - [3.2 + 5.6] \\
&= 10.2 - 8.8 \\
&= 1.4
\end{aligned}
$$

The word "pseudo" is used because the 3.2 percent and 7/10 change over time. The above equation essentially gives what is commonly accepted as the Fosback Index.

In the case of a particular fund with assets of $100 million, then cash on hand for:

1. *redemptions* is (0.032)($100 mill) = $3.2 mill
2. *stock purchases* is (0.056)($100 mill) = $5.6 mill
3. *mad money* in excess of numbers 1 and 2 above is (0.014)($100 mill) = $1.4 mill

The amounts above represent just one fund out of about 1000, so that excess cash on hand to buy stocks and drive prices up is:

$$(1000 \text{ funds})(\$1,400,000) = \$1,400,000,000$$

You can see how things mount up!

Suppose the LAR increases to 10.6 percent while the CP rate decreases to 7 percent. Then the FI shoots up:

$$
\begin{aligned}
FI &= 10.6 - [3.2 + (0.70)(7.0)] \\
&= 10.6 - [3.2 + 4.9] \\
&= 10.6 - 8.1 \\
&= 2.5
\end{aligned}
$$

This is very bullish because it means that mutual funds (which have about 20 percent of the action in all stock markets combined) have, on the average, more cash to buy stocks with than they expected to need. When you consider that there are hundreds of billions of dollars in mutual funds generally, 2.5 percent of this amount waiting to be invested is nothing to sneeze at.

Bearishness occurs when the LAR decreases as the CP is increasing. This causes FI to decrease:

$$
\begin{aligned}
FI &= 8.5 - [3.2 + (0.70)(9.0)] \\
&= 8.5 - [3.2 + 6.3] \\
&= 8.5 - 9.5 \\
&= -1.0
\end{aligned}
$$

You can see that, when FI turns negative, funds must sell stocks, or at least refrain from buying stocks, so that they can pay for redemptions. If FI = 0.0, then mutual funds on the average have exactly the right amount of cash on hand.

Norman Fosback, president of the newsletter *Market Logic*, developed the real Fosback Index. The real FI is one of the best overall technical indicators available. This doesn't mean that you should rush out, get a lot of LARs and CPs for the last several years, and base your whole investment philosophy on this one index. It is never wise to do that, no matter how good an index is. When FI is bigger than 0, you should be in a stock NLF because this means, on the average, funds have an excess of cash over and above what they typically need for redemptions. When this occurs, funds have extra cash to buy stocks with. If the FI turns negative (or less than zero), you should be invested in a money NLF because funds will probably need to cash in stocks in order to make redemptions.

Figure 7-1 shows a graph of the Pseudo Fosback Index for May 1982 to July 1988, with MMP interest rates replacing CP rates. MMP and CP are almost exactly the same mathematically, so MMP can be used to replace CP. This replacement shows you how useful tracking your money NLF can be. (Your money NLF represents a lot more than what you are making in it; it represents all shorter-term interest rates quite well.) Switching based on the FI gained an average of 17.0 percent per year, while Buy/Hold gained 22.3 percent. As usual, we are using Windsor and MMP for switching. Buy/Hold in MMP for this time period was 8.2 percent per annum.

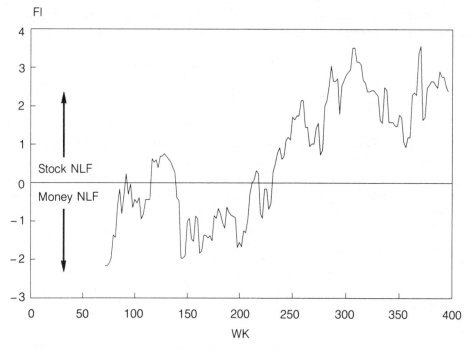

Fig. 7-1. Psuedo Fosback Index (May 1982 to Jul 1988).

I purposely chose the FI as the first index to show you because it beautifully demonstrates how one of the best technicians approaches the problem of how to understand the market. Fundamentals are nicely linked with technical aspects in the FI. The LAR by itself is not enough to explain what the market is doing. The important factor is the link between the LAR and the CP rate. Fine-tuning is done with the constants 3.2 and 7/10. This is important, because no matter how impressive fundamentals by themselves may be, they aren't worth much unless you can attach numbers to them and unambiguously determine what to do with your money.

Fundamentalists tend to shy away from equations to begin with and would not go through the trouble of finding the constants 3.2 percent and 7/10. These constants took some work to come by, and that work was of a technical nature. In addition to all this, fundamentalists would not go out of their way to mathematically verify that the FI really works. In conclusion, though the FI is based on fundamentals, it requires TA to make it useful.

FEDERAL DISCOUNT RATE

Suppose that a bank you do business with requires a minimum deposit of $200 for free checking. The bank pays you 0 percent on any money in your checking account, even on money in excess of $200. Being astute, you don't want to have one penny more than $200 in your checking account. On the other hand, you don't want your balance to fall below $200 because you would lose that free checking. This calls for some financial planning on your part.

Your paycheck is deposited on Friday and you have $700 in your account then. You pay a few bills, take out some pocket money, and still have $300 left in your account. Based on some projections, you feel that you won't need to write any more checks until next payday, so you mail a check for $100 to your favorite money NLF in order to make some interest on that $100. This leaves the minimum $200 in your checking account.

Oops! Best laid plans and all that. You soon find you have to write an unexpected check for $50. The bank is only too glad to make you a quickie loan at 5.5 percent, but there's all that paperwork, parking, and waiting in line. A friend will loan you the $50 at 6 percent with no trouble (your friend is just as astute as you are). To keep the free checking, you borrow $50 from the friend until next payday. It is usually less messy to arrange for a quickie loan from a friend than it is to go to a bank.

The Federal Reserve System (FRS) is *the bank* for certain important banks across the country. View these banks as friends of one another. The Fed (that is, the FRS) requires these important banks to keep a reserve requirement on deposit at a regional FRS bank (roughly equivalent to the $200 minimum for free checking). This reserve requirement is equal to a fixed proportion of cash which a bank has to lend. Since banks make money lending money and the reserve required by the FRS gains them 0 percent, they want to come as close to that minimum required reserve as they can without going under it at accounting time.

Accounting time is close of business each Wednesday. When a bank falls short of meeting this reserve, it has two places from which it can borrow: the FRS and other banks. The Fed's price for lending money to other banks is called the *federal discount rate* (FDR). The price other banks charge each other (on a friendly basis, naturally) is called the *federal funds rate* (FFR). The mightiest interest rate in the entire Milky Way is the FDR. It is impossible to overstate that fact. As you proceed, you will see why this is true.

As of August 1988, the FDR = 6.5 percent and the FFR is about 7½ percent. The FFR fluctuates daily, especially on Wednesday when all those important banks do all that borrowing from each other and from the Fed. The FDR remains constant for long stretches of time, until it is changed by an FRS edict. The fundamentals in this situation concur with the analogy you just saw on free checking where the bank charged you less than a friend, but the friend was nicer to borrow from. For the important banks, their "friends" are other important banks, but the Fed is "the Bank."

Figure 7-2 uses the weekly MMP rate as a proxy for the FFR. This is fine, because mathematically speaking, these two interest rates are almost exactly the same. The switching rule is: Be in a stock NLF when FDR minus MMP plus

1.00 is positive (bigger than zero); otherwise, be in a money NLF. Doing this, you would have averaged 16.0 percent per year instead of the Buy/Hold of 20.5 percent. Why are you shown such a poor switching strategy? Because it is necessary to do this now so that a point can be made in the next section.

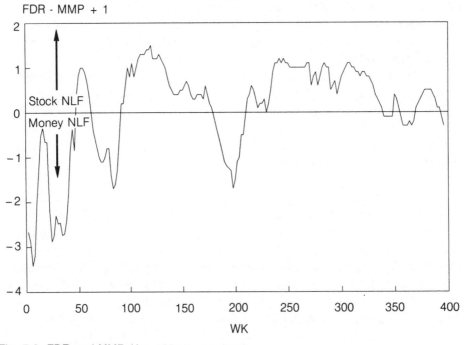

Fig. 7-2. FDR and MMP (Jan 1981 to Jul 1988).

Like the Pseudo Fosback Index, the FDR − MMP + 1 is but one of dozens of indices which could be taken into account when devising a switching strategy. Sometimes a few switching indices which don't stand well by themselves can be combined to give one number on which to base NLF switching. The best way to do this is by using a math process called *regression*, which will be explained in Chapters 10 and 11. All you have to know about regression right now is that it is like a big mixing bowl into which you pour just the right amounts of all the right ingredients to end up with a gourmet meal. Projectors are the TA pros who use regression. Trend followers would combine several indices by confirmation or resistance/support levels as discussed in Chapter 6.

TWO TUMBLES AND A JUMP

Let's use the same $200 minimum checking situation as in the FDR example, except this time the bank charges 14 percent. The bank rate has jumped from 5.5 percent to 14 percent because there is an all-around shortage of money to lend. When things of value become scarce or are expected to become scarce, their price goes up. How about some sweet revenge on your part? That friend who gave you 6 percent has a shortfall of $50. You are only too glad to loan your friend the $50 at 14.75 percent (yearly rate) for a 1-week period. Your friend should be much more careful about not being caught short when interest rates are so high, due to a scarcity of money to lend.

When a bank raises its lending rate, it is said to be tightening its monetary policy. The Fed can tighten monetary policy for the U.S. (in fact, for the whole world) by raising the FDR. It can also loosen its monetary policy by lowering the FDR. When the Fed lowers the FDR twice in a row, the market jumps upward a while later. This is the reason Norman Fosback, who developed this method, gave the name "two tumbles and jump" to this index. Remember the S & P 500 and MMP? When MMP is in a downtrend, the S & P 500 goes into an uptrend. As interest rates fall the stock market rises, because it is cheaper for businesses and individual people to go into debt. Businesses can expand and advertise more because money is cheaper. Everyday citizens can buy that new car because they will pay 8 percent on the balance instead of 13 percent. Therefore, when interest rates fall, more money is lent out.

Raising or lowering the FDR has a tremendous effect on the stock market and it is done infrequently. This is so, because many important financial factors have been taken into consideration over a period of months or years before such a move is made. A change in the FDR affects much more than the U.S. stock markets. World stock and financial markets respond as well. Be clear on one point, however. The reason that the Fed manipulates the FDR is not to control the stock market. The Fed's main concern is to manage inflation. What happens in the stock market is a direct result of the FRS's discount rate manipulations, but it is not a big consideration when the Fed actually decides to raise or lower the FDR.

Changing the FDR is one of three ways that FRS decisions have an impact on the economy, and hence, affect the stock market. The other two ways are the *margin requirement* and the *reserve requirement*. The margin requirement tells investors (you as well as the big institutions) how much money they need up front to buy stocks. Think of buying a car. Far fewer cars would be sold if the only financing policy was "cash on the barrelhead." It's the same with stocks. If stock buyers can only buy $10,000 worth of stock with $10,000 (minus commissions of course), then they will not be nearly as eager to buy stocks as they would if they could "margin" and buy $15,000 worth of stocks for $10,000. For a downpayment of $10,000, a person can buy $15,000 worth of stocks.

The reserve requirement tells banks they must keep a certain percentage of cash on hand to meet daily obligations. This is like the FRS dictating a liquid asset ratio to banks, or a bank dictating a $200 minimum for free checking to you. This minimum percentage is multiplied by the bank's total assets to obtain the amount which must be kept in reserve. This amount gains 0-percent interest. The larger the percentage, the larger the amount. So, when the reserve requirement is raised, there is less money available from all banks to loan out. This puts a damper on things. When the reserve requirement is lowered, the economy heats up.

Far and away, the most frequently used tool the Fed uses to tweak the economy is the FDR. If a bank borrows directly from the Fed's lending window to meet reserve requirements, it borrows at the FDR. In summary, there are three ways the FRS manipulates the U.S. and world economies:

They ease the . . .	*So that . . .*
1. FDR	banks pay less for money needed to meet the reserve requirement
2. margin requirement	investors can buy more stocks with less cash
3. reserve requirement	banks have more money to lend

When the FDR drops, banks can borrow money more cheaply at the Fed window, and by golly, when the FDR drops, you better believe that all other interest rates drop down the road. Lowering the margin requirement allows investors to put less of a downpayment on the line to buy stocks. If the reserve requirement is eased, banks need to tie up less of their cash at an FRS bank; this way, they have more money available to lend.

An easing in any one of those three Fed levers makes more money available to businesses, investors, and consumers, and so the stock market rises. Usually the FDR is the one which is manipulated by the Fed because it is the least risky of the three. It turns out that, when any combination of those three levers fall twice in succession, investors wake up and the market trends upward a short while later. This is where the terminology for this TA method, "two tumbles and a jump," comes from. Two tumbles (in any of the three levers) and a jump (in the stock market).

Figure 7-3 shows the FDR for January 1981 to July 1988. The first time two tumbles occur causes a move into Windsor. If the FDR drops again after this, you just stick with the stock NLF. Whenever the FDR rises, exit to MMP and start the game all over again. Buy/Hold gain for Windsor was 20.4 percent and the switch gain was 21.3 percent. Recall that reference in the last section to a point which was to be made in this section. Figure 7-2 showed a more elaborate index which got a much worse return (16.0 percent) than the plain "two tumbles and a jump" strategy. You could play with the FDR and MMP numbers all day long and not come close to 21.3 percent. Even if you did come close or

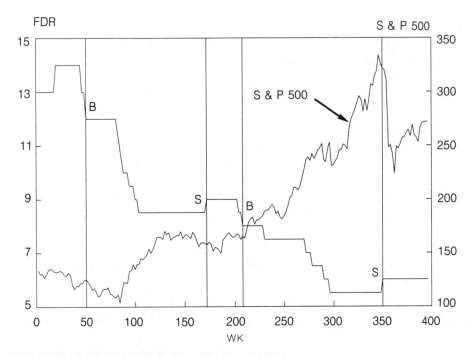

Fig. 7-3. FDR with S & P 500 (Jan 1981 to Jul 1988).

beat 21.3 percent by a touch, it is always better to stick with the simpler index than to perform gyrations and complicate matters.

"Two tumbles and a jump" makes a lot of fundamental sense. The first tumble wakes investors, large and small, out of their stupors. At this point, investors don't really believe the Fed is serious about easing its policy. The second tumble gets investors excited because they sense that the FRS means business and they don't want to be left out of the action.

YIELD CURVES

If your friend wants $100 till payday next week, you would say, "OK, but you owe me $100.27 then." If he or she agrees, it is a deal. (This is about a 15-percent rate, annualized.) Same friend now, but he or she wants the $100 for 1 year. A lot can go wrong in a year that can't go wrong in a week, so you demand $120 at the end of the year. Another deal has been made, but this one is for a 20-percent annual rate over a longer period of time. (This period of time is called the *maturity* of the loan.) It is only normal to demand a higher rate of interest on a loan with a longer maturity because the loan entails more risk for the lender.

Interest rates fluctuate. Today it might be 7.53 percent, tomorrow 7.51 percent, 10 years from now 17.53 percent. The longer money is loaned out, the more risk is taken by a lender that the same money could have been loaned out at a higher rate or that the borrower could default. When you buy a 30-year treasury bond and get 8 percent from the federal government in interest, you would think it abnormal if you could, at the same time, buy a 6-month certificate of deposit and be paid 9 percent for it.

In fact, you would take the higher rate for one 6-month period after another until the 30-year bond rate attracted you. Four 6-month periods down the road, the 6-month rate might be 8.5 percent, and the *long bond* rate (another term for "30-year bond") might be 11.5 percent. The best way to play this game is to put your money in a money market NLF and let them get the highest rates for you. The point is that there are thousands and thousands of debt instruments like bonds, notes, commercial paper, and so on. Each one has an interest rate and a maturity attached to it. It is only normal that longer maturities go with higher interest rates.

A yield curve (YC) is a graph of interest rates over maturity. When people say that a YC has a "positive" or "normal" slope, they mean that, when a straight line is drawn through the middle of the mass of points which make up one of the monthly curves in Fig. 7-4, this line slopes upward. This shows that as maturities increase, so do interest rates. You can see that interest rates for all maturities are increasing up to the point of the Crash in October 1987. July's curve is lower than August's curve. The graph for August is beneath the one for September. October is the highest of all. Fig. 7-4 has an X-axis which is not

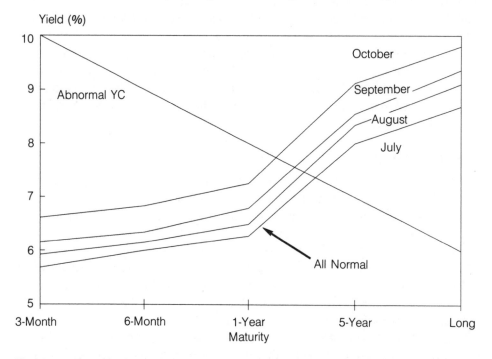

Fig. 7-4. YCs Up to The Crash of '87 (All appears "normal").

to scale. It is easier to get an initial feel for the interest rate versus maturity relationship using this graph.

The graph in Fig. 7-5 is a collection of real YCs because the X-axis is ticked in a much more realistic fashion than is the X-axis in Fig. 7-4. This, in a fundamental sense, is the normal situation for maturities and rates. You would expect larger interest rates to go with longer maturities. When the line slopes downward, analysts say the slope is "abnormal" or "negative." This indicates that there is something screwy going on with interest rates. If you could make a 10-percent annual rate by tying your money up for only 6 months, why would you tie your money up for 30 years in a treasury bond and receive only 8 percent?

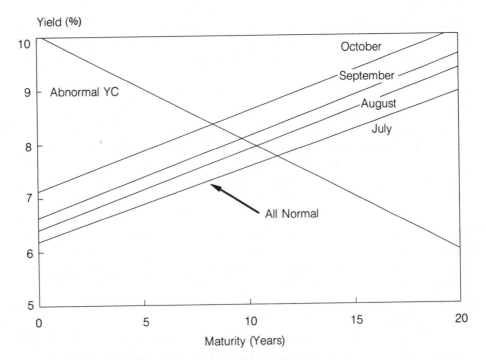

Fig. 7-5. YCs with Numeric X-Axis (as used in practice).

A positively sloped YC is simply a picture of the normal, healthy interest rate versus maturity situation, while a negatively sloped YC graphically illustrates that something might well be wrong. Figure 7-4 shows four YCs in 1987 for the first week in July, August, September, and October. You know what happened in October about 2 weeks after that YC was made public. But there is nothing abnormal about any of those YCs! So there was no abnormality to signal the crash. You *can* see interest rates rising before the crash, however. As the curves go from July to October, they rise above one another in succession. In spite of missing this call, YCs are much used by technicians and fundamentalists alike. YCs, like any other TA index, are only one part of the picture. Many other parts need to be considered to get the whole view.

Figure 7-5 shows the 4 months of YCs replaced with "regression lines." These regression lines are made to pass through the center of the masses of points (five points for each month) depicted in Fig. 7-4. The X-axis has been changed to a numeric axis to better illustrate how the actual numbers relate to one another. All regression lines are normally sloped, so there appears to be nothing out of kilter. The 3-month and 6-month X-axis points in Fig. 7-4 wind up very close to the Y-axis in Fig. 7-5.

SUMMARY

Remember MMP (representing interest rates) and the S & P 500 (representing the stock market)? You've come a long way since you first saw this relationship in a graph near the end of Chapter 4. In Chapter 7, you experienced some relationships which linked fundamental notions like interest rates with the stock market. These fundamental notions were expressed technically by graphs of actual values, or by straight lines passed through a mass of actual points. Maybe you didn't notice, but there were no MAVs in this chapter. Isn't it interesting that the fundamental meaning of a situation can be pictured by graphing the numbers and not using even one MAV? Simple graphs are very important in understanding the stock market. MAVs are useful, but not always required. You will see some more MAVs in the next chapter.

You learned about the Fed (that is, the FRS) and its discount rate, the FDR. The importance of the liquid asset ratio for stock mutual funds was examined. Numbers for important fundamental notions were graphed, and insights were obtained into how the stock market is affected by monetary considerations. The notion of a sloped line was introduced to show you what a normal yield curve looks like. You also saw some good TA in action and learned a few fundamentals about the banking system.

Good TA must link fundamental notions (like the FDR expressed in human language without numbers) with technical concepts (like how to switch using the FDR in the two tumbles and a jump method), to produce a concise visual summary which gives insight about stock market behavior. Without a basis in fundamental analysis, TA would be hogwash. Without TA we would not be able to unambiguously and consistently recognize important trends and relationships. In fact, without TA, we might not see these relationships at all.

8

How Trading Volume
Affects the Market

MONETARY INDICES ARE ULTIMATELY BASED UPON INTEREST RATES WHICH RE-flect, to a large extent, what the FRS does. Monetary factors are one of the most important driving forces of the market. You saw how monetary fundamentals were considered first, before technical factors, when trying to understand market behavior. Fundamental factors are not the foremost consideration however. Both fundamental and technical factors are foremost considerations. Fundamentals tell you "why" and technicals tell you "how much." Lacking either side of the coin, you can't cash in.

Volume refers to the number of shares bought or sold. Volume might at first appear to be more of a technical concept but, just like interest rates, there are underlying fundamental factors at work. After volume, we will look at price. Then you will have seen the three basic factors which give you insight on how the market works: monetary, volume, and price factors.

Investor interest in an individual stock or in a group of stocks, like the 2,000 NYSE stocks, can be gauged by volume and price. When volume in trading a stock is increasing, this indicates that interest in that stock is increasing. If the price of that stock rises on rising volume, you have a hot stock. If the price falls on rising volume, you have a turkey. At least that is what the fundamentals say. In this chapter we will see what the technicals say; that is, we will attach numbers to reasonable-sounding statements about volume and then determine if those statements make much sense.

SHORT INTEREST RATIO

You have a friend who wants to buy 100 cans of water-packed tuna fish of a certain brand. This friend doesn't like shopping for tuna (just a personality quirk), so you offer to deliver the 100 cans for $70 within 2 months. Why wait? Because another friend (who works at a supermarket) advises you that tuna will fall in price in the next couple months. You reason, "If it falls to 50 cents a can, I can buy it for $50 and sell it for $70." This would mean a 40 percent profit for you!

So you wait. One month goes by and the price falls to 59 cents. Should you buy now? You give it a little thought as you go on a 2-week vacation. When you are gone, a tuna famine occurs. The price shoots up to 85 cents. Only 2 weeks until the delivery date. You panic. It will cost $85 to actually buy the tuna, and you will only get $70 for it! (A 17.6-percent loss in 6 weeks.) This process is called "selling short."

When a trader sells a stock short, he or she expects the price of that stock to fall. Short sellers are selling something they don't own. Before the end of a specified time period, a short seller must make good on his or her contract by actually purchasing the stock involved. There are wise and not-so-wise short sellers. Both types are in hock to the market. The amount they are in hock is called the *short interest* (SI). SI is the volume of stocks sold short and not yet purchased to make good on those contracts. SI is measured each month about the middle of the month.

Let DVOL be the average daily volume for the market during the 4 weeks of a mid-month to mid-month period. Then the short interest ratio is:

$$SIR = SI \div DVOL$$

"Interest" does not connote "interest rate" here. "Interest" means "how anxious would short sellers become if, heaven forbid, the market went up?" When the market rises, short seller anxiety changes to panic because the rising prices of stocks (just like the price rise of tuna fish) is going to cost short sellers very dearly. Short sellers begin a rush to purchase the shares that they don't own but need to buy to make good on their contracts. This tends to drive the market up even further than that nasty jump in stock prices which started the short sellers' nightmare.

A short seller's fear is directly proportional to SIR. When the SI and DVOL are equal, $SIR = SI \div DVOL = 1.00$. What this means is that there are enough short sellers out there to account for 1 whole day's worth of trading volume all by themselves. An SIR of 2.00 means that jittery short sellers have 2 days of volume worth of bets on the line. High SIR values are generally bullish because short sellers are, for the most part, wrong. They have faith that a raging bull is going to faint dead in its tracks.

The SIR, like almost all market indicators, bounces around quite a bit. The SIR for the NYSE is given in Fig. 8-1. This is one of those rare graphs where the time units are months and not weeks. The time period for this graph runs from January 1981 through July 1988. The assumption upon which switching will be based, using the SIR, is that as long as the SIR is above 2.00, the market will probably be strong down the road. As you have seen, Buy/Hold has been a pretty good strategy so far when compared to switching based on just one TA indicator. Buy/Hold will usually lose to occasional switching in the long run, but frequent switching generally loses to occasional switching.

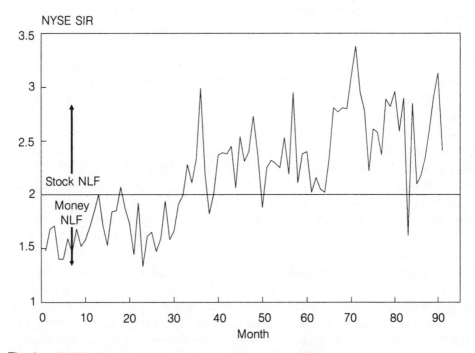

Fig. 8-1. NYSE Short Interest Ratio (Jan 1981 to Jul 1988).

When the SIR is above 2.00, you are in the market. Otherwise you are in a money NLF. Using this strategy, an annual gain of 16.2 percent is achieved, but using Buy/Hold in the Windsor NLF, an annual gain of 20.4 percent is realized. What you see here is a good index, the SIR, which is not good by itself for switching. The SIR is a much-watched index by professionals, both fundamentalists and technicians on Wall Street, because it gives an indication of latent buying power in the market.

ODD LOT SHORT SALES RATIO

You go to a convenience store with $1 and buy a can of cola for 55 cents. This is all you can afford at the time. Next time you have $3 and buy a six-pack for

$1.98 and a single can for 55 cents. You still pay a 22-cent premium for that single can (33 cents per can in a six-pack but 55 cents per single can). When you ask the clerk why this is so, he tells you, "We can't split six-packs."

Stocks are sold in "round lots" of 100 shares each. If you buy 100, 200, 1,500, or 10,000 shares, you don't pay a premium. If you buy 241 shares, you pay a premium for the "odd lot" of 41 shares. (Two 100-packs and 41 single cans.) There is a good reason for a premium being charged. Most buying and selling of stocks (about 70 percent of the action) is done by big to gigantic investors. To these biggies, a mere 1,000 or 2,000 shares is child's play. Your odd 41 shares have to wait (and be accounted for while waiting) for 59 shares to come by so that a round lot transaction can be made with the biggies. On a high-volume day, large block transactions (these are transactions of 10,000 or more shares) can number over 3,000. This alone accounts for more than 30 million shares traded. Your 200 shares would fit well into this picture, but those 241 shares make things difficult for the people who keep track of things at the stock exchanges.

People who do a lot of odd lot trading are necessarily small investors. These people are called "odd lotters." This is the small-time investor who can't afford to buy 1500 shares at a crack. He or she can afford 57 shares at $21.87 per share, though. Odd lotters will pay premium brokerage commissions for odd lots as their price for playing the game. Some odd lotters do very well because they can maneuver more quickly than big institutions. There is a subset of odd lotters which does a consistently poor job of calling shots in the stock market. This masochistic subset of odd-lotters is called the "odd lot short sellers."

One reason this subset finds life so difficult is because buying 41 shares you don't have can be more difficult than selling 41 shares you do have. Odd lot short sellers keep coming back for beating after beating. Odd lot short sellers not only pay higher brokerage commissions, but most of them are wrong about what the market will do. This makes odd lot short sellers good contrarian indicators of market direction. Some technicians call indices like the one you are about to witness "sentiment indicators." A sentiment indicator is supposed to gauge how a particular group of people feel about what the market is going to do.

Let OLSS be odd lot, short sales volume. This volume represents the number of stock shares sold short by odd lot players. OLTP stands for odd lot total purchases. OLTP is the grand total of shares bought by odd lotters. Finally, OLTS is the odd lot total sales or the number of shares sold by odd lot people. When you add up all sales and purchases of shares done in the odd fashion, you get total odd lot shares traded. Divide the total odd lot shares traded into the number of odd lot short-sales made and you get the odd lot short-sales ratio, OLSSR:

$$OLSSR = OLSS \div (OLTP + OLTS)$$

OLSSR is the proportion of all those odd lotters who also like to toy around in the risky business of short selling. OLSSR is taken only with respect to odd lotters, so it is a gauge of the size of that masochistic subset of small-time players. The OLSSR shows how big a group of people odd lot short sellers are compared to all odd lotters. The OLSSR is graphed in Fig. 8-2 for September 1983 through July 1988. When the OLSSR goes up, it indicates that the odd lot short sellers are happy because they expect the market to go down. Since odd lot short sellers make up a contrarian indicator, you would expect the market to go up when the OLSSR goes up. This is because the odd lot short sellers expect to be blessed with a falling market but usually wind up getting burned.

Similarly, you would expect the market to go down when these people pessimistically expect the market to go up. When odd lot short sellers expect the market to go up, they do less short selling and the OLSSR goes down. As luck would have it for this group of people, when they expect the market to go up, it goes down. When odd lot short sellers expect the market to go up, they do much less short selling and the OLSSR goes down.

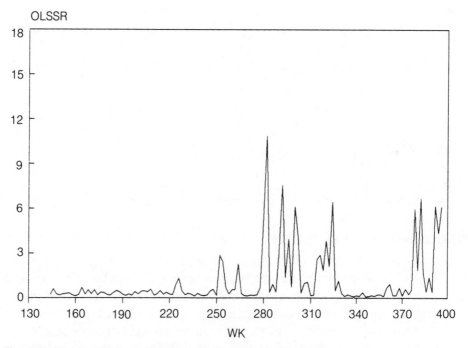

Fig. 8-2. Odd Lot Short Sales Ratio (Sept 1983 to Jul 1988).

Using a 20-MAV of the OLSSR and the strategy "be in a stock NLF when the 20-MAV of the OLSSR is greater than 0.75" gives a Windsor gain of 18.0 percent versus a Buy/Hold gain of 19.6 percent. (See Fig. 8-3.) The OLSSR went up just before the Crash of '87 (about Week 335) and so would have appeared to signal a surge in the market because, it is assumed, odd lot short sellers are generally wrong about the market's direction. Just before the Crash (about Week 355) the OLSSR fell below 0.75. This fall demonstrates technically that, since odd lot short sellers are bullish (that is, less interested in selling the market short), the market should decline. The OLSSR also jumped up significantly a few other times in the years before the crash.

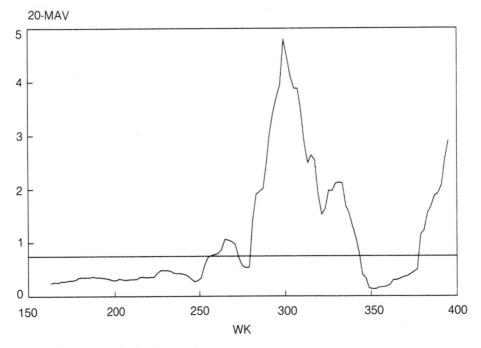

Fig. 8-3. 20-MAV OLSSR (Feb 1984 to Jul 1988).

NEGATIVE VOLUME INDEX

When volume rises from week to week , the crowd starts getting excited. Maybe the crowd thinks that the market is going up, so it buys stocks and pushes prices higher. The opposite happens on rising volume when the crowd thinks the market is going down, because then they sell and prices fall. Besides the crowd, there are huge dividend plays made and these plays can increase NYSE volume by as much as 30 or 40 percent on a daily basis. Another factor that increases volume are stock buybacks and takeovers. A company's management might want to buy back stock to gain more control over the company. Volume increases on takeover activity when individuals outside the company want to take it over.

When the crowd leaves and dividend players don't want to capture dividends, management doesn't want to gain control in a company, and takeover artists don't have the yen to take over a company, then the activity of a few people, called "the smart-money people," becomes apparent. These people should be watched because their sole purpose is to buy or sell a stock, focusing on the inherent value of that stock. Collectively refer to the crowd, dividend players, company management, and takeover players as "the crowd" in what follows. The rest of the investors will be referred to as "smart money."

When volume goes down on successive weeks, this signals that the crowd is leaving the market, which should make more apparent the moves of the smart money. As volume falls, you should pay attention to the direction the market is taking. As volume rises, you should ignore the direction that the market is taking, because you want to do what the smart money does and not what the crowd does.

Let:

V = average weekly NYSE volume
P = percent weekly change in the S & P 500

Don't go through the trouble of graphing P as you first might expect to graph it. The problem will be that this kind of P will fluctuate up and down so rapidly on a week-to-week basis that the curve will hide a lot of its flow from you. There is a more revealing way to look at P. Look at Table 8-1.

——— **Table 8-1. Calculating the Negative Volume Index** ———

WK	V	V up/down?	S & P 500	P(%)	NVI
1	41.90	—	136.34	—	100.00
2	73.60	up	133.48	-2.10	100.00
3	48.70	down	134.77	0.97	100.97
4	44.70	down	130.23	-3.37	97.60
5	44.30	down	129.55	-0.52	97.08
6	51.70	up	130.60	0.81	97.08
7	42.50	down	126.98	-2.77	94.31

Take Week 1 (this is January 2, 1981) as the base week to define a different kind of P called the *negative volume index* (NVI). Define NVI to be 100.00 for Week 1. In Week 2, even though the S & P 500 fell 2.1 percent, we ignore this activity because V went up—remember, we don't want to follow the crowd. For Week 3, V went down, the S & P 500 went up almost 1 percent (0.97 percent), and so we add P to the NVI. Week 4 has another declining volume and the NVI for this week is calculated:

$$NVI = 100.97 - 3.37$$
$$= 97.60$$

Keep doing this for hundreds of weeks and use the trend defined by the 50-MAV to determine if smart money has been buying or selling on declining volume.

Figure 8-4 shows that smart money, as indicated by the NVI trend, went on a powerful buying spree in the fall of 1986 (about Week 310). This spree lasted until the spring of 1987 (about Week 330). Just looking at the 1986 to 1987 period, the NVI trend seems to have done an outstanding job of predicting market direction. Previous to 1986, however, the NVI trend would have told you to be out of the market and caused you to miss much of the 1982 to 1987 bull. This means that you shouldn't interpret the NVI and its 50-MAV as a good trend for timing the market. The NVI did indicate one of the most powerful surges in stock market history (during 1986). It even got you out before the Crash. Buy/Hold gained 20.7 percent per year and the trend of the NVI and its 50-MAV gained 10.9 percent.

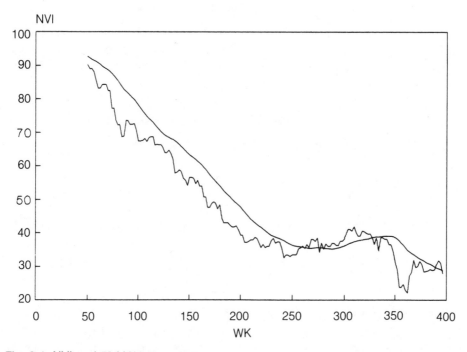

Fig. 8-4. NVI and 50-MAV (Jan 1982 to Jul 1988).

ARM'S INDEX

Suppose a real wealthy person holds a garage sale. This sale can tell a lot about what buyers are interested in. If the buyers buy a lot of old pots and pans, they are more interested in cheaper items. If they buy those old paintings (Rembrandts, Picassos, and the like), then they are interested in higher-priced items. Of course, the wealthy person's garage is huge and contains all sorts of cheap, higher-priced, and in-between items which buyers will haggle over.

Pots and pans might start the day at $2 a throw, but then drop to 50 cents apiece. Picassos might start at $2 million each and fall to a miserable $1.75 million. In either case, these are called "decliners." The opposite could just as easily happen. Pots and pans and Picassos could increase in price. We would call these items "advancers." The rich person holding the garage sale tells you that she will give you a goodly sum of money if you can demonstrate to her whether this garage sale is a buyers' or a seller's market. If you tell her that it is a buyers' market, she will kick everyone out of her garage and shut the sale down. (That is probably one of the big reasons she became wealthy in the first place.) If you tell her that it is a seller's market (that is, "her" market), then she will lock the doors to keep anyone from escaping. If you are wrong, she will find some-one else to pay for the advice she wants.

Average price per item wouldn't do the trick of determining whether her garage sale is a buyers' or a seller's market, because items vary so widely in price. You can rest assured that the rich woman will not get as much for a 1978 vintage pot as she will get for a 1920 Picasso. This garage sale woman wants to know overall how her sale is going. If a Rembrandt fetches only $5 million instead of $5.5 million, that ½-million decrease in the price of one item makes up for an awful lot of pots and pans. What if you ignore price and just split the items into three sets?

One set would be those items advancing in price, another set would be those items declining in price, and there would be a third set of items unchanged in price. Ignore those unchanged items because they don't have anything to do with the up-and-down price activity in which you are interested. If she is selling more items advancing in price than items declining in price (that is, the haggling is going the seller's way), she is doing well overall, because the buyers are willing to pay higher prices whether for pots or pans or Picassos. If the opposite is occurring, then she should shoo people out of her garage and shut the doors for another day more favorable to her. What is important here is the volume of items advancing in price relative to the volume of items declining in price.

Buyer interest in advancing stocks can be measured by looking at the average volume per advancing stock. So when the average volume per advancing stock is larger than the average volume per declining stock, buyers are in more of a buying mood. This is to say that buyers are more eager to pay the rising price for advancing stocks than they are to get bargains on declining stocks.

You have probably seen a number on T.V. called the TRIN or *trading index*. This is also called the Arm's Index after the man who invented it. Each week you can observe the number of advances, A, and the number of declines, D. With A and D we can associate volumes, VA and VD, respectively. VA is the volume of stocks advancing, and VD is the volume of stocks declining. Now look at how these four numbers can be used to gauge whether or not it is a good time to buy into a stock NLF.

Let:

$$A = \text{number of stocks advancing}$$
$$D = \text{number of stocks declining}$$
$$VA = \text{volume of advancing stocks}$$
$$VD = \text{volume of declining stocks}$$

Then the Arm's Index is:

$$\text{ARMS} = \frac{(VD \div D)}{(VA \div A)}$$

What do you have here? Look at the top part of this ratio first:

$$VD \div D = \text{average volume per declining stock}$$

If there were 60 million shares traded in 600 stocks declining in price, then:

$$VD \div D = 60{,}000{,}000 \div 600$$
$$= 100{,}000$$

This shows that, on the average, 100,000 shares per declining stock were traded.

Similarly, for the bottom part of the ARMS, if there were 60 million shares traded in 600 advancing stocks, then:

$$VA \div A = 60{,}000{,}000 \div 600$$
$$= 100{,}000$$

This shows that there were also 100,000 shares per advancing stock traded. Now we can calculate the ARMS:

$$\text{ARMS} = 100{,}000 \div 100{,}000$$
$$= 1.00$$

This is a neutral reading because there is exactly the same interest shown in declining as in advancing stocks. It is a technician's dream to see all those millions and thousands reduced to a manageable 1.00. This meaningful little number is much lighter baggage to carry around than those numbers with all the goose eggs in them.

What if the top of the ARMS was bigger than the bottom of the ARMS? This would mean that there is more interest in declining than in advancing stocks. This would be interpreted as a bad omen for the market. For example:

$$\text{ARMS} = 150{,}000 \div 100{,}000$$
$$= 1.50$$

This could happen if VD = 60 million shares traded in D = 400 declining stocks and if VA = 80 million shares traded in A = 800 advancing stocks:

$$VD \div D = 60,000,000 \div 400$$
$$= 150,000$$

$$VA \div A = 80,000,000 \div 800$$
$$= 100,000$$

Notice in the last ARMS calculation (as compared to the ARMS = 1.00 calculation) that heavier volume was traded on the average in declining stocks because the same volume took place in 400 such stocks instead of in 600 stocks. Also notice that there were twice as many advancers as there were decliners. Even with a big excess of advances to declines, ARMS tells us that things don't look too bright.

In the same way you reasoned that an ARMS bigger than 1.00 means the market is going sour, you can reason that an ARMS of less than 1.00 is a bullish indication for the market. Now, if you run into that rich woman, you can do a job for her. Don't sell yourself short! See Fig. 8-5 for a picture of the ARMS on a weekly basis from September 1983 to July 1988.

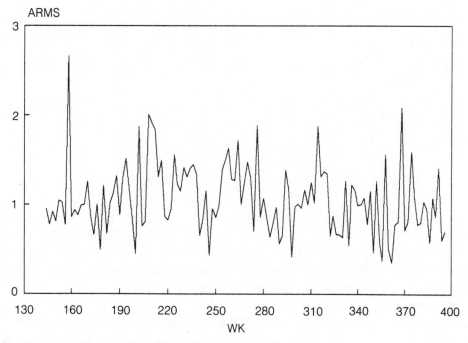

Fig. 8-5. Arm's Index (TRIN) (Sept 1983 to Jul 1988).

Here is another good example of not basing a strategy on one index, no matter how good that index appears to be fundamentally. Remember, fundamentals and technicals are two sides of the same coin. Fundamentally the ARMS is a very good index. When the ARMS is evaluated technically for NLF switching, it is seen that Buy/Hold in Windsor was 21.2 percent; but, switching into Windsor when the 50-MAV of the ARMS was less than 1.00, gives a gain of only 14.9 percent. Of course the ARMS, like most of the indices you have been looking at, was designed for a specific purpose. That purpose was short-term, or daily (even hourly), trading. Figure 8-6 shows the trend of the ARMS and its 50-MAV.

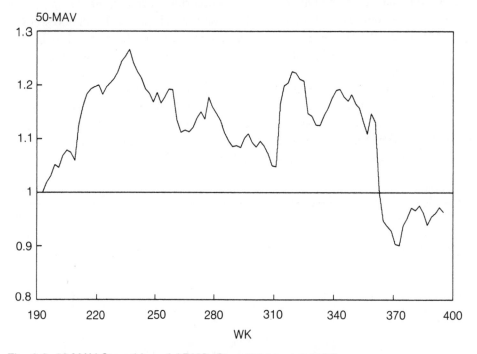

Fig. 8-6. 50-MAV Smoothing of ARMS (Sept 1984 to Jul 1988).

It's fun to watch the ARMS change every few minutes if it is displayed on a ticker you have access to. Since volume is not settled officially until the end of a trading day, the ARMS keeps bouncing around as it is reported on a ticker tape every 15 minutes. The numbers which make it up change so the ARMS fluctuates as its components change. The ARMS is a much-watched index by very short-term traders.

Compared to the wild gyrations of the graph in Fig. 8-5, in Fig. 8-6 the ARMS is quite smooth. The 50-MAV of the ARMS would not have signaled an exit to you before the October 19, 1987 debacle (Week 356). In fact, it would have told you to get out just before Christmas of that year. You must always find out what the underlying purpose of a stock market indicator is before you put it to use.

Start with the fundamentals of a situation to see if those fundamentals make sense. Then evaluate an index based on the technicals involved.

SUMMARY

As you go more deeply into these three chapters on factors affecting the stock market, you can see more how TA and fundamental analysis are related. Some things sound really good fundamentally but fail miserably when put through a TA examination. Some things, like Daily Temp. and Weekly Bonanza price, could not be surpassed for TA validity, but, because they are unrelated fundamentally, they should be shunned by anyone in his or her right mind.

You have added an understanding of volume to your understanding of money and interest rates. The picture of what is really going on in the stock market is clearer because you have donned TA spectacles. Your view of Wall Street has changed for the better.

One note on trend-followers versus projectors. The Odd Lot Short Sales Ratio graph, Fig. 8-2, has an abundance of wild up-and-down variation. Such highly variable graphs bother the heck out of trend-followers, so these types of technicians do a lot of graph smoothing. Smoothing makes nicer-looking graphs but destroys some of the information contained in the actual data. Graphs that jerk up and down don't bother projectors at all. Projectors use a math process called *regression* which can extract meaning from numbers quite well (if any meaning is there to begin with), without smoothing information out of the data.

Notice that, so far in Chapters 7 and 8, Buy/Hold generally runs about 20 percent while the various switching strategies run about 16 percent. When you hear claims something like ''using my method would have gained you 35 percent per year over the last 10 years'' or ''you can count on about 25 percent per year if you listen to me,'' just remember what you've seen here. It is much easier to make claims like that than it is to back them up.

To beat Buy/Hold is tough to do in a consistent, safe fashion over the long haul. Remember that table at the end of Chapter 5 showing how investing in the S & P 500 and reinvesting dividends beat the CPI by a factor of about 2.4 (average S & P 500 return of about 15.3 percent per year) over the 10-year period? You can reasonably expect to do about 20 percent per year in good growth-type NLFs if you follow a good market timer who has a proven, long-term track record. Shade the 20 percent to 15 percent if you go into ultraconservative funds or put something like half your money in money NLFs. Shade the 20 to 25 percent if you pay very close attention to your newsletter and track your NLFs like your life depended on it. Don't believe someone who tells you that a consistent 30 percent or more a year is possible. Even 25 percent per year is tough to accomplish. The 15 to 20 percent per year is probably a lot more than you are now getting. Even if you have been gaining 15 to 20 percent per year, chances are that you can do it much more safely and cheaply by investing in NLFs.

9

How Stock Prices
Affect the Market

YOU HAVE JUST SEEN HOW MONETARY AND VOLUME FUNDAMENTALS ARE TRANS-
lated into technical indices. Along the way you picked up some fundamental
information about the banking system and the Fed, volume and short selling.
All is not money and volume, however. Price is also important. In fact, some
people define TA as "using price alone to determine current and future market
conditions." These people are dead wrong. As you have seen, a good technician
uses numbers that are related to any kind of meaningful fundamental situation
to arrive at a prediction about how the market will be performing. Technicians
don't just base what they do on price fundamentals alone. Good TA combines
monetary, volume, and price factors to indicate what will be happening in the
stock market.

One important point you have noticed in the last two chapters is that relying
upon only one TA indicator is not the best way to proceed when investing your
hard-earned money. Many of the indices covered were just so-so when viewed
in isolation. Such will also be the case in this chapter. So you will see further
examples in Chapter 9 of two TA truisms: good TA indices are always based
on solid fundamental reasoning; and only one index, no matter how good it is,
can't do a proper job of projecting market behavior or determining current market
health.

What makes TA so successful is the translation of human, qualitative notions
about the stock market into numbers that don't lie. Different individuals might
interpret stock market numbers differently, but the numbers themselves can't

be disputed. Gut feeling and human language are all very good but, when you throw in numbers as well, ambiguity about what to do is thrown out the door and consistency let in. There is no guaranteed method, be it fundamental or technical, which can predict what the stock market will do all of the time. One important thing that good TA provides for you is the unambiguous, consistent advice which is so essential to good long-term success in investing.

ADVANCE/DECLINE LINE (ADL)

A stock starts a trading week at an NAV equal to the previous trading week's closing NAV. If at the close of this week's trading, the stock's NAV is higher than last week's NAV, that stock counts for one advance. A declining stock is one whose NAV at the end of this week's trading is less than its closing NAV from the previous week. An unchanged stock is one which hasn't changed in price during the last week. Count all advancing stocks and you get the advances for the week. Same goes for declines and unchanged stocks. One would think that an up-week on Wall Street should always be associated with more advances than declines. This is true most of the time.

Since it is not always true that the market goes up when advances beat declines, you need to have a way to look at the flow of advances and declines so that you can discern over a period of time whether or not advances are dominant. Then you need to relate this to market behavior in general.

Let:

$$ADV = \text{total number of advancing stocks}$$
$$DECL = \text{total number of declining stocks}$$
$$UNCH = \text{total number of unchanged stocks}$$

Then:

$$ADL = 1.00 + \frac{(ADV - DECL)}{(ADV + DECL + UNCH)}$$

Notice that UNCH appears in the bottom of this equation. This gives ADL (advance/decline line) values in terms of total shares traded. Out of about 2000 total shares traded on the NYSE, it is not uncommon to see 400 or so shares unchanged in price from what they began the week at. Since any stock must be either an ADV, DECL, or UNCH, the total number of shares traded is the sum given in the denominator.

In the above equation, when ADV beat DECL, the top is bigger than zero. The reverse is true when DECL beat ADV. When DECL and ADV differ from each other by only a small amount, the decimal fraction added to or subtracted from 1.00 is very small so the ADL value is very close to 1.00. When the ADL value is much above 1.00, this means that ADV kicked the heck out of DECL for that week. When the ADL value is far below 1.00, DECL obliterated ADV. The hypothesis is that ADL values much above 1.00 are good and those much below 1.00 are bad.

Here are a few sample calculations for ADL values:

$$\begin{aligned} \text{ADL} &= 1.00 + [1100 - 500] \div 2000 \\ &= 1.00 + 600 \div 2000 \\ &= 1.30 \end{aligned}$$

$$\begin{aligned} \text{ADL} &= 1.00 + [400 - 1200] \div 2000 \\ &= 1.00 - 800 \div 2000 \\ &= 0.60 \end{aligned}$$

In order to keep the numbers nice and round here, the assumption that UNCH = 400 has been made. This eases the calculations and gives a good idea of what is going on.

The ADL is used to determine what is called "market breadth." You will also hear "market momentum" applied to the ADL. To add to the confusion, there are many different ways to calculate the ADL, none of which is equivalent to the way it is calculated here. The above equation is a perfectly valid way to look at the ADL but, as usual, a graph is the preferred way.

One of the wildest graphs you will ever see is the unadulterated ADL graph. The gyrations in this graph force the use of the 50-MAV of the ADL to see how the ADL relates to stock prices. The graph in Fig. 9-1 looks like a lie detector test gone haywire; however, it is always nice to see a graph of the actual data.

As you can see in Fig. 9-2, when the 50-MAV of the actual A/D line (this is another common way of abbreviating "advance/decline line") is pictured, the resulting smoothness allows the use of this graph as a trend. When the 50-MAV of the A/D line is bigger than 1, you should be in a stock NLF. Whenever the ADL is smaller than 1, the market should be weak according to this indicator. When the A/D line is approaching 1 from a position above 1 and the market is going strong, technicians say "there is a lack of confirmation between the market and the Advance/Decline Line." This worries technicians because it shows that decliners are starting to win over advancers. This particular phenomenon began occurring several weeks before the Crash of '87.

If every good technician knows about the ADL and it warned about the October massacre, why didn't all good technicians warn their readers to bail out? Because the ADL is not infallible when viewed in isolation. Yes, there were some good calls by the ADL, but there were also some horrible ones. It is almost as sickening to miss a 30 percent winning year in the stock market as it is to hit a 30 percent losing year. No one technical index (or fundamental notion) exists which can steer you in and out of the market at exactly the right time, 100 percent of the time.

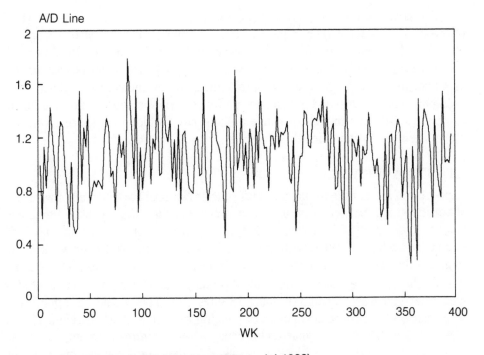

Fig. 9-1. Unadulterated A/D Line (Jan 1981 to Jul 1988).

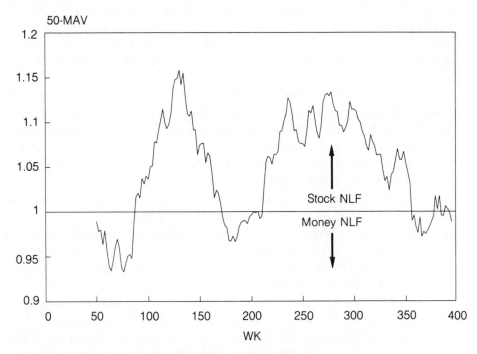

Fig. 9-2. 50-MAV of A/D Line (Dec 1981 to Jul 1988).

The strategy defined above keeps you in a stock NLF when the 50-MAV of the ADL is above 1.00 and puts you in a money NLF otherwise. Using this strategy, the gain achieved was 17.8 percent per year versus a 20.7 percent per year for Buy/Hold. The ADL is like your blood pressure. It can indicate whether or not there might be a serious problem, or it can indicate that there is no problem. When your blood pressure is up (or the ADL is approaching 1.00 from above 1.00—this is enough to cause a slight rise in blood pressure), you pay more attention to your health.

UTILITY AVERAGE

Suppose you are getting in shape to visit Glacier National Park instead of worrying about the stock market. You are up to walking around the block 10 times and want to keep track of your progress. Each week you hope to add one block till you get to 25 blocks. What with the weather and all (too tired after work, need to go get the car fixed, et cetera) you don't always strive onwards and upwards.

You hit upon the idea of comparing how many round trips you can make today with what you were capable of doing 13 days ago. This would be a good way to measure your progress. Instead of jumping right in and calculating a 13-day MAV, you decide to use what technicians call an *oscillator*. Taking as a base how many trips around the block you walked 13 days ago, you can find out how you are doing now compared to then by dividing two numbers. Suppose you completed 10 circuits 13 days ago and completed 10 today. Your progress is $10 \div 10 = 1.00$ or, in other words, you are doing the same now as you did about 2 weeks ago. Maybe 13 days from now you will walk 15 times around the block. This means that you will be achieving $15 \div 10$ or 1.50 (50 percent better) of what you are now achieving.

Utility stocks are extremely sensitive to interest rates because utilities commonly operate with a large portion of debt. They have to borrow money constantly to finance expensive long-term operations like new generating plants, air pollution scrubbers, purchase of coal or fuel oil. Utilities can't shut off the juice to their customers and are publicly regulated so they operate on a shoestring. The better they are at forecasting what the price of fuel will be to them, the better they can buy their fuel at a low price. Utilities must also be extremely good at predicting whether interest rates will rise or fall because they do so much long-term financing. So utilities need to be very smart about the direction in which interest rates and oil prices are headed, and these two factors are important components of the CPI. When the DJUA goes down, this bodes ill for inflation and therefore for the stock market.

Utilities form the biggest industry group, in terms of the number of companies, on the NYSE. The 15 utilities that comprise the Dow Jones Utility Average (DJUA) offer a good and readily available substitute for following the almost 200 utility companies on the NYSE. The DJUA is available daily in every major newspaper.

The DJUA has a very high predictive value for the stock market in general. The reason is that utility prices move in anticipation of interest rate changes so they give a better indication of future market trends.

You have already seen the trend of the DJUA and its 50-MAV in Chapter 5, so for this visit with the DJUA, you will see another way technicians analyze the stock market using the DJUA. Technicians like to use an oscillator, which we briefly discussed earlier in the chapter. Specifically, an oscillator is the ratio of some stock market index, in this case the DJUA, to its previous value, say, 13 weeks ago (see Fig. 9-3). The 13-week time period can be varied. Technicians pick the period that works best. When the DJUA is greater than its value 13 weeks ago, this ratio is bigger than 1.00 and the market is said to be in a bullish uptrend. When this ratio is less than 1.00, the market is bearish.

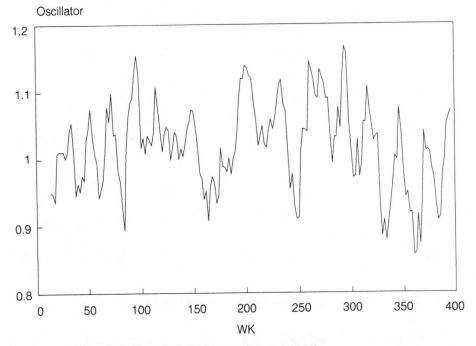

Fig. 9-3. 13-WK Oscillator of DJUA (Apr 1981 to Jul 1988).

The MAV in Fig. 9-4 is an MAV of the actual values of the 13-week oscillator of the DJUA shown in Fig. 9-3. An oscillator gauges how well a technical index is doing now compared with how it was doing some fixed distance in the past. The 13 weeks chosen in this example is not sacred. Some other fixed period could have been used. Just as with MAVs, oscillators don't have some magic period that works best. Again, the variability had to be smoothed out of the actual data using an MAV to get a trend. As in the Advance/Decline line, you didn't use the trend but used a cutoff point (in both cases 1.00) to determine when to be in or out of the market.

Switching based on the trend of the 30-MAV of the DJUA 13-week oscillator and the horizontal line emanating from 1.00 on the Y-axis in Fig. 9-4 would have gained 18.7 percent, as opposed to a gain of 21.1 percent in Windsor over the period indicated. Calculating an oscillator is more work than following a trend of price alone and doesn't necessarily result in any more earnings. Oscillators can be useful tools but, just as you wouldn't build a good sundeck using only a hammer, you can't use just one kind of index to build a good investment strategy.

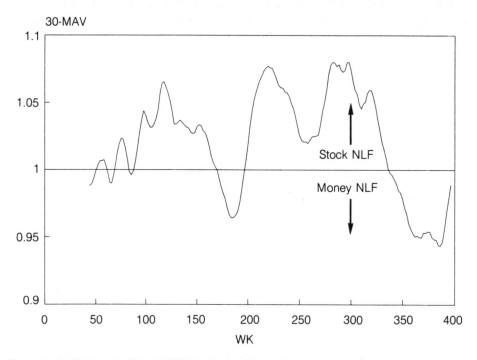

Fig. 9-4. 30-MAV of DJUA 13-WK Oscillator (Nov 1981 to Jul 1988).

SIMPLIFIED DOW THEORY

You have no doubt heard about "Dow Theory." Dow Theory is a reasonably successful trend-following strategy which uses several MAVs in its construction. Dow Theory provides an example of how multiple indicators can be used to confirm one another to produce Buy/Sell points.

The idea behind Dow Theory is that the trend of the DJIA determines the trend of the whole market. Dowists believe that a Buy/Sell signal given by the trend of the DJIA is not enough to act upon all by itself. They require also that this Buy/Sell must be confirmed by a corresponding Buy/Sell in either the DJUA or the Dow Jones Transportation Average (DJTA). Either one will do the trick.

Dowists consider the DJTA important because, as it rises, this usually indicates the economy is starting to boom, what with all the transport required to move goods to market and to move salespeople and executives around the country on business trips.

If you want to follow Dow Theory, you need to follow the three 39-MAV trends of the DJIA, the DJUA, and the DJTA. The main one is the DJIA. It must make its move (a buy or a sell) first. When that happens, wait for a confirmation from either of the other two trends. When the DJIA move is confirmed, you buy (or sell) your stock NLF. This is the simplified version of Dow Theory.

There are other conditions put on Buy/Sell signals by Dowists. Some say that the DJIA has to penetrate a previous high or low before a buy or sell signal is given. This is an application of the concepts of resistance and support you saw in Chapter 6. There are many variations of Dow Theory, and each Dowist will argue that his or her type of Dowism is the best type. Dow Theory uses more than one stock index and has a long-term outlook. Dow Theory usually depends on a lot of "seat of the pants" tweaking to make things work reasonably well.

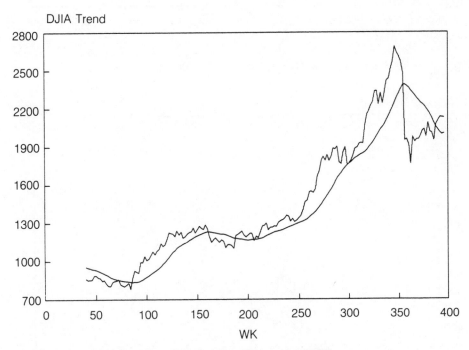

Fig. 9-5. DJIA Portion of Dow Theory (Oct 1981 to Jul 1988).

Using only the confirmation aspect of the DJIA and not the resistance/support part of Dow Theory, Windsor gain is 26.1 percent. Buy/Hold gain is 21.4 percent. Gains for the DJIA, DJUA, and DJTA 39-week trends are, respectively, 23.7 percent, 20.7 percent, and 21.4 percent.

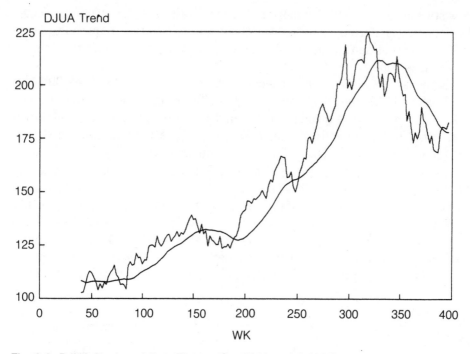

Fig. 9-6. DJUA Portion of Dow Theory (Oct 1981 to Jul 1988).

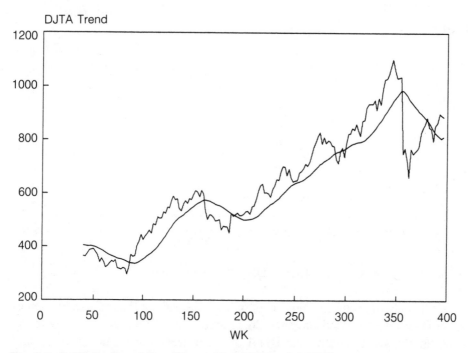

Fig. 9-7. DJTA Portion of Dow Theory (Oct 1981 to Jul 1988).

GOLD FEVER

Generally speaking (watch out for exceptions to this one!), gold stocks go opposite the stock market. The main factor that makes that heavy, yellow metal so precious to people is concern about inflation. When people expect inflation to creep up, gold prices go up and so do the NAVs of gold mining stocks. However, from the spring of 1986 through the spring of 1987, one of those exceptions just mentioned occurred. The stock market kept intact one of its most impressive bull markets while, at the same time, good gold mutual funds doubled their NAVs! You could have been in a balanced stock NLF, made about 30 percent and slept at night, or you could have spent a year tossing and turning while you were in a good gold fund and made 100 percent.

If you want to have a chance of cashing in on this phenomenon in the future, follow what good technicians who dabble in gold projections say. When you are in any type of aggressive NLF, you must constantly call your letter's hotline. Then expect to pick up on maybe 30 to 40 percent of that surge in a good gold fund in about a 6-month period, if you are very lucky. Of course, if you are unlucky, then you could just as well lose 30 to 40 percent. When you've stood it for that long (if you can), you can go grab another 15 to 20 percent in a stock NLF for the remaining 6 months. In other words, gold fund investing is not for the faint of heart or faint of stomach, but it can be very rewarding if you do it right and are lucky. On the other hand—well, just be very careful and stock up on Bromo Seltzer.

Gold funds can be a very good alternative to a part of your investment bankroll when the market is in a long-term downtrend. To buy and hold a gold fund over the years is not too exciting because they average about 5 percent per year when used this way. But when the market is trending downwards, there is a feeling of security knowing you have a small part, say 5 to 10 percent of your total investment money, in a good gold fund. Gold is known as an inflation hedge, so you can use it in your portfolio of NLFs to guard against hyperinflationary times like those in the late 1970s and early 1980s. Using a gold fund in this way means that you don't time it. Even for conservative investors, putting 5 percent of a big nest egg in a gold fund can be reassuring.

Don't use the trend you see in Fig. 9-8 for your own investing. This graph is meant for explanatory purposes only. In the graph, the price of gold and its 30-MAV are shown. You are in Windsor if gold is below its 30-MAV and in MMP otherwise. The reason you are in a stock NLF when the actual gold is below its MAV is the same as the reason you would be in a stock NLF when using a trend of interest rates. Gold and interest rates tend to rise when the stock market is falling and vice versa. Using just one trend in switching aggressive or sector funds can magnify many times the bad effect of relying on just one trend because aggressive and sector funds are so risky.

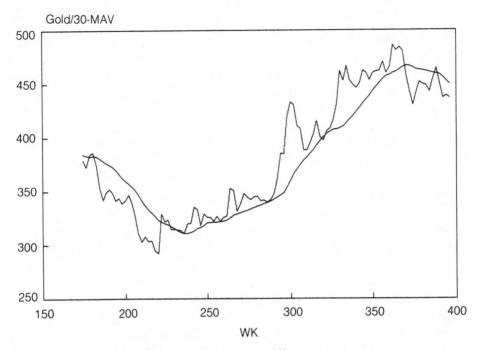

Gold/30-MAV

WK

Fig. 9-8. Gold Fever (AVOID) (Apr 1984 to Jul 1988).

Gold and precious metals funds generally purchase stock in mining companies and not in the metals themselves. Precious metals stocks usually oscillate in value much more than the actual metals, so you can get quite a ride for your money. Windsor gained 12.6 percent based on gold trend switching while Buy/Hold in Windsor attained 20.7 percent. Over significant portions of the 4-year time period depicted in Fig. 9-8, gold and the market made healthy gains at the same time. This explains why this particular trend didn't work too well. Using a gold price trend to switch a stock NLF would have had you out of the stock NLF most of the time that the fund was going up. This is because, when gold was rising in price, so was the stock market for many periods shown in the graph.

WINDSOR GAIN

When strength or weakness were discussed in this book, so far all references have been to the stock market in general. What about when a particular stock NLF is strong or weak? Because of ex dividend days, a straightforward trend of a stock NLF is out of the question. What is needed is to track the actual weekly gain of a stock NLF. As long as that gain is above one of its MAVs, the fund is going strong and you stay in it. When the gain curve falls below the MAV, you exit to a money NLF.

Look at Windsor and calculate its gain. The base week used ends Friday, January 2, 1981. This is Week 1 in most of the graphs you have seen in this

book. For Week 1, Windsor closed at $10.47. The gain for Week 1 is
$10.47 ÷ $10.47 = 1.0000 or 0 percent. Even though the 1.0000 means you have
100 percent of what you started out with, the gain is 0 percent because there
was no increase above that original 100 percent.

For Week 2, Windsor closed at $10.68 for a gain of $10.68 ÷ $10.47 = 1.0201
or 2 percent above the NAV you started with in the base Week 1. For all the
396 weeks, Week 1 will be used as the base week. This is important to keep
in mind. For Week 3, the Windsor closing value was $10.65 so the gain is
$10.65 ÷ $10.47 = 1.0172, or 1.72 percent gauged from the initial entry into
Windsor. Compared to Week 2, there was bit of a loss (28 one-hundreds of 1
percent), but compared to Week 1, there is still a gain of 1.72 percent.

As a final calculation, look at Week 18. In this week, Windsor closed at $11.42.
However, the gain is *not* $11.42 ÷ $10.47 = 1.0907 or 9.07 percent. As of Week
18, Windsor had gained 15.66 percent because it paid a dividend of 69 cents in
this period. This 69 cents represents about a 6-percent distribution and must
be included in the gain calculation. Calculating gains like this is fairly tricky and
you don't need to get into the details. If you basically understood the last few
paragraphs, that is all you need to know for what follows.

Look at Fig. 9-9, which shows the graph of Windsor's gain along with the
30-MAV of that gain. This defines a trend upon which a switching strategy is
based. Should Windsor's gain be above its 30-MAV, you would be invested in

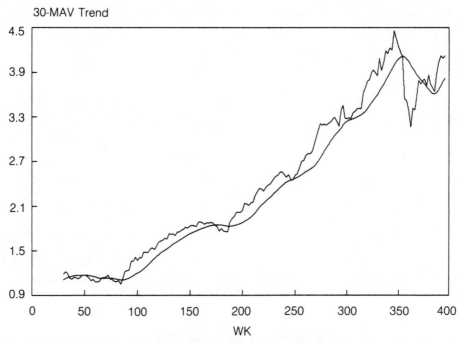

Fig. 9-9. Windsor Gain and 30-MAV (Aug 1981 to Jul 1988).

Windsor. Otherwise you would be in MMP. Using this strategy, the gain averages 22.3 percent per year. Buy/Hold for Windsor during this time was 19.3 percent per year. By beating Buy/Hold by only 3.0 percent per year over this 7-year period, your money mounts up much more quickly. Starting with $10,000, Buy/Hold would have fetched $34,628. Switching on the trend in Fig. 9-9 would have given you $41,243 for a $6,615 increase. That 3.0 percent per year can make quite a difference!

BAD SWITCHING

It is easy and enlightening to give an example of bad switching. The first thing somebody should do when concocting a bad market timing scheme is to ignore fundamental common sense. Possibly the person concocting this bad scheme remembers hearing somewhere that "transportation stocks are related to a quarterly business cycle." This causes the trend of the DJTA and its 13-MAV sound enticing to that person. Technically, 13 numbers are much easier to add up than are 45 or 50 numbers, so this trend sounds even more attractive. Look at Fig. 9-10.

There are two problems here. One problem is that this trend generates 47 switches in a 5-year period. This implies more than eight switches per year! Way too much switching going on. The other problem is that Windsor gain for this

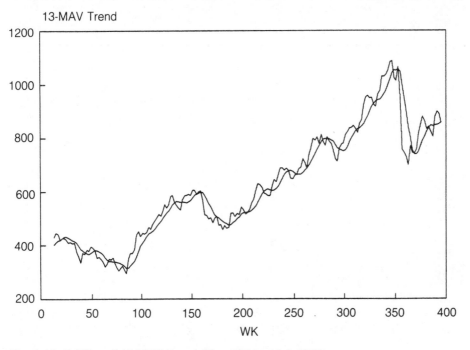

Fig. 9-10. DJTA and 13-MAV Trend (May 1981 to Jul 1988).

trend is only 19.8 percent per year, while Buy/Hold in Windsor averages 19.6 percent per year. What is bought with all that switching? Not much. And the odds on getting whipsawed are greatly increased.

The only selling point of this trend is that it bailed you out before the crash. Big deal! There cannot be enough importance attached to switching infrequently between a stock NLF and a money NLF. One essential component of a good switching strategy (and there were good ones which would have had you in a stock NLF during the crash) is that it does not switch too frequently. At most a good strategy for conservative investors should call for a switch once every year or 2 on the average. There may be a couple of switches in a given year, but, on the average a conservative timing strategy doesn't call for much switching at all.

An aggressive timing strategy might call for half a dozen switches in a given year but might average one or two switches per year over the long haul. Once you start to switch so aggressively, you have to watch your investments very closely. Some NLF groups allow a maximum of two switches per year, so if you are going to follow a letter which calls for more than a few switches in a particular year, you need to choose a different fund group for your more aggressive switching.

SUMMARY

Price has brought you that last step out of the woods. Many mysteries of the stock market and of TA have been cleared up in the last three chapters. It turns out that things weren't all that mysterious to begin with. Price was the easiest to understand of the three major fundamental market factors: price, volume, and money. There are good newsletters which base their switching strategies totally on price trends.

An important result of the first nine chapters has been that you have developed enough TA sophistication to understand what technicians (good and bad) are saying to you. Knowing the basics, you can intelligently pick a good newsletter and track your NLFs so that you can increase your investment success and enjoyment in an easy and safe manner. Talk of oscillators, trends, correlations, and the like sounds impressive, but the bottom line is finding out if these things can do the best job for you.

Right now you are able to understand most of the TA you will ever see. The next two chapters will explain that small but important part of TA which is not based on trend-following. If you find Chapters 10 and 11 a bit difficult, just skim them and go on to the last chapter in the book. Chapter 12 will tie everything together for you and give you a few more insights to put into your bag of investment tricks.

10

Predicting the Future with Straight Lines

IF YOU THINK THAT CORRELATION MEANS ONE ACTIVITY HAS AN EFFECT ON ANother activity, then you are right. Think of the year-end holidays. As these happy periods go by, people gain weight. Weight gain is correlated to how many calories people eat and drink during Thanksgiving, Christmas, and New Year's. Infamous resolutions are made after that last holiday, "I will eat less and lose weight!" This calories/weight relationship is an example of correlation because one activity, weight gaining, does what the other activity, increasing calories, does. If calories go up, so does weight. If calories decrease, so should weight.

The calories/weight example is an example of positive correlation because when one activity is increased, the other activity is also increased. Positive correlation also means that, when one activity decreases, so does its related activity. Correlations can also be negative. If interest rates go down, stock prices should go up, and if interest rates rise, stock prices are expected to fall. You have been seeing this example of negative correlation throughout the book. "Negative" doesn't have a bad connotation here because this interest rate versus stock market relationship is valuable to you for making money in NLFs.

If you understood those two examples of correlation, then you should be able to easily pick up on the TA concepts in this chapter. To know what correlation means in a TA sense, you need to have a little knowledge about straight lines, scatterplots, correlation coefficients, and regression. The 10 percent of technicians called "forecasters" live by regression. Regression is one of the math biggies that make modern life possible. There are thousands of examples of successfully applied regression in engineering, biology, health science, and so on. Basically, regression replaces a mess of data points scattered all over the place by a nice, neat, straight line. This allows all sorts of designing, planning, and monitoring to go on which would not be possible without regression.

Trend-followers replace actual data of something like the DJUA with an MAV. Then trend-followers watch for when the DJUA goes above or below its MAV. Forecasters replace actual data with straight lines called "regression lines." Then forecasters project those lines into the future and use them to make guesses about what some stock index will be down the road. Mathematically speaking, regression is much more sophisticated than smoothing with MAVs, but you needn't become an ardent regressionist to appreciate what stock market forecasters do for a living. In this chapter you will be given the basics needed to understand how the stock market is predicted. In Chapter 11 you will see how regression is actually applied to forecasting the market.

STRAIGHT LINES

Besides replacing a table of data with a graph, you can replace that table with an equation. The table below gives guidelines for how many calories per day are required for a moderately active, healthy 20- to 29-year-old person to maintain his or her desired weight. There are three ways that this table will be obliterated by the much more efficient graph/equation team. Table 10-1 has 31 lines in it, but a 20-year-old individual only needs one line. Like most tables, it doesn't give a good idea of how things flow or are related. Finally, what if someone wanted to be 112 pounds? There is no line in the table corresponding to that weight.

————Table 10-1. Weight/Calories————

Weight Desired	Calories Required
100	1500
105	1575
110	1650
...	...
245	3675
250	3750

All three defects of Table 10-1 can be remedied by replacing the table with a graph and an equation. The graph is shown in Fig. 10-1. Here is the formula:

$$C = 15W$$

where C is "calories required" and W is "weight desired." For example, let's help out that 112 pounder:

$$C = 15W$$
$$= (15)(112)$$
$$= 1680 \text{ calories/day}$$

These are guidelines for the other age groups:

$$C = 14W \text{ (30-39 years)}$$
$$C = 13W \text{ (40-49 years)}$$
$$C = 12W \text{ (50-?? years)}$$

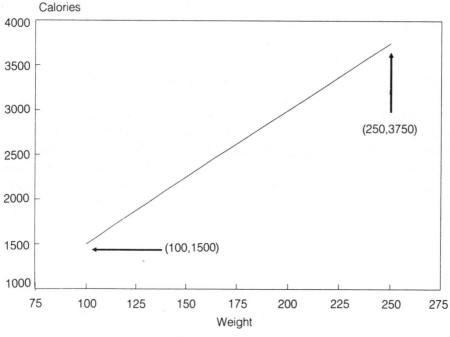

Fig. 10-1. Calorie/Weight Relationship (C = 15W).

In Fig. 10-1 you see a picture of the fundamental relationship: as weight desired increases, so do calories required. The flow in this picture is from lower left to upper right. This flow is like the flow you saw in Chapter 7 for normally (or positively) sloped yield curves. The relationship there was: as maturity increases, so should interest rates. What if you pigged-out over the holidays and lost 10 pounds? Would you be shocked? You should be just as shocked if interest rates go down when maturity goes up. One reason to graph two variables that are highly correlated is to keep track of their relationship so it can be seen when this relationship goes haywire.

Two points are marked in Fig. 10-1. Unlike other relationships you have graphed, you only need graph two points for this one because it only takes two points to draw a straight line. Suppose you wanted to draw the curve in Fig. 10-1. The best way to do it would be to choose the biggest and smallest X-axis values and plug them into the formula, C = 15W. Using the smallest X-axis value, you get:

$$\begin{aligned} C &= 15W \\ &= (15)(100) \\ &= 1500 \end{aligned}$$

Using the biggest X-axis value, you get:

$$\begin{aligned} C &= 15W \\ &= (15)(250) \\ &= 3750 \end{aligned}$$

The X-axis is made to go from 75 to 275 in Fig. 10-1 so that you can see the straight line more clearly. You will be returning to this graph frequently in the next section.

SCATTERPLOTS

Did you notice that the graph in Fig. 10-1 doesn't have weeks or months or days on its X-axis? Didn't bother you a bit, did it? Before this, you were always graphing temperature over day, the S & P 500 over weeks or the Short Interest Ratio over months. Days, weeks, and months are all time-related variables. Figure 10-1 relates calories to weight. Neither of these variables involves time. The graph in Fig. 10-2 is like the first graph, but points are used instead of a line connecting those points. Neither of these two graphs are true "scatterplots." Later on, you will be shown a graph which illustrates how scatterplots got their name. Right now you will be focusing on how to replace those points in Fig. 10-2 with the straight line in Fig. 10-1. Don't fret about any equations. The graphs are what are important.

The second graph contains 31 points which strictly stick to a straight line. Figure 10-1 replaces all those 31 data points in Table 10-1 and replaces the graph of the table (Fig. 10-2) with one straight line. This was easy because those 31 points actually fell on that straight line. Unfortunately, this is a rare occurrence in the real world. It occurs in the calories/weight graph due to the fact that this situation has been idealized. By "idealized" I mean that all the inherent variability present in the real situation that could have been included wasn't included.

In a real-world calories/weight relationship, there would be a fair amount of variability between different people. For instance, you have a friend who eats like a horse and doesn't gain an ounce. People like your friend throw the weight/calorie relationship off. She weighs 100 pounds and eats 4000 calories

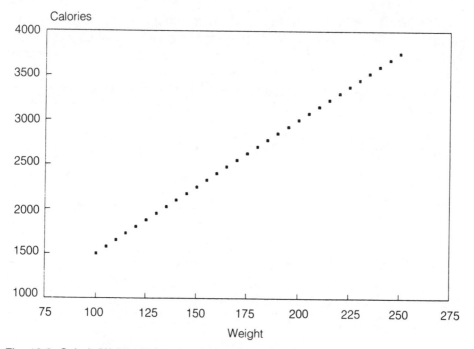

Fig. 10-2. Calorie/Weight Points (can't see in Fig. 10-1).

every day. If you wanted to graph her on Fig. 10-2, her point would fall in the upper left corner area of that graph. When dietitians gather data for graphs like Fig. 10-2, they assemble hundreds of data points and these points don't fall on one nice, straight line. However, even though real-world points don't usually fall exactly on a straight line, it can make sense to replace a bunch of points scattered all over the place with one straight line. This is the situation you will see next.

Interest rates and S & P 500 values furnish a good real-world example of replacing points with a straight line. This time all the variability will be included. There is variability because the S & P 500 doesn't jump up or down each and every time in perfect concert with interest rates. Most of the time when MMP goes up, the S & P 500 will go down, and vice versa. But there are many times when both variables rise and fall together. All in all though, whichever way MMP goes, the S & P 500 goes the opposite way. Look at Fig. 10-3. This is the real world.

Lower interest rates usually, but not always, correspond to higher stock prices and vice versa. The phrase "but not always" in the last sentence is vital. Around the 6 to 6½ percent region for MMP, there correspond S & P 500 values ranging from 250 to 350. High, low, and in-between values of the S & P 500 occur at the single value of 6½ percent for MMP. Unlike Fig. 10-2, Fig. 10-3 shows several different Y-values (S & P 500 values) corresponding to the same

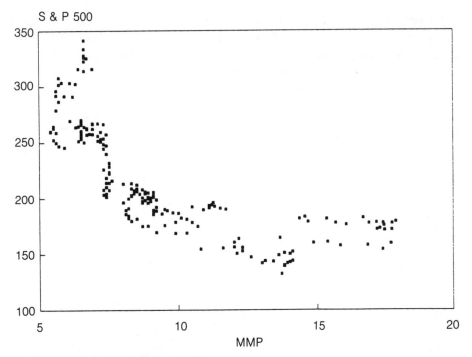

Fig. 10-3. Scatter S & P 500 on MMP.

X-value (MMP value). This is what is meant by "scatter" and this is how scatterplots got their name. Scatterplots commonly have more than one point on a graph over a single X-value. The graphs you saw before in this book were all based on time. Since the S & P 500 had only one value at the end of any given week, all those graphs you saw before were not scatterplots.

Scatter can't be seen in Fig. 10-2 because there is no scatter there. If you pick one X-axis value in Fig. 10-2, you can find only one point lying above it on the graph. There is a fair amount of scatter in Fig. 10-3 because many times, when you pick one X-axis value, you see several points on the graph above that single X-axis value. Figure 10-2 is like planting a garden by first staking it out into nice neat rows with strings and stakes. Figure 10-3 amounts to closing your eyes and heaving a bucket full of assorted seeds in the general direction of the proposed garden. The graph in Fig. 10-2 looks like the person who made the graph had some predetermined notion of what it should look like. Figure 10-3 looks like the person who made the graph didn't care much about how it would look.

Imagine that, while looking at Fig. 10-2 with its individual points displayed, you closed your eyes. When you opened your eyes again, you saw the straight line of Fig. 10-1, instead of the individual points in Fig. 10-2. Now imagine the same thing happening with Figs. 10-3 and 10-4. Figure 10-4 replaces that scatter of points in Figs. 10-3 with a straight line. It was easy to replace the points in Fig. 10-2 with the straight line in Fig. 10-1 because all the points actually did lie on that line. To see how the line in Fig. 10-4 replaces the scatter in Fig. 10-3, you need to learn a little about correlation (in the next section).

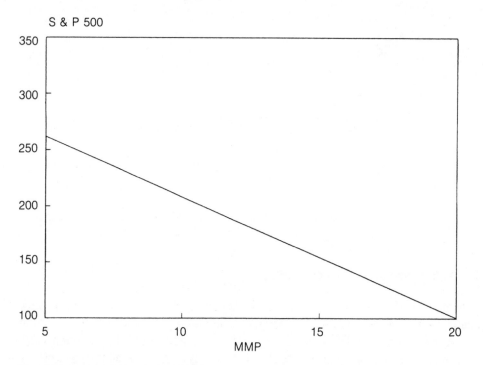

Fig. 10-4. Straight Line S & P/MMP.

Both Fig. 10-3 and 10-4 say that interest rates and the stock market are out-of-sync with one another, but Fig. 10-4 says it more succinctly. You can't just run around and, at random, throw away hundreds of actual data values like those appearing in Fig. 10-3 and replace them with one of those nice, neat straight lines you see in Fig. 10-4. If you were allowed to do this, you would soon lose the handle on how well or poorly two variables relate to one another. Someone else could happen along and, with just as much justification as you used, replace the scatter in Fig. 10-3 with their own straight line.

To keep control of the situation when replacing a scatter of points by a straight line, some mathematical sense must be made of this situation. Using a mathematically sound approach, it will be possible to determine when it makes sense to replace a scatter of points (not to mention all that ugly variability) by one straight line. Remember in what follows that there are two sides to the coin of understanding the stock market. Both sides, fundamentals and technicals, must make sense; otherwise, you might be fooling yourself. Though you are about to enter the realm of TA, you must maintain a handle on the fundamentals, as well.

CORRELATION

You have a basic idea of what correlation is all about. Let's attach a number to that idea. The way this number, called the *correlation coefficient*, is attached to the relationship between two variables is by using a lot of addition, subtraction, multiplication, and division. This means that my trusty PC will do the calculations for you. Calculations will only cloud the issue anyway. What you need to know is how to interpret the correlation coefficient. And that is as easy as knowing the difference between positive and negative.

Rest assured that for any two variables, a correlation coefficient can be calculated. This number will never be less than −1, nor will it ever by more than +1. Look at the figure below. Recall from the introduction to this chapter that there are basically two types of correlation: positive and negative. The best possible correlations (labeled "Fantastic" in the figure) are +1 and −1. This means that the two variables are perfectly related. In fact, it means that one variable can be used in place of the other one with absolutely no loss of information. For purposes of working with the variables, one is exactly like the other.

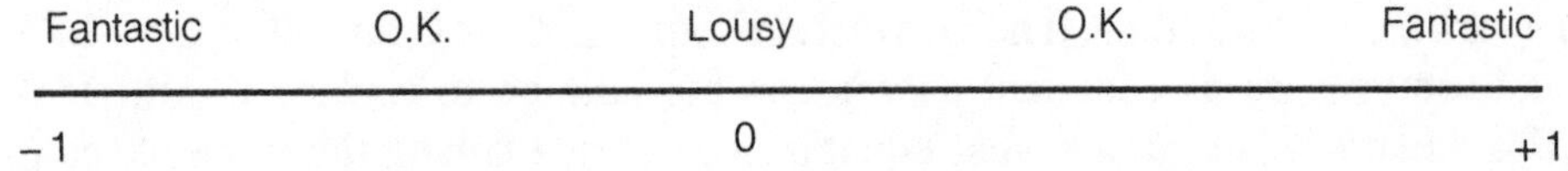

Fantastic	O.K.	Lousy	O.K.	Fantastic
−1		0		+1

Fig. 10-5. Good/Bad Correlation.

Perfect correlation is exemplified in Fig. 10-1 where you can actually substitute, in all confidence, 15W for C. If that 112 pounder asks "How can I maintain my current weight," you can answer with infinite assurance "Eat on the average 1680 calories per day." The calorie/weight relationship is a positive one so that the correlation coefficient in this idealized case is +1.

An example of an idealized situation in which the correlation coefficient is −1 would be the relationship between your heating bill and the outside temperature. Suppose you have a special gas meter attached to a furnace in your home which is used only for heating. This furnace is not used to wash or dry your clothes, heat your bath water, or dry your dishes. Then you would know for a fact that 100 percent of that gas bill was used for heating your house. Now all you would need to do is to take that special gas bill, record the average monthly temperature, and graph the amount of the gas bill over the temperature. As the temperature rose, your heating bill would tumble. As the temperature dropped, your bill would climb.

An example of zero correlation would be when you relate the monthly average price of tea in China with the monthly average number of Italian governments.

Needless to say that, in the real world, correlation coefficients don't land right on $+1$ or -1 very often. In fact, out of every 1000 relationships for which a correlation coefficient is calculated, you might see 50 coefficients fairly close to either $+1$ or -1 and, maybe, 400 fairly close to 0. The other 550 correlation coefficients will lie between -0.70 and -0.30 or between 0.30 and 0.70. With these ideas in mind, the following figure (Fig. 10-6) is a refinement of Fig. 10-5.

Very Strong	Strong	Poor	Strong	Very Strong
-1 $-.70$		$-.30$ 0 $+.30$	$+.70$	$+1$

Fig. 10-6. More Refined Interpretation.

For the S & P 500 and MMP, the correlation coefficient is $-.78$. This would be called a very strong relationship because of the correlation coefficient. The strength of a relationship increases as the correlation coefficient approaches $+1$ or -1. The relationship is considered very weak if its correlation coefficient is close to 0.

The stronger the correlation, the more confident you feel about replacing one variable with another. The correlation coefficient for C and W in C = 15W is $+1$, so you are as confident as you can possibly be to replace C with 15W in this situation. No matter what equation you derive linking the price of tea in China with the number of Italian governments, you wouldn't trust it at all because the correlation coefficient is 0.00 there. You are in an "in-between" type of area when it comes to the S & P 500 and the MMP. Here the correlation coefficient is $-.78$, which is just inside the "very strong" range.

You will be seeing several correlation coefficients in Chapters 10 and 11. Usually, when someone tells you "Those two variables are correlated," they mean that the correlation coefficient is non-zero. Sometimes people throw correlation jargon around trying to impress you in their advertisements. Now that you know enough about correlation coefficients, you needn't be hoodwinked. Just because someone says that two variables are correlated, doesn't mean too much unless they give you a numerical value for the correlation coefficient. Even if a correlation coefficient is non-zero, there is still lot of room out there between -1 and $+1$.

What you've been exposed to so far in this chapter is new, challenging, and crucial to understanding regression. You've seen two scatters of points replaced by two straight lines, and one of the scatterplots had an equation attached to it. In the case of the calorie/weight relationship, the points didn't scatter too much. In fact, the correlation was the strongest possible. For the S & P 500/MMP situation, correlation was very strong. What you should have right now is a general idea of how a straight line can replace a scatterplot of points. You should also have a good feel for what strong and weak correlation coefficients mean for this replacement. When it comes to replacing a scatter of points with a straight line, the bottom line is given by the answer to the question: "How strong is the correlation?" The stronger the correlation, the more confidently can this replacement be made.

REGRESSION

Regression is the mathematical process of replacing a scatterplot of two variables with a straight line. Regression is quite firmly based in math theory, so its validity is unquestionable. This process involves an awful lot of arithmetic. The arithmetic will be ignored, because you only need to get a feel for what regression can do for you when used as a TA tool. You already have nearly all of the knowledge you'll need to understand regression. Just one more piece of information and you will be home free.

You will see for the first time a scatterplot with the regression line drawn through the middle of its mass of points. This is done in Fig. 10-7. For each of 10 major-league baseball games, the number of strikes called by a certain umpire against the home team was recorded by a vigilante group of bleachers fans. These fans also rigged up a laser beam in center field to accurately measure the number

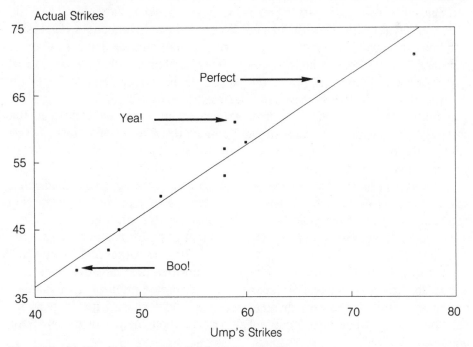

Fig. 10-7. An Umpire's Accuracy (strikes per game).

of actual strikes which should have been called by that ump against their beloved team. The bleachers coalition was out to get the goods on the umpire.

A husband-wife combo in the bleachers gang were PC addicts, so they brought their portable PC to the tenth game in order to perform an on-the-spot regression analysis of the umpire's alleged bad calls. After the last strike of the game was called, the wife announced that the ump had a correlation coefficient of 0.9737. The vigilantes adjourned to the nearest bar to drown their sorrows. The ump was extremely accurate in his calls against the home team. No longer could the group rant and rave and boo him with gusto. Regression spoiled their fun.

You see two things graphed in Fig. 10-7: the regression line and the actual data points. In one game, the umpire called 44 strikes when the laser beam picked up only 39. This was his most biased performance against the home team, but it is only one data point and not enough to hang him with. In another game, he called 59 strikes when he should have called 61. This gives an advantage to the home team. One time he was perfect and called 67 out of 67.

Unlike the calories/weight example, the actual data points vary about the regression line. If the correlation were 1.00, as in the weight/calorie example, then the 10 points would all fall on the regression line. The correlation in this case is 0.9737, which is just a bit off of perfection. You can see that many of the points fall a little off the line. For the most part, though, the points cluster pretty tightly around the regression line. If the points had an awful lot of scatter to them, the correlation coefficient would be much closer to 0.00.

Since 0.9737 is such a strong correlation, you could confidently replace the scatter of points with the straight line. When you hand someone a regression line, you can convince them of its validity with another number that is even more revealing than the correlation coefficient. This number is called the *coefficient of determination*, and it is simply the square of the correlation coefficient. In the current example, the coefficient of determination is $(0.9737)(0.9737) = 0.9480$. The reason that the coefficient of determination is more revealing than the correlation coefficient is because it can be interpreted as a percentage. If you multiply the coefficient of determination by 100 and tack on a percent symbol, you get 94.8 percent in this example.

The 94.8 percent tells you that, if you throw away the actual data and count solely on the regression line, the line explains about 95 percent of the relationship between reality and the umpire's calls. Important as the correlation coefficient has been for the discussion so far, the coefficient of determination will be even more important for you in studying regression. The correlation coefficient is still needed to indicate when the relationship is a positive or a negative one. This is because when you take the square of any negative number, that number becomes positive. If you were given a coefficient of determination of 95 percent, you couldn't tell whether it arose out of a correlation coefficient of 0.9737 or one of $-.9737$.

The graph in Fig. 10-8 shows the scatter of the S & P 500 over MMP and the regression line passing through those points. There are two things to notice: time has apparently been eliminated from the picture, and there is a lot more scatter than in the baseball example. (Time is still lurking in the background, and it will reappear in a new exciting way in the next chapter.) The increased scatter is apparent when you consider that the correlation coefficient is − .78. This means that the coefficient of determination is (− .78)(− .78) = 0.61 or 61 percent. Recall that a drop from 100 to 95 percent in the baseball example (compared to the calorie/weight example) showed up as a little bit of scatter about that regression line. Here the drop is from 100 percent down to 61 percent and the scatter is much more evident.

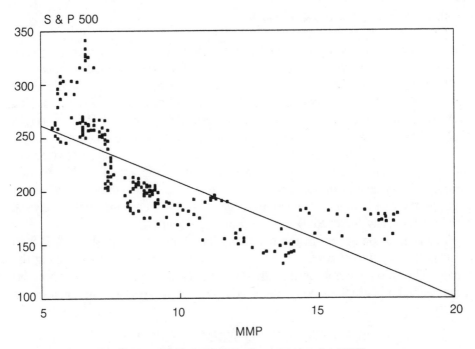

Fig. 10-8. Line with Scatter for S & P/MMP (Jan 1981 to Jul 1988).

What you now have is a conclusion which states "61 percent of the ups and downs in the S & P 500 can be explained by the ups and downs in the MMP." Though 61 percent is not all that close to 100 percent, it is still a healthy percentage. Look at the next figure. Just like you call correlation poor when the coefficient falls between 0.00 and 0.30 or between 0.00 and − .30, you call a regression line a "poor fit" for the data when the coefficient of determination falls between 0 and 9 percent. A regression line is a good fit for the data it replaces if its coefficient of determination shows it explains between 9 and 49 percent

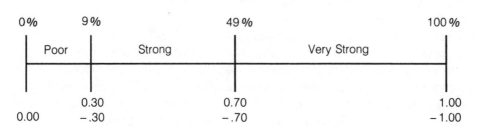

Coefficient of Determination

Correlation Coefficient

Fig. 10-9. Interpreting the Two Coefficients.

of the relationship. A very strong fit occurs when the coefficient is bigger than 49 percent. It is always nice to have at least half an idea of what is going on.

Naturally, the goal of regressionists is to explain as much as possible about the relationship between two variables like the market and interest rates. You now have a line which explains over half the variability of the S & P 500 in terms of MMP rates. This is pretty good for using only one variable to explain another. There is still 39 percent of S & P 500 ups and downs going unexplained, but to explain anything near 100 percent of a variable in a real-world situation is rarely, if ever, achieved. Once you get close to 90 percent, things usually start to get pretty sticky. In fact, even 90 percent is usually not attained unless several variables (possibly hundreds!) are used in one equation.

In a regression equation, the main variable of interest (like the S & P 500) is called the *dependent variable*. The dependent variable is graphed along the Y-axis. The other variable in a regression equation is called the *independent variable*, and it is graphed along the X-axis. Here is the regression equation for Fig. 10-8:

$$S \& P\ 500 = -10.459MMP + 311.496$$

The S & P 500 is the dependent variable because its values depend on values we substitute for MMP in the above formula. MMP is the independent variable. If you ignore the scatterplot and use this equation to estimate what the S & P 500 will be when MMP is at 10 percent, you will get an S & P 500 value of 206.91 because:

$$
\begin{aligned}
S \& P\ 500 &= -10.459MMP + 311.496 \\
&= (-10.459)(10) + 311.496 \\
&= -104.59 + 311.496 \\
&= 206.906 \\
&= 206.91 \text{ (rounding to pennies)}
\end{aligned}
$$

Projectors develop such equations for you and plug numbers like "10" into them, and then tell you in their newsletters that the S & P 500 should be 206.91 plus or minus some tolerance factor.

When you follow a projector, all that has just occurred and more is involved behind the scenes. Trend-followers smooth information out of the data by using MAVs. Projectors enter thousands of numbers, decimal points and all, into their computers, and the computers apply regression procedures to that mountain of detailed data and spit out regression equations. Projectors look at many things to judge whether or not an equation fits the data well. The coefficient of determination is one of the most important things they look at to decide the question of whether or not a regression equation is worth using.

SUMMARY

Has this chapter given you more insight into what the word "correlation" means? It wasn't so bad learning about correlation in a TA sense. The correlation coefficient is just a number between -1 and $+1$ which tells you how strong or how weak a relationship between two variables is. The correlation coefficient arose because scatterplots were being replaced by straight lines, so you needed to have a good idea of how valid this replacement was. Some relationships are more valid than others, and some aren't valid at all. This is just real life imitating mathematics.

Regression is the math method that calculates equations for those straight lines which replace scatterplots. A very revealing number, the coefficient of determination, arose when you were learning about regression. This coefficient tells you the percentage, between 0 and 100 percent, of the dependent variable's ups and downs, which are explained by the independent variable. Variability is an omnipresent thing so, when we try to explain it, we would like a firm handle on how good our explanation is. That handle is the coefficient of determination.

Good trend-followers are as successful at switching NLFs for you as are good projectors. Why do projectors get so much more involved with their math if they accomplish no more than do trend-followers? For the same reason that master craftspeople do a higher-quality job than do run-of-the-mill artisans. It is simply in them to do work of a higher quality, even if the rewards are no greater. Be it furniture or a handmade suit, you can get the same use out of a well-made item as you can get out of a master-crafted item, but the pleasure and assurance you have knowing that special care was taken with the master-crafted item adds to your enjoyment of that furniture or piece of clothing.

11

Examples of
Market Forecasting

THE RELATIONSHIP BETWEEN TWO VARIABLES OVER TIME WAS EXCLUDED FROM consideration in Chapter 10. Time must be returned to the picture in order to discuss forecasting. To know whether or not to be in a stock NLF now, you need to have some idea of what the future holds. This means that anyone who gives you advice on when or how much to be in the market is making forecasts about future market behavior. So far you have looked at the S & P 500/MMP relationship as if the two indices were moving lock-step through time. Whenever you saw a graph of these two variables, each S & P 500 value and each MMP value emanated from the same week in the data table.

Soon you will see a graph that has MMP values in the present paired with S & P 500 values in the future. One important consideration in determining the validity of this new kind of relationship is the strength of the correlation. If correlation is strong, then it can make sense to use a current MMP value to predict a future S & P 500 value. Other important considerations about when forecasting makes sense will also be discussed.

MMP is a monetary index. You will also see the S & P 500 predicted from a volume index and a price index. In fact, all three types of indices will be thrown in the same pot to stew up a prediction for the S & P 500. The sole intent of all these predictions is to show you how TA forecasters do their job. Don't use the predictions for your own investing. Seeing an example of how forecasting the market is accomplished will help you develop a feeling for what good projectors do. This feeling will give you confidence in their forecasts.

Trend-followers and forecasters don't usually land right on the money, but they do usually make specific statements about what they expect the market to be doing. There is no one who can be right all of the time. A good success rate is calling three out of four shots right. That is simply in the nature of the game. If someone has a worse long-term success rate, then that person is below par at calling turns in the market. If someone tells you that they have a better long-term track record than three out of four, then they are trying to pull the wool over your eyes.

LEAD/LAG

It is April in northern Minnesota and you see a robin. Ah! Spring can't be far ahead. Next thing you know, it is 10 above zero and that bird flew into your cabin and perched on the fireplace mantel. Back to the drawing board? No. Things like this happen. Same goes for groundhogs. Robins and groundhogs are "leading indicators" of spring. The stock market also has fallible leading indicators. In fact, when it comes to predicting the weather or the stock market, there don't seem to be any infallible indicators. That doesn't mean you should ignore weather reports or stock market forecasts. You should heed their prophecies with a grain of salt, however.

One index leads another when it is a portent of things to come. In biological parlance, the robin is said to "lead spring," or spring is said to be "lead by the robin." Spring is also said to "lag the robin." When the robin arrives, then, at some near future time, spring will have sprung. If interest rates go up, then, at a future time, stock prices will fall. No fundamentalist or technician would dispute this fact. The arguments arise when two questions are probed: How much is up, and how far in the future is the time?

To get a feel for what projectors do, imagine the following situation. Suppose you are given an MMP value for this week, and in return you have to guess the S & P 500 value 1 year from now based on that MMP value. Sounds tough, doesn't it? That is what projectors do. All you would have to work with would be a data table like the "usual" one below (Table 11-1). If you proceed in the

_____Table 11-1. Usual Data Table_____

WK	S & P 500	WK	MMP
1	136.34	1	16.3
2	133.48	2	16.7
..	...	..	...
53	122.55	53	12.1
54	119.55	54	12.0
..	...	..	...
395	263.50	395	7.2
396	272.02	396	7.3

usual fashion, you would plot both variables over time by pairing off values from the same line in the table. Don't plot anything just yet, though.

You are accustomed to this type of plotting. There has to be a little twist thrown in because there is a more productive way of arranging the table. First you should try to play the forecasting game with the table as it stands. This will help you find out what "leading" and "lagging" mean to a forecaster. If you tried to forecast an S & P 500 value 1 year from now based on a current MMP value, you probably found yourself looking ahead 52 weeks in the table. Besides being a pain in the neck to have to look ahead 52 values all the time, you might have felt guilty because you thought you were cheating. This wasn't really cheating on your part. After all, how can you guess at a future value unless you get a feel for the data?

You necessarily have to look at S & P 500 values 52 weeks in the future. Based on the feeling you get from the data, you will be ready when the real fun begins. That happens when someone calls you right now and says: "Interest rates are at 9.2 percent this week. What do you think the market will be doing next year?" When you play this forecasting game, you find yourself ignoring the first year of S & P 500 values because they don't fit in the picture anymore. If MMP is to be a leading indicator of the S & P 500, then you have to determine the effect an MMP value in the 1st week has on an S & P 500 value in the 53rd week. You wind up no longer caring about S & P 500 values for the first 52 weeks.

The same thing happens to the last 52 weeks of MMP data you have available. The S & P 500 data end at Week 396. To predict that week's S & P 500 value, you need to use the MMP value from Week 344. Values for MMP for Weeks 345 through 396 don't matter anymore. You wind up no longer caring about MMP values for the last 52 weeks.

Stock market forecasters have a way of solving the problems you just ran into. What they do is arrange the "usual" table into the "unusual" table. The forecaster's intent is to line up current MMP values with future S & P 500 values. This table ignores the first year of S & P 500 data and the last year of MMP

———Table 11-2. Unusual Data Table———

WK	S & P 500	WK	MMP
53	122.55	1	16.3
54	119.55	2	16.7
..	...	..	...
152	167.18	100	9.2
..	...	..	...
313	246.92	261	7.5
..	...	..	...
395	263.50	343	6.6
396	272.02	344	6.6

data. Not only that, but, after chopping off 1 year of data apiece, the S & P 500 column is jammed upwards so that Week 53 coincides with Week 1 for MMP. What is going on here? The forecaster is making like a robin or a groundhog and leading the S & P 500 by the MMP. When the forecaster aligns the weeks that are 1 year apart, he or she is getting ready to project the future. A few pictures of what is going on will help you visualize the situation.

Look at the graph in Fig. 11-1. This graph is the result of graphing both curves in the "usual" table and then erasing one portion from each graph. Erase the first year of the S & P 500 and the last year of MMP. This leaves you with the same numbers which appear in the "unusual" table but does not give you the arrangement of that table. To get the arrangement of the "unusual" table you need to move the S & P 500 column upward. The same thing can be accomplished in the graph if you shove MMP to the right 52 weeks. This has been accomplished in Fig. 11-2.

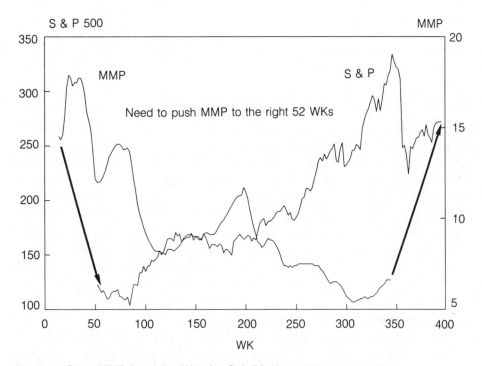

Fig. 11-1. Does MMP Lead the Way for S & P? (Jan 1981 to Jul 1988).

What allows you to do all this pushing, erasing, and jamming? Your imagination. Why do you bother doing it? Because you want to develop a relationship between current MMP values and future S & P 500 values. You can't do that unless you generate the right pairs of numbers. In practice, the first thing forecasters do when developing a relationship is calculate the correlation coefficient. This

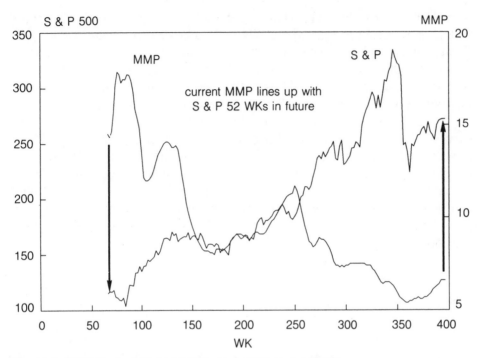

Fig. 11-2. MMP Pushed Right 52 WKs (Jan 1981 to Jul 1988).

tells them whether it will be fruitful or not to go through the trouble of scatterplotting the points. A scatterplot of points for the "usual" table is given in Fig. 10-8, Chapter 10. The graph in Fig. 11-3 shows a scatter of points for the "unusual". Both these scatterplots look quite a bit alike. The main difference is that the correlation coefficient for Fig. 11-3 is – .81 while the correlation coefficient for Fig. 10-8 is – .78.

A regression line is passed through the scatter in Fig. 11-3. In the same fashion you replaced C (calories required) with 15W (weight desired) in Chapter 10, you can replace the scatter of points in this graph with the formula for the regression line. When you replace the points with an equation, this is called *projection*. In projection a current value for MMP is plugged into the regression equation and out pops a future S & P 500 value.

From now on just think of forecasting (or projecting or predicting) as leading the S & P 500 by the MMP, scattering their pairs of points and passing a regression line through that scatterplot. This is how forecasters do their job. They look at dozens of monetary, volume, and price indices and then look at hundreds of ways of transforming those indices (by multiplying them, dividing them, taking square roots, and so on) to try to come up with regression lines that have strong correlations to a stock index like the S & P 500. One important transformation projectors use is leading one variable by another. Leading variables is not at all

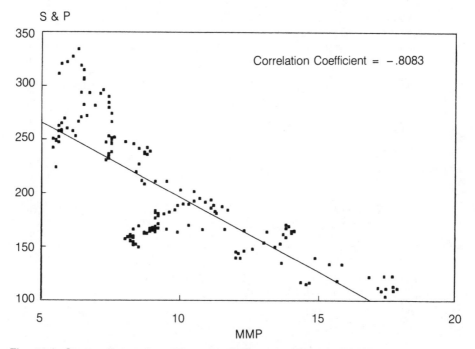

Fig. 11-3. Scatter Future S & P/Current MMP (Jan 1981 to Jul 1988).

unusual for forecasters. Good forecasters are even more successful than groundhogs.

WITH MONETARY INDICES

You first need to make a note of one thing about the rest of the graphs in this chapter. The rest of the graphs run from April 1981 to July 1988. These graphs start in April because the DJUA 13-week oscillator is used for the price index. The 13-week oscillator isn't defined until Week 14. This is the reason that the correlation coefficient in Fig. 11-4 is different from the one in Fig. 11-3. The graph in Fig. 11-4 contains 13 fewer points than does Fig. 11-3. Now that you have that cleared up, it is time to proceed.

Someone with a black belt in regression analysis can look at Fig. 11-4 and dream up some nifty ways to transform the numbers represented there. You will concentrate on the basics like scattering one variable over another, passing the regression line through the scatterplot and interpreting the correlation coefficient. Fig. 11-4 does all of these things for you. It gives you a good picture of the situation at hand, which is what graphs should do. The correlation coefficient is – .78, so the regression equation will give strong predicted values of the S & P 500 from corresponding MMP rates.

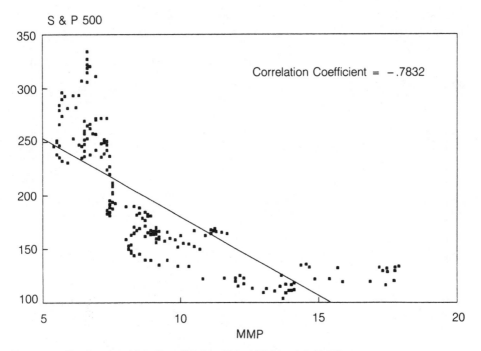

Fig. 11-4. Regression Line thru Scatter (Apr 1981 to Jul 1988).

Now look at Fig. 11-5. The regression equation obtained from the scatterplot in Fig. 11-4 was used to calculate the "Predicted" curve. The "Actual" curve is composed of S & P 500 values for Weeks 14 to 396. It is exciting to see these two curves when you realize that the "Predicted" curve mimics the "Actual" curve by using only MMP values. The coefficient of determination is 0.61, so that 61 percent of the up and down motion in the "Actual" curve is accounted for by the up and down motion of the "Predicted" curve. This is pretty good. Even though the relationship between these two variables is a strong one, predicted values aren't always that close to actual values. This is because 39 percent of the variability in the S & P 500 is due to factors other than MMP rates.

Now consider how predicted values are used to mimic actual values. Suppose that the current MMP value is 7.2 percent. Plugging that value into the regression equation gives an S & P 500 value of 236.19 for 1 year in the future. This guess is based on the regression equation and won't be exactly on target. Trend-followers say that "the market is in a strong uptrend," meaning "it looks like stock NLFs are a good bet because we don't see the market falling any time soon." Projectors say "the S & P 500 is expected to increase to (about) 236.19 in 1 year, so it is good to stay in your stock NLF." The business of projectors is to say "how much" and "how far in the future." They don't have to be right on the mark to be successful.

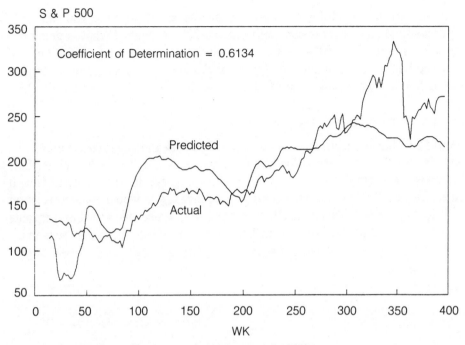

S & P 500

Coefficient of Determination = 0.6134

Predicted

Actual

WK

Fig. 11-5. Predicted versus Actual (Apr 1981 to Jul 1988).

Another important use for developing a prediction equation is to know technically that interest rates and stock prices, for example, are strongly related. Fundamentalists knew this for a long time before technicians came along. Technicians verify that this relationship is true and state how true it is via the coefficient of determination. Remember way back in Chapter 4 when you first saw the S & P 500/MMP relationship? You could sort of see the variables moving along through time and out of sync with one another. Figure 11-4 shows you exactly how MMP and the S & P 500 move along out of sync and Fig. 11-5 shows you how you can make use of this fact. The regression line slopes downward (it has a negative correlation coefficient) in Fig. 11-4. This is what is meant technically by "out of sync." The relationship is a strong one (coefficient of determination is 61 percent), so there is strong TA verification for the fundamental notion represented here.

Something else quite important is demonstrated by Fig. 11-5. The mathematically sophisticated method of regression can't predict the S & P 500 right on the nose. In light of this fact, how can any other method be expected to do better? In other words, since the best method around isn't perfect, you must beware when someone sounds like he or she has a lock on predicting future stock prices. In all the universe, the absolute best method of predicting the S & P 500 from MMP is regression. Ouija boards, astrology, goat entrails, and tea leaves are no match for regression analysis. Since the best you can do is regression and since regression can't explain 100 percent of what is going on, you now have one, big fat secret of the universe: anyone who comes on as if he or she has a monopoly on investment truths is either fooling you, or fooling him- or herself, or fooling both of you.

WITH VOLUME INDICES

Figure 11-6 shows a scatterplot of the S & P 500 over the negative volume index (see Chapter 8). The correlation coefficient for this graph is $-.77$. Note that, shape-wise, the graph looks an awful lot like the graph in Fig. 11-4. In fact, if you scattered MMP over the negative volume index, you would get a correlation coefficient of 0.8247. This means that either one of these two variables explains about 68 percent of the other one. This fact is interesting for two reasons.

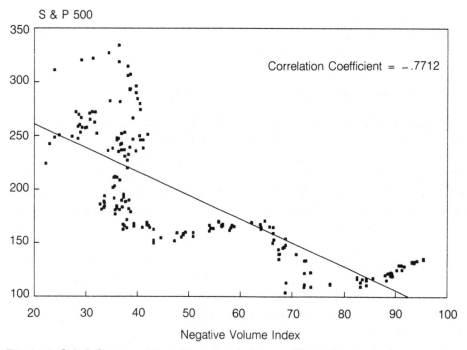

Fig. 11-6. S & P Scattered over Volume (Apr 1981 to Jul 1988).

One reason is that MMP values are arrived at in a fashion totally unlike negative volume index values. This is an example of regression demonstrating relationships which would have otherwise been hard to spot. MMP values are obtained by taking a weighted average of interest-bearing certificates held by the NLF and then extracting fractional roots. Sounds fancy but, with computers, the hardest part is making sure the data are o.k. Negative volume index values change only when volume falls and are calculated on a percentage basis anchored at some arbitrary point in the past. Nonetheless, when these two variables are regressed, a strong link is shown between them. The uncovering of hidden relationships makes regression analysis a powerful research tool both inside and outside of TA.

The other reason that the 68-percent coefficient of determination between MMP and the negative volume index is interesting is because both these variables are strongly related to the S & P 500. The MMP/S & P 500 relationship has a coefficient of determination of 61 percent and the negative volume index/S & P 500 relationship has a coefficient of determination of 59 percent. (See Fig. 11-7.) What this means is that forecasters would choose either one, but not both, of these two variables to predict S & P 500 values. Why? Because using both of them would be like carrying extra baggage and, when traveling the math route, it is always best to travel light. This is shown in the "Real Situation" (see Fig. 11-8).

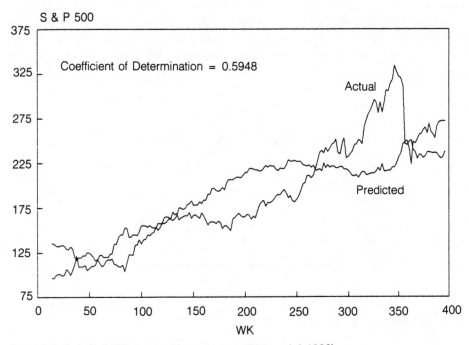

Fig. 11-7. S & P Predicted by Volume (Apr 1981 to Jul 1988).

What regressionists dream about when trying to explain something like the S & P 500 are two variables (call them the "XXX Index" and the "YYY Index") which explain all about the S & P 500 and don't interfere with each other (that is, XXX and YYY have zero correlation). Look at the "Unreal Situation" below (Fig. 11-9). Out of hundreds, even thousands, of possible independent variables,

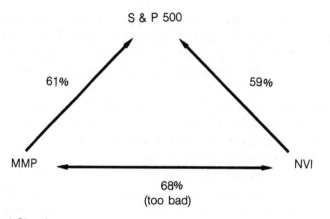

Fig. 11-8. Real Situation.

if just two would explain the dependent variable in this fashion, then forecasters would be ecstatic. Their dream is unrealistic because explaining one variable by two other variables is such a rare phenomenon that they don't even consider the possibility. Most of the time projectors settle for one or two dozen independent variables to do a decent job of predicting the future. XXX and YYY merely offer a nice target at which to aim.

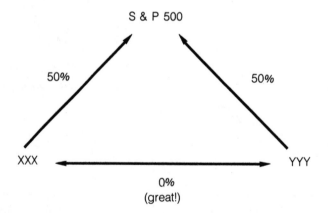

Fig. 11-9. Unreal Situation.

WITH PRICE INDICES

The example of zero correlation you saw in Chapter 10 was rather hokey. It got the idea across, but correlation had not been discussed enough at that point to give you a more solid illustration of a really weak relationship. Now for the worst real relationship you will probably ever see. Look at Fig. 11-10. When you see a joke like this, you don't even have to bother calculating a correlation coefficient (it is − .0762). Draw a vertical line through "1" on the X-axis. There are eight points on that line and not one of them comes anywhere near the regression line. But don't get the impression that price indices are bad to use in predicting the stock market. For instance, the DJUA/S & P 500 relationship has a correlation coefficient of 0.9516 and a coefficient of determination of 91 percent.

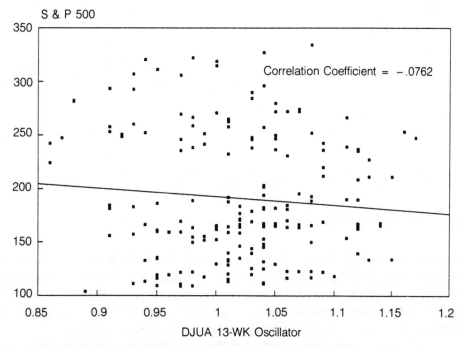

Fig. 11-10. Worst Real Correlation in Book! (Apr 1981 to Jul 1988).

To see what kind of predictive power you achieve when you use such a weak relationship, look at Fig. 11-11. The DJUA 13-week oscillator explains about 6/10 of 1 percent of the S & P 500. You could do better drawing S & P 500 numbers out of a hat. Yet there are oscillators that are good predictors. The reason you are seeing this one is because it is so poor and its parent, the DJUA, is so good. This comparison should make you wonder. It is the same old story of life imitating math. Good parents don't always have good progeny. You still have solid information here, though. Now you can avoid the DJUA 13-week oscillator for forecasting the S & P 500.

Before projectors do their first regression, they look at all the correlations involved to pick out miserable performers and exclude them from analyses. If this wasn't done, a lot of wasted motion would occur. For example, if a forecaster was handed eleven independent variables with which to predict a dependent

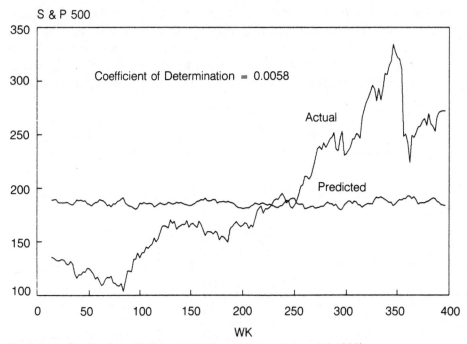

Fig. 11-11. Predict from DJUA 13-WK Oscltr (Apr 1981 to Jul 1988).

variable, there would be 66 correlations to examine. Calculating 66 correlation coefficients involves hundreds of thousands of nit-picking additions, subtractions, divisions, and so on. One glance at those 66 correlation coefficients is usually enough to eliminate at least half a dozen independent variables from consideration because they don't correlate strongly with the dependent variable.

Another reason projectors look at all the correlation coefficients before they regress is to see which independent variables are strongly related to each other. As you saw in the last section, this helps to get rid of excess baggage and sometimes opens your eyes to unexpected relationships. You might have a good relationship now; but you are always looking for a better one or a different one to put a different slant on things.

WITH ALL THREE

Figure 11-12 shows the "Predicted" curve obtained by using all three indices (even that bogus oscillator) considered in this chapter. The "Predicted" curve explains 67 percent of the "Actual" curve. You should prefer the "Predicted" curves in Figs. 11-5 or 11-7 to this one. Though 67 percent is larger than the 61 percent and 59 percent of the two previous graphs, there are two too many independent variables used. One variable to dump right away is the oscillator since it doesn't predict anything. The other variable to eliminate depends on those

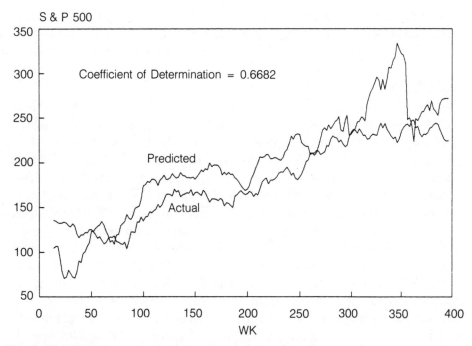

Fig. 11-12. Prediction from All Three (Apr 1981 to Jul 1988).

other considerations alluded to in the introduction to this chapter. Let's discuss these considerations now.

Which of MMP and the negative volume index is the easiest to calculate? Since you can get MMP rates out of a newspaper each week, MMP is the easier of the two to come by. It is also the simplest of the two to understand. If you were bent on projecting only the S & P 500, then, by all means, use MMP. What if you were in the habit of projecting a lot of different things: the price of gold, the strongest sectors to invest in with sector NLFs, what percentage of your investment dollars should be in a money NLF and what percentage in a stock NLF, the price of oil, and so on. You might well find that in some of these cases the negative volume index does a better job for you than MMP. Professionals follow these same guidelines: use the simplest index, the easiest index to obtain, or the most meaningful index.

By far the most important attribute an independent variable should have is to be fundamentally related to the dependent variable. If this isn't true, then you will get burned somewhere down the road. Once you get cooking with a neat relationship, you tend to start taking it for granted. It has worked for you in the past, you update the data every week, and everything seems fine. But without a sound fundamental basis, the relationship could well fall apart on you overnight. You won't see it coming or know why it dissipated. When a relationship is soundly based in fundamentals and it starts to come unglued, you can go back and examine what went wrong and maybe set it right again. If you can't set it right, then you will have ideas about what to look for in the next relationship.

SUMMARY

Projectors lead one variable, say the S & P 500, by another variable, say MMP, and then find the regression equation which ties these two variables together. To forecast the stock market, projectors repeat this plan of attack with dozens of variables playing the role of MMP and come up with dozens of different equations. The first consideration in all of these regressions is that the S & P 500 be fundamentally related to MMP or to any of the other independent variables. After fundamental significance is established, TA significance can be investigated.

When these regressions have been accomplished, the projector's job is not yet done. With only a dozen variables, there are 66 relationships to consider. Now ponder the fact that each of the 11 independent variables (the twelfth variable is the dependent variable) is made to lead the S & P 500 by 1, 2, on up to 12 months. Instead of 11 independent variables, there are now $(11)(12) = 132$ independent variables. These 132 variables can be transformed by multiplication, division, rooting, and all sorts of other types of mathematical machinations. This could easily result in thousands of regressions when it all started with only 12 variables!

Even with all this regressing going on, only a few equations might result which provide meaningful predictions of what the stock market will do in coming months. These predictions are good ones if they are in the ballpark three out of four times. "Ballpark" here refers to "the predicted value, plus or minus a tolerance factor." For example: "The S & P 500 six months from now will be 300.00 plus or minus 30.00." Only one-tenth of technicians are projectors because forecasting statements look like "the S & P 500 will be between 270 and 330 six months from now." Trend-followers and fundamentalists don't have to lay it on the line like that.

No matter who is predicting the future, the fact is that no method is more accurate and consistent than one using regression analysis. If someone predicts the future and doesn't use regression analysis, those predictions may be heavily dependent upon which side of the bed the person got out of that morning. Using regression analysis, numbers are crunched by mathematically proven techniques to arrive at consistent and fairly accurate estimates of future market conditions.

Just like correlation is the gauge of strength for a relationship, a projector's track record is the gauge of how much you can trust him or her. Long-term records are the only ones worth paying attention to, which implies that you should stick with your pro's advice through good and bad times over the long haul. If you choose a good pro, he or she is consistent. If you don't follow that pro's advice, *you* become inconsistent.

12

No-Load Profits
and You

INVESTMENT ADVICE IS NOT GIVEN TO YOU, IT IS SOLD TO YOU. THE REASON YOU buy that advice is because the future is uncertain and you want the guidance that a professional advisor can give. As good as the pro's advice is, it does you no good unless you follow it. Assuming you follow the advice of a good professional, how well can you expect to do? That depends partly on the type of risk-taker you are. There are objective standards upon which you can base your investment success. A good TA pro will give you clear and consistently good advice which, if you follow it over the long run, will help you reach your investment goals.

Since you are being sold investment advice, beware of perfume-mouthed alligators. Over the last 10 years, the S & P 500 with dividends reinvested has gained an average of 15.27 percent per year. Choosing good NLFs and following the advice of a good TA professional could allow you to beat that performance by a few percent per year. This gets you to the 18-percent to 20-percent range. When you hear claims bordering on 25-percent average yearly return on investment, chances are that a snow job is being performed on you. Advertising is like letting students grade their own tests. Grades will tend to be quite inflated and even the best students are forced to go along with the crowd lest they gig themselves. What you need is a good idea of what kind of returns you can expect.

There are do's and don'ts for any activity you take part in. It is best to fix these in your mind early in your investment experience because it takes practice to form the right habits. Many such guidelines are common sense, so it seems innocuous to mention them. But sure enough, you go fishing with someone in a canoe and that person, against all warnings, will stand up. "Dumb" does not begin to describe such an act. Hopefully you won't lose any of your favorite lures. (You can always find another fishing partner.)

Two hot ways of investing in NLFs have emerged in the last few years. One is making a portfolio of funds and the other is sector fund investing. Some NLF advisors are for these methods and some are against these methods. Both types of advisors want your business, so don't listen to what they say. The basics of these two types of NLF investing will help you make up your own mind.

HOW WELL CAN YOU DO?

You need to relieve yourself of fantasies before you can come down to earth. Go back in time to October 3, 1980 and imagine you are going to be stranded on an island for 3 months. You will be given plenty of things for a relaxing, comfortable stay, but you are allowed only one personal item and you can't bring that item back with you. What would that item be? Yes! A sheet of paper giving weekly closing values and ex dividend dates for the Windsor NLF from January 2, 1981 to February 26, 1988. Three months should be enough time to memorize it. You return home and begin investing with $1000 at the end of the first week.

You put your money in Windsor when it is going to go up the next week, otherwise you switch to MMP. Windsor will rise from $10.47 to $10.68 from Friday of Week 1 to Friday of Week 2, so your $1000 goes into Windsor that first week. Windsor will drop to $10.65 at the end of Week 3, so you switch to MMP at the close of Week 2. Proceed like this for 372 weeks and the initial $1000 grows to $32,256 during the 7-year period (62.7 percent per year). This would have involved only 185 toll-free switches and would have beat the pants off of Buy/Hold which gained a paltry 20.2 percent per year over that same period.

Now for the real world. Table 12-1 is the same as the "Beating the CPI" table (Table 5-4) that appeared in Chapter 5, except for a few rearrangements of lines. For the last 10 years, this table represents reality as opposed to

─────── **Table 12-1. Real World Situations** ───────
(1978 to 1987)

Situation	Gain (%)	Factor
Inflation	6.39	1.00
Money Market	9.97	1.56
S & P 500 wo/divs	10.02	1.57
Fixed Income/Income	13.13	2.05
Balanced	14.53	2.27
S & P 500 w/divs	15.27	2.39
Growth	15.45	2.42
Aggressive	16.38	2.56

advertising claims. Use the table so you can reduce some of the uncertainty about the future when you plan your NLF investments. This won't be as simple as "I am the fixed-income-type of person, and so can expect to gain 13.13 percent per year before taxes over the next 10 years." Using the table as a planning tool will be easy for you once a few things are set straight.

You already know two things you need to use the "Real World" table: your risk tolerance and various investment objectives. Assuming a balanced risk tolerance and the three investment objectives of an IRA, a new car and Las Vegas money, you can invest the three available amounts in an income NLF, a balanced NLF, and a growth fund, respectively. Many, varied, confusing and unsubstantiated tweakings of this method will be cast at you by investment "professionals." For free, you can do your own tweaking and invest the money you saved in a good NLF.

The IRA adjustment comes when you begin to approach the golden years. Looking ahead to retirement time, you will have time on your hands, won't have a job, and won't have kids. Without offending too many thousands of people, you should begin tweaking your IRA about the age of 40. Maybe put half in an income fund and half in a money market fund. The new car money can go in a balanced NLF, because being a balanced person, you can sleep at night knowing your money is in that type of fund. If the new car is looming on the not-too-distant horizon and if your newsletter tells you the market is strong, then you can put half or all of your new car investment in a growth fund. A few years down the road, this might allow you to buy a luxury car instead of a compact. If you are going to Las Vegas (pronounced "Lost Wages") and the market is strong, you might feel like putting half or all your Las Vegas money in an aggressive NLF.

You can be charged a $500 initial fee plus 2 percent of the amount you will invest in those three NLFs for the guidance in the last paragraph. Instead of being just a tad wishy-washy (by saying "might" or "half or all"), people charging you those fees will come on as if they know what they're talking about. Talk to three different investment professionals and you will get three different answers. These three answers won't vary all that much from each other or from your own common sense and will amount to what I just told you. If absolute tables exist that state exactly what percentage should be invested in what type of investment by people of a certain age and risk tolerance, then they are a big secret.

The returns in the above table are just guidelines. You have heard, and correctly so, that "future returns cannot be guaranteed based upon past performance." This does not imply that you throw the Real World table in a wastebasket and bite your fingernails wondering what will happen to your investments. How well you do will be gauged in 10 years by another Real World table, with a future decade at the top. Whether you will significantly beat the new table or lose out to it depends on how closely you follow the advice of your newsletter and how well you track your NLFs. You know how to choose a good letter and how to choose good funds. The rest is up to you.

The 1978–1987 Real World table suggests that, depending on your risk-level and investment objectives, you can expect about 10 to 16 percent per year over the next 10 years, if you just park your money in some NLF and forget about it. Following a good newsletter and choosing good NLFs should get you about 10 to 20 percent per year. The low-end figure is still 10 percent because you might be just a money NLF-type person. If you are, you have plenty of company because 80 percent of the money invested in mutual funds goes into money market or bond funds. Only 20 percent of mutual fund money goes into stock funds. The 20-percent gain at the upper end of the next 10 years is thrown in because some of you may invest aggressively in good NLFs.

Over that 10-year period, your newsletter will make some good calls and some bad calls. A good newsletter expects to be right 70 to 80 percent of the time. A bad call doesn't necessarily mean disaster, and a good call doesn't necessarily mean success (see the discussion of the Crash of '87 in Chapter 2). You will cause your own disaster over the next 10 years if you don't beat the CPI by at least a couple of percent a year. If inflation goes at 6.39 percent per year, you most certainly need to gain a minimum of 9 or 10 percent per year to keep your head above water (the extra few percent are tacked on to account for taxes in this one case). That is just what most small investors do when they invest in money or bond funds, there is nothing wrong with investing in this safe manner.

Those who dabble in stock NLFs want to beat the CPI by a bigger margin than a couple of percent. Some of these people have half their money in a money NLF and put the other half in some stock NLF. Because tying or losing to the CPI spells disaster, the CPI is one of two elemental gauges of how your investments are doing. The other gauge is the S & P 500 with dividends reinvested. People who stay 100 percent in money NLFs have no hope of beating this standard in the long haul. People who invest some or all of their money in stock NLFs want to beat the reinvested S & P 500 by at least a few percent per year.

For aggressive investors doing what a good TA newsletter tells them to do and paying very close attention to their NLF's performance (sometimes on a daily basis), the breaking of the 20-percent barrier is likely. With some luck, even 25 percent per year on a sustained basis can be reached. You need a stomach for this type of investing. You need the inclination to spend the time required to monitor things. But anyone with enough money can do it for kicks. If you have $30,000 invested in various NLFs outside an IRA, then there is nothing wrong with putting $1500 of that money into an aggressive growth fund. This is only 5 percent of your total investment money, so if you lose one-third of it, you can retreat to safer waters.

What you have just seen is an interpretation of the Real World table for 1978–1987. Realistic annual rates of return on investments ranged from 10 to 20 percent in the discussion. Most of you will have a lot of your money, if not all of it, in money or bond NLFs. There are good newsletters (see Appendix C), which deal with investing like this. Why should conservative investors bother with letters that talk about stock NLF investing?

If you are a conservative investor, you might want to increase your returns by a few percent a year without incurring much more risk. You are already beating inflation by 3 percent per year, so why not take some of your money, purchase a good TA newsletter, and beat the CPI by 6 to 7 percent per year? Suppose you take half your money and put it into a good balanced NLF. What the table says is that, without any switching, you can expect to achieve about 15 percent per year with that half and about 10 percent per year with the half you kept in a money or bond NLF. Ten years from now, this translates to $33,197 assuming you have $5,000 in a money NLF IRA and $5,000 in a balanced NLF IRA. Compare this with the $25,937 you would have in 10 years if you keep the whole $10,000 in a money NLF. The difference is $7,260.

Now into this stew, throw a good TA newsletter and a little switching. You still start with $5,000 in a money NLF and let it ride at 10 percent per year. You still invest the other $5,000 in a balanced NLF, but because of switching, you make 17 percent per year instead of 15 percent for the Buy/Hold strategy. After 10 years, you wind up with $37,003 in your IRA instead of $25,937, for a difference of $11,066. The switching with half your money in a good, safe balanced NLF gets you $3,806 more than buying and holding the balanced fund. Like I said before, you are the boss of your investment dollars. The more you crack the whip, the harder they work for you. And it doesn't have to be a Bret Maverick adventure either.

Finally, let's close this discussion of what to expect with some advice to bank CD devotees. There was a time, about 1979 to 1981, when banks were offering 5-year CDs at a guaranteed 15 percent per year. If you bought one of these (say $10,000 worth) in early 1981, you got locked in until early 1986. Your average rate of return for those 5 years was 15 percent per year. MMP averaged 16 percent for the early 1981 to early 1982 period. For this one year, MMP beat the banks by 1 percent. Should you have put your $10,000 into MMP for that year instead of a bank CD, you would have made out by much more than the 1 percent because after that year expired, you could have entered Vanguard Windsor.

Because of the super-liquidity you have in NLFs, you can switch some or all of your money when market conditions warrant such a move. Banks (insurance companies, stock brokers, and financial planners) are quite proficient in playing "gotcha," which means they drain your investment money of most of its liquidity. They cramp your style and you can't maneuver like the finely tuned investment machine that you have become after reading this book. So, in early 1982, you move from MMP to Windsor and hold on to Windsor until early 1986. Again let's assume an IRA investment so we don't have to mess up calculations with tax rates and the like. In those 5 years, the bank CD lost to the NLF switch by $7,904. The score was "Bank: 20114, NLF: 28018."

The great shoot-out you just took part in between NLFs and banks covered a 5-year period from early 1981 to early 1986. The Real World table covered January 1978 to December 1987. The fantasy you acted out at the beginning of this chapter went from January 1981 to February 1988. Time periods, players, and games changed in all three cases but one thing remained constant: The more you work on becoming a better NLF investor, the more you stand to gain. You can perform significantly better than the averages depicted in the Real World table by investing ½ hour per week of your time. It is not unrealistic to expect thousands or tens of thousands of dollars for this effort, as compared to passively investing in CDs, in money funds, or by allowing those alligators to shear you.

WHAT TO DO

My first piece of advice shouldn't surprise you one bit: Avoid stock brokers, banks, insurance salespeople, and financial planners. They all want a piece of your action, and you can only lose out. Handling your own investments via the NLF switch route is something you can do for yourself with the help of a good technician. Stock brokers charge commissions so you start out 4.5 to 8.5 percent in the hole. There is no way you can achieve the diversity an NLF gives you unless you have about $50,000 to invest in at least 15 stocks from different industry groups. If you pay full-service broker commissions (about $2000 to $4000 on $50,000 worth of transactions), the broker will be only too glad to help you pick those stocks. Where is your broker's long-term track record? Is it verified by an independent third party? (There is no EPA-type rating agency for brokerage houses.) You wind up paying more for something of very questionable value. NLFs are your best bet.

Bankers want to lock you into things which, it always seems to turn out, significantly reduce your yearly gain—even when compared to investing 100 percent in a money NLF. Bankers sell security, but do you need 16 tons of security in a bank CD or just 15.9 tons in MMP? Besides, if that $100,000 insurance policy on your deposits ever needs to be called upon, you will be waiting in line with tens of millions of other people for the Fed to give out the money as promised. Only 1 percent of those promises are backed up with actual cash or equivalents. You would do much better to stock up your pantry with tuna fish and beans. The Crash of '87 didn't bother money NLFs one bit. Spread your money around only a few of the hundreds of good money NLFs available and beat the bank rates by a couple percent per year to boot.

You probably don't need insurance people for insurance because you have enough already. If this isn't the case, forget about NLF investing for now and contact a good insurance agent. If you totally lack the discipline to sock some money away on a regular basis, then look into insurance annuity plans for your retirement. Notice that nothing has been said about investing in the stock market through an insurance company so far. If you want a good hunk of prime rib to cook for dinner guests, you don't go to a health food store. Don't invest with insurance companies.

I've saved financial planners for last because they come on as Jacks and Jills of all trades. They will offer to be your stockbroker, CD purchaser, insurance agent, tax planner and estate planner. They will even offer to buy your NLFs for you if: 1) you pay a $500 fee up front to let them plan all your finances; 2) you pay a 2-percent load to them for purchasing your NLFs; and 3) you don't touch the money in those funds (switch it, redeem it or anything else). So, for only $500, you can sign a contract with a financial planner and ignore all your personal finances. Two-thirds of us fill out a short form so we don't need tax planning. If you don't like to do your own taxes, go to a professional tax preparer and pay that person $50. You don't need estate planning unless you are a cattle baron or a Citizen Kane. Pay a lawyer $100 to make a valid will out for you. Now you can answer the question: "Why in the world would I ever want to use the services of a financial planner?"

So much for my favorite people to avoid.

Appendix E has an annotated bibliography which will help you get started reading about investing in general and NLFs in particular. Read newspapers, magazines, and books. Listen to radio and watch T.V. talk shows. Become informed about investing and make it a hobby. Explain things to friends and, when you argue with them about the best strategy to follow, stand your ground. In arguments like these, no one can prove once and for all that he or she is right, but standing one's ground shows confidence. Confidence is important to good investing. The more knowledge you gain, the more you will get out of your investment experience. An important and enjoyable source of information is your newsletter.

There are two groups of people you should become quite intimate with: a good TA newsletter pro and some good NLF groups. This returns you to the Three-Step Process: 1) pick a good newsletter; 2) pick good NLFs; 3) track your NLFs. The first two steps are simple, and once done, are pretty much set in stone. Step Three requires a few minutes of your time each week; it is fun, easy, and keeps you involved and aware of what is going on. You are fighting a war for your financial security. The newsletter is your commanding general, the NLFs are your troops. You furnish the ammunition (cash). As commander in chief; if you ignore what is happening, you become decadent. Remember what happened to the Roman Empire!

WHAT NOT TO DO

Don't get scared or overly enthusiastic by what you see on T.V., read in newspapers or magazines, or overhear at work. It is good to pay some attention to these sources because it shows you are interested and you can gain some knowledge about the stock market. But when it comes to executing your plan, the only source you listen to is your newsletter. The next couple of paragraphs give an example of what not to listen to.

There was an article in the business section of a local newspaper that slammed mutual funds by mentioning tax consequences of investing in them. The article implied that copious, complicated records have to be maintained, and that mutual fund investors were singled out by the IRS in 1987 to have accounting nightmares. A few gory specifics were given and would have scared the uninitiated. If the words "mutual funds" were replaced by the words "individual stocks" in that article, the nightmare would have been magnified by 15 times, assuming a diversified portfolio of 15 stocks. Fifteen times the horror and you pay only $2000 to $4000 more for it. What a bargain!

If you do a lot of redeeming and have none of your dividends reinvested, you will create a lot of entries on your tax form. This problem is easily solved by paying $50 to a professional tax preparer. When you invest in NLFs, you receive detailed, easily understood statements of every transaction. All you need do is shoebox these and keep them in some kind of order. If you deal in individual stocks instead of NLFs, you will need 15 times the number of shoe boxes. If you park your money in a bank, your accounting is much simpler, but you average 8 percent per year instead of 10 to 20 percent per year. The columnist sounded like he wanted to help out some stockbroker buddies by slamming mutual funds. The local paper and its business section are reputable, but that particular column was very misleading.

Don't change your newsletter unless something calamitous warrants it. Changing newsletters every year is like buying a different brand of lawn mower every year—an unnecessary expense. Also, you lose the consistency you would achieve if you follow the same letter over a period of years. No matter what game you might play, you improve your performance by improving your consistency.

For younger investors (these are the ones who are apt to put off investing because they are not yet running scared like the rest of us), don't wait to begin your investment experience. Start now. You will spend $15,500 on your first new car with wing flaps and pinstriping. Why not forget either the flaps or striping, pay only $15,000, and put the other $500 into an IRA in a good NLF. You will get a tax refund of $100 to $150 which you can use to pay speeding tickets.

Don't start off fancy. Get into one good stock or money NLF, depending on what your letter tells you. Once you've been at it for a while, you can branch out to muni bond funds, Ginnie Mae funds, sector funds, Pacific Basin funds, and the like. If someone tells you that Ginnie Mae funds are the best place to be and you are just starting your NLF trip, don't listen to them. Ginnie Mae funds may be a good parking place for some of your money down the pike, but start in the meat or potatoes stock or money NLFs before you partake of gourmet dishes. Even then, that is all that will happen—you will be in a muni bond NLF making no larger a gain (and possibly smaller) than you would have made in a plain old money NLF. Specialty funds like muni funds always have some gimmick attached to them. In the case of muni funds, it is the tax-free angle. I've seen people go into muni funds (and into the municipal bonds themselves), simply because they were completely free of federal and state taxes and wind up getting a smaller return than if they had invested in a taxable money NLF.

Don't get discouraged at the apparent slow pace of accumulation of your wealth. Trying to make a quick killing in the market is like going on a crash diet. It may work briefly, but shortly after that, you are back to where you started. Chipping away consistently over a long period of time is a guaranteed winner. The way to think about slow, unexciting gains and hence, to keep the faith, is given to you in the next few paragraphs.

Suppose you had $10,000 in an IRA NLF a couple of months ago, and that fund gained 2.5 percent during that time period. Ho-hum, only $250 was added on to your $10,000 retirement nest egg. This is definitely the wrong way to view that gain. Make three reasonable assumptions: 1) you will begin to cash in the IRA in 20 years; 2) inflation will run about 7 percent a year; 3) you will average 16 percent per year in this IRA investment.

Does $1,257 sound better to you than $250? That is what the $250 equals in 20 years with inflation at 7 percent per year and your IRA gaining 16 percent per year. This is how you should think of your investments growing. Look at the long-term picture. What you see as only a few dollars now can easily become hundreds or thousands of dollars down the road if you just stick with it. One note is that, when you see these calculations performed by others, the CPI is generally ignored because it inflates the $1257 to $4865. Since I am not grading my own test here, you get to see things as they should be seen. After all, can you still buy a new Cadillac El Dorado for $10,000?

Don't get discouraged if you aren't achieving your investment goals. Maybe they weren't realistic to begin with, or if they were realistic, the normal ups and downs of the stock market are temporarily doing you in. Like all long-range plans, your NLF investment plan needs to be flexible. Investment goals and risk levels will change. Economic conditions will change. Everything will change. So how can you expect to make up a plan now that will be a good guide for the next 10 years? You can't, and no one else can either. You plan so that you have some good direction. Otherwise you float about aimlessly, trying some of this and some of that. Without direction, you easily get lost and waste time when you should be accruing good, steady returns.

Don't wait to get started. There are good NLFs out there with no minimum initial investment or just a small initial investment. Even a 12-year-old who rakes leaves can scrape up $50 and have his or her parents invest it in an NLF. You spend hundreds of dollars on toys for your kids, why not invest $50 in an educational NLF for each of them? While you are doing that, start a Virgin Islands NLF for mom and dad. One reason people put off investing is because they feel they need a good reason. Getting in the habit of putting a few dollars into an NLF on a regular basis is one of the best reasons to invest in an NLF. Try it. It might catch on.

PORTFOLIOS AND SECTORS

You can, and probably will, make your own portfolio of NLFs. A natural reason this happens is because you have different investment objectives. You don't want to mix up rainy day money with Las Vegas money because you have different levels of risk for those two types of investments. Even when you have a lot of money in an NLF for one specific objective, it makes sense to diversify. For example, suppose you and your spouse are both working and have $20,000 in one balanced IRA NLF. No good! Diversify into the balanced funds of two or three good NLF groups. Put $10,000 in one group and $10,000 in the other group. For further diversification, you can switch $2,000 to $5,000 from each of the two balanced NLFs into their corresponding money NLFs.

There are NLFs which are "funds of funds." Vanguard Star is an example. It invests in Windsor, Windsor II, Explorer, Explorer II, Morgan, GNMA (a Ginnie Mae NLF), Investment Grade Portfolios and MMP. Some of these NLFs are closed to new investments by individuals, but you can get into them by going through Star. The idea behind NLFs like Star is to achieve a better return than you would get from an income NLF with about the same risk. There are professional advisors who are reptiles and will invest you in a portfolio of NLFs for a fee. This is just another sales gimmick, and you can do it yourself for nothing by investing in NLFS like Star. If you have $10,000 and want to diversify across a few different types of NLFs, then find out what your newsletter writer has to say first. If it isn't in the letter, then write your own letter to the publisher of the newsletter and ask for advice.

Another method of diversification is the *percent allocation* method. Some newsletters use this method instead of pure market timing, wherein you are put either 100 percent in a stock NLF or 100 percent in a money NLF at any given time. A "percent allocation" newsletter might tell you to have 60 percent in a stock NLF, 30 percent in a money NLF, and 10 percent in a gold NLF. A couple months down the road (remember to call the hotline every week or two), your letter might change to 80 percent in a stock NLF and 20 percent in a money NLF.

Another way to diversify is to use more than one newsletter. You have no doubt noticed on Sunday morning talk shows that experts frequently disagree.

How can you tell when one expert is right and one expert is wrong? You don't have to determine that. Believe both of them. Using two newsletters, allocate half your money to the advice of one and the other half to the advice of the other. There were two newsletters, both high in Hulbert's rankings, one that avoided the Crash and one that didn't. You don't have to know which one will be right the next time. Had you been diversified among those two letters before October 16, 1987, you would have lost 10 percent instead of 20 percent.

There are a few newsletters that give advice on sector fund investing. You need one of those letters if you are going heavily into sector NLFs. Sector funds are much more volatile than the average growth fund. This means they can go way up very rapidly, but they can also go way down just as rapidly. Sector fund investing is a good way to go if you are an aggressive-type investor. You absolutely have to track them very closely, as you would with any highly aggressive fund. Unless you have 10 spare hours per week, the inclination, a PC and the know-how, don't invest in sector NLFs unless you subscribe to a good sector fund letter.

The only time you should do your own sector fund investing is when you are using a gold or precious metals sector NLF as a hedge against inflation. If you have at least $30,000, it is fine to take 5 to 10 percent of it and keep it in a good gold NLF. You might put $3,000 in the gold fund on Friday, a calamity could ensue during the weekend, your gold fund would double to $6,000, while the $27,000 you left in the stock NLF would fall to $24,000. The idea is that you have protected your overall investment by betting a little bit of your money on an unlikely outcome. For the same reason, you might want to put 5 to 10 percent of your money in a long-term bond NLF to guard against deflation.

GOOD LUCK!

You should know by now that good investing is not 100 percent luck. It is 95 percent sticking to a good investment plan and 5 percent luck. Hopefully, this book gave you the knowledge to formulate your own investment plan, to gather the forces you need to improve your investment performance, and to make sure that the plan is going as scheduled. Don't worry about the 5 percent of investing that is pure luck. Like anything else in life, you mostly make your own luck and that isn't being lucky at all—it's being wise.

Appendix A
Glossary

aggressive growth fund—(Chapter 1). Growth for growth's sake. The riskiest type of NLF. Almost 100 percent of gain comes from an increase in NAV.

balanced fund—(Chapter 1). Stable, middle-of-the-road fund. Halfway between ultraconservative and ultrarisky, but tending more to conservative. There will be some NAV type gain but there is a hefty amount of dividend and interest gain. Good protection in down markets.

buy/hold—(Chapter 2). The total lack of market timing. Buy into an NLF and never sell it—no matter how the stock market is faring. This can be a successful method for some of your money if you invest it in an index NLF.

certificate of deposit or **CD**—(Chapter 1). Certificates of deposit are what you usually buy from a bank. Maturities generally range from 3 months to 5 years and interest rates, in the long haul, will get beat by money fund rates.

coefficient of determination—(Chapter 10). The square of the correlation coefficient. This is a number between zero and one. If multiplied by 100 percent, it gives you an idea of how well a regression line replaces the scatter of points.

commercial paper—(Chapter 7). Short-term debt notes issued by private enterprises to accrue cash for expansion.

confirmation—(Chapter 6). Using two trends to mutually confirm buys and sells.

consumer price index or **CPI**—(Chapter 5). One of the two rates to beat with your stock and money market gains. The other rate is the gain from the S & P 500 with dividends reinvested.

correlation coefficient—(Chapter 10). A number between plus and minus one which says exactly how related two indices are to each other. The closer to plus or minus one, the stronger the relationship. The closer to zero, the worse the relationship.

dividends—(Chapter 1). Money taken out of profits by a company to keep shareholders happy. Blue-chip companies make a much bigger point of paying dividends than do smaller, more aggressive companies. Same goes for NLFs. This is one of three ways an NLF or an individual stock makes money for its shareholders.

Dow Jones Industrial Average or **DJIA**—(Chapter 2). The most popularly known stock index of all. Taken over 30 stocks which were originally in the industrial sector but now cover more sectors because some of the original stocks have been replaced.

Dow Jones Transportation Average or **DJTA**—(Chapter 9). An average of airline, railroad stocks, and the like.

Dow Jones Utility Average or **DJUA**—(Chapter 4). An average of utility stocks. Utilities are very good at predicting what long-term interest rates will be. If used in addition to the S & P 500, the DJUA gives a very good indication of what will be going on in the stock market.

Environmental Protection Agency or **EPA**—(Chapter 2). An agency of the federal government which regulates pollutants of all kinds and also regulates auto emissions. Sets industry standards for companies to meet. If standards aren't met, many times companies are penalized.

ex dividend—(Chapter 5). The day on which your NLF removes money from share value and puts it aside to pay dividends to you later on. Your fund's NAV will probably drop sharply on this day, but don't worry. You will get the money in new shares, a check, or a combination of both.

federal discount rate—(Chapter 7). The Godzilla of interest rates. When this rate goes up or down, the rest of the world (not necessarily immediately) reacts in a like fashion.

Federal Reserve System or **FRS**—(Chapter 7). Keeper of the monster FDR. Unleashes the FDR's fury or tames the FDR, depending on how its members feel inflation is going. The stock market has little to no effect on FRS decisions.

fixed-income fund—(Chapter 1). The least risky fund type around, except for money market funds. Many retired people keep some of their money in these funds, have the dividends automatically mailed to them, and use those distributions to finance their retirement.

growth—(Chapter 1). Usually refers to an increase in gain due to an increase in NAV. Sometimes referred to as "paper gain" or "paper loss."

growth fund—(Chapter 1). This is a broad category of NLFs which borders on balanced NLFs on the one hand and on aggressive NLFs on the other. Just because an NLF is called a growth fund doesn't mean it is risky NLF.

growth income—(Chapter 1). That portion of gain which is totally due to an increase (or a decrease) in the NAV of an NLF.

income fund—(Chapter 1). Between a fixed income and a balanced fund in terms of risk and return. Is used by some people for what the name implies: income. One of the safest type funds around.

index NLF—(Chapter 3). Instead of buying into several dozen stocks, index NLFs buy into several hundred. This is done by purchasing, for example, all the stocks in the S & P 500 index. This is how index NLFs got their name. These NLFs are good investments for long-term investors because the overall stock market beats inflation by a factor of three-to-one.

Individual Retirement Account or **IRA**—(Chapter 1). Individual Retirement Account. Whether the money you invest gives you a tax refund or not, this is absolutely one of the best investments going. When you gain 15 percent per year in an IRA, you gain exactly that. In a taxable account, your 15 percent drops to 10 percent, after you pay taxes.

interest income—(Chapter 1). Income like you would gain in a CD or a savings account. The only type of income that money market NLFs have.

lead/lag—(Chapter 11). What robins and groundhogs do for spring and what projectors try to do successfully for the stock market. When one index, say MMP, leads another index, say the S & P 500, then whatever happens to MMP now has an important bearing on what will happen to the S & P 500 in the future.

money market fund—(Chapter 1). The safest of all NLFs. Just about any one of the hundreds available will beat bank rates in the long run and your money will be liquid to boot. Money and bond NLFs are by far the most popular way to invest in NLFs.

money market prime or **MMP**—(Chapter 3). One of the Vanguard money market NLFs. Used in numerous examples throughout this book.

moving average or **MAV** or **??-MAV**—(Chapter 5). An average of a series of numbers over a certain time period. For example, the 50-MAV of the DJUA for this week would be the average of the most recent 50-week values of the DJUA. Use in trend-following.

net asset value or **NAV**—(Chapter 1). Net asset value. This is the price tag per share for an NLF or a stock. Determines the growth component of gain.

New York Stock Exchange, NYSE—(Chapter 2). The best known of all stock exchanges. Also called the "big board."

no-load fund or **NLF**—(Chapter 1). Cooperative owning of many, many stocks and/or CD-like investments by thousands of individuals. Stocks and CDs bought and sold by managers of the NLF. No commissions charged (except for low-loads). Are the absolute best bet for small (less than $1 million) investors.

oscillator—(Chapter 9). A ratio of a current value to some past value. This ratio is calculated as one means of determining how an index is going compared to some historical value.

paper gain—(Chapter 1). An idiom for "NAV gain." This gain is only worthless (not guaranteed) until you cash it in. See also *growth income.*

percent allocation method—(see *timing*).

price-earnings ratio or **P-E value**—(Chapter 2). Divide the expected earnings of a stock into its current price. When P-E values approach 20, stocks are said to be "over valued." This happened just before the Crash of '87.

pure timing—(see *timing*).

regression line—(Chapter 10). The straight line that replaces a mess of points scattered all over the place.

resistance and support—(Chapter 6). Upper and lower bounds, respectively, put on a stock index. When an index goes through its resistance, some technicians say happy times are in store. When the index falls through its support, it is time to head for a money NLF.

scatterplot—(Chapter 10). A graph where more than one point can appear over a specific X-axis value.

sector NLF—(Chapter 1). An NLF which invests in only one sector of the stock market (precious metals, health, utilities, paper products, technology, and so on).

Securities and Exchange Commission or **SEC**—(Chapter 1). Securities and Exchange Commission is the watchdog for investors. Makes sure that fund managers do a reputable job. An arm of the federal government that actually works!

special purpose NLF—(Chapter 1). An NLF which uses leverage (borrows money to invest), invests using options (pays for insurance in case it is wrong) and the like. Look at these types of funds closely since they can be very speculative.

Standard and Poor's 500 Index or **S & P 500**—(Chapter 3). One of the best stock indices to follow because it represents the average of 500 stocks and so gives a really good indication of how the whole market is going.

strategy or **plan**—(Chapter 6). This is one thing you need to be a success whether it is making money in the market or not getting soaked in a thunderstorm. To plan you must have predictions of what the future holds in store.

technical analysis or **TA**—(Introduction). Using math to analyze numbers related to stock market behavior to determine when to be in or out of stock NLFs.

Technique for Order Preference by Similarity to Ideal Solution or **TOPSIS**—(Chapter 2). Math method used to rank alternatives like newsletters and NLF groups.

three-step process—(Introduction). Choose a good newsletter, choose a good NLF, and track that NLF. Follow this process, and you should get more out of your investing than you now do.

timing or **switching**—(Chapter 6). The attempt to be in a stock NLF when the market is due to rise and to be in a money NLF when the market is due to fall. Pure timing is when a letter writer has you either 100 percent in a stock NLF or 100 percent in a money NLF at any given time. The percent allocation method of timing splits your percentages between stock and money NLFs at any given time (that is, you are not necessarily 100 percent in either type of NLF).

trend—(Chapter 6). A combination of an index and one of its MAVs used to determine whether the market is in an uptrend or a downtrend.

uptrend or **downtrend**—(Chapter 6). Trend-following terminology used to describe the direction the stock market will be taking. Trend-followers who don't like projectors will emphatically state that "the market is currently in an uptrend (or a downtrend) but this has no bearing on what the market will be doing in the future." The best question to ask these people is "If I blink, will the trend change direction?"

week or **WK**—(Chapter 4). Most of the graphs in this book are over time periods whose unit is in terms of weeks, hence the acronym "WK."

whipsaw—(Chapter 6). The uncomfortable feeling you experience on a roller coaster or when you switch between a money and stock NLF too frequently. When whipsawed, it seems like you are always in the wrong kind of NLF. You are in a stock NLF when the market is caving in and in a money NLF when the market is soaring.

Appendix B

NLF Groups

- The raw data for this appendix come from the *1988 Handbook for No-Load Fund Investors*, but my own calculations led to the numbers you see in the tables. Write to Sheldon Jacobs of the *No-Load Fund Investor* for details of how to get this valuable yearly publication (see Appendix C for address).
- Information on funds has a cutoff date of December 31, 1987. You must call the NLF groups to get the most recent prospectus on an individual NLF. This is especially important because some NLFs have "N/A" (meaning "Not Available") in the Gain column. By the time you read this book, many of the NLFs will have 1986–1988 gains, and so the N/A would disappear from the Gain column.
- For NLF TYPE, these are the meanings of codes in column 2 below:

> A is Aggressive
> G is Growth
> B is Balanced
> I is Income
> M is Money Market

There is no listing for fixed-income funds because there are so many of them. If you are interested in fixed-income funds, call the fund group for information.

- Don't go for a group because its money market fund has a high gain. Some of the money funds deal in federal government bills and notes and so have a lower gain. These funds are safer than the other money funds but all the money funds listed here are very safe.

• Don't go for a group because it is higher in the list. Scudder is tied for tenth out of twelve places but it has special NLFs (not listed here) which are advertised through the American Association of Retired Persons. These special NLFs have much lower risk than the rest of Scudder's NLFs.

• Some NLFs might be closed to new accounts. A few NLFs don't allow switching between other NLFs in a group. You need to check these two items out also. You don't necessarily have to do any switching, so if you are interested in such funds, call the group and ask for the information.

• After the name, address and phones of the groups are given and before the listing of individual NLFs in that group, there is some other information of use. The average gain for 1985–87 for the group as a whole is given. This average can only be taken over listed NLFs with track records for these three years. Average risk and expense ratios for each group is also given.

DREYFUS

666 Old Country Road
Garden City, NY 11530
(718) 895-1206
(516) 794-5200
(800) 645-6561

• 1985–87 Gain = 12.9%, Risk = 0.77, Expense Ratio = 0.97
• Unlimited switching permitted.
• No telephone redemptions.
• Minimum $2500, subsequent $100 non-IRA.
• Minimum $750, subsequent $0 IRA.

Name	Type	1985–87 Gain
New Leaders	A	N/A
Growth Opportunity	G	17.2
Third Century	G	11.6
Convertible Securities	I	16.0
Liquid Assets	M	6.9

FIDELITY

82 Devonshire Street
Boston, MA 02109
(617) 523-1919
(800) 544-6666

- 1985–87 Gain = 17.0%, Risk = 1.00, Expense Ratio = 0.78
- Reserves right to limit switches to four.
- Some telephone redemptions.
- Minimum $1000, subsequent $250 non-IRA.
- Minimum $500, subsequent $250 IRA.

Name	Type	1985–87 Gain
Freedom	A	17.0
Trend	G	11.6
Contrafund	A	12.1
Value	A	8.6
Puritan	I	15.0
Fidelity Fund	B	15.1
Convertible Securities	I	N/A
Cash Reserves	M	6.9

FINANCIAL PROGRAMS

6312 S. Fiddler's Green Circle
Englewood, CO 80111
(303) 779-1233
(800) 525-8085

- 1985–87 Gain = 11.7%, Risk = 1.06, Expense Ratio = 0.81
- Four switches permitted per year.
- No phone redemptions.
- Minimum $250, subsequent $50 non-IRA.
- Minimum $250, subsequent $50 IRA.

Name	Type	1985–87 Gain
Dynamics	A	12.5
Industrial	G	11.5
Industrial Income	I	16.2
Daily Income Shares	M	6.7

FOUNDERS

3033 East First Avenue, Suite 810
Denver, CO 80206
(303) 394-4404
(800) 525-2440
(800) 874-6301

- 1985–87 Gain = 12.8%, Risk = 0.91, Expense Ratio = 1.16
- Unlimited switches permitted.
- No phone redemptions.
- Minimum $1000, subsequent $100 non-IRA.
- Minimum $500, subsequent $100 IRA.

Name	Type	1985–87 Gain
Frontier	A	N/A
Special	A	12.9
Growth	G	19.3
Blue Chip	B	16.4
Equity Income	I	9.6
Money Market	M	6.4

NEUBERGER & BERMAN

342 Madison Avenue
New York, NY 10173
(212) 850-8300
(800) 367-0770

- 1985–87 Gain = 12.8%, Risk = 0.95, Expense Ratio = 0.84
- Switches are "monitored."
- No phone redemptions.
- Minimum $1000, subsequent $100 non-IRA.
- Minimum $250, subsequent $50 IRA.

Name	Type	1985–87 Gain
Manhattan	G	17.2
Partners	G	16.7
Guardian Mutual	B	11.5
Government Money	M	6.1

T. ROWE PRICE

100 E. Pratt Street
Baltimore, MD 21202
(301) 547-2308
(800) 638-5660

- 1985–87 Gain = 11.2%, Risk = 1.02, Expense Ratio = 0.95
- Three switches per year.
- Telephone redemptions.

- Minimum $1000, subsequent $100 non-IRA.
- Minimum $500, subsequent $50 IRA.

Name	Type	1985–87 Gain
New Horizons	A	4.7
Capital Appreciation	A	N/A
New Era	G	18.9
New America	G	N/A
Growth Stock	G	19.4
Growth & Income	B	7.2
Equity Income	I	N/A
Prime Reserve	M	6.8

SAFECO

SAFECO Plaza
Seattle, WA 98185
(206) 545-5530
(800) 426-6730
(800) 562-6810 (WA)

- 1985–87 Gain = 10.7%, Risk = 0.94, Expense Ratio = 0.86
- Unlimited switching.
- Telephone redemptions.
- Minimum $1000, subsequent $100 non-IRA.
- Minimum $250, subsequent $100 IRA.

Name	Type	1985–87 Gain
Growth	G	9.5
Equity	B	12.5
Income	I	14.2
Money Market	M	6.7

SCUDDER

160 Federal Street
Boston, MA 02110
(617) 439-4640
(800) 225-2470
(800) 225-5163

- 1985–87 Gain = 12.3%, Risk = 1.07, Expense Ratio = 1.05
- Four switches per year.
- Telephone redemptions.
- Minimum $1000, subsequent $0 non-IRA.
- Minimum $240, subsequent $0 IRA.

Name	Type	1985–87 Gain
Development	A	8.3
Capital Growth	A	16.5
Global	G	N/A
Growth & Income	B	17.8
Equity Income	I	N/A
Cash Investment Trust	M	6.8

STEIN ROE & FARNHAM

P.O. Box 1143
Chicago, IL 60690
(312) 368-7826
(800) 338-2550

- 1985–87 Gain = 13.1%, Risk = 1.08, Expense Ratio = 0.95
- Four switches per year.
- No phone redemptions.
- Minimum $1000, subsequent $100 non-IRA.
- Minimum $500, subsequent $50 IRA.

Name	Type	1985–87 Gain
Special	A	15.3
Discovery	A	10.7
Universe	A	12.8
Capital Opportunities	A	16.6
Stock	A	15.8
Prime Equities	G	N/A
Growth & Income	B	N/A
Total Return	I	13.8
Cash Reserves	M	6.7

TWENTIETH-CENTURY

605 W. 47th Street
P.O. Box 419200
Kansas City, MO 64141
(816) 531-5575
(800) 345-2021

- 1985–87 Gain = 18.2%, Risk = 1.36, Expense Ratio = 1.00
- Eleven switches per year.
- Telephone redemptions.
- Minimum $0, subsequent $0 non-IRA.
- Minimum $0, subsequent $0 IRA.

Name	Type	1985–87 Gain
Vista	A	17.9
Ultra	A	14.1
Heritage	G	N/A
Growth	A	21.6
Select	G	19.4
Cash Reserves	M	N/A

VALUE LINE

711 Third Avenue
New York, NY 10017
(212) 687-3965
(800) 223-0818

- 1985–87 Gain = 11.8%, Risk = 1.06, Expense Ratio = 0.86
- Eight switches per year.
- No phone redemptions.
- Minimum $1000, subsequent $100 non-IRA.
- Minimum $1000, subsequent $100 IRA.

Name	Type	1985–87 Gain
Leveraged Growth	A	17.1
Special Situations	A	4.9
Value Line Fund	A	18.5
Income	I	12.1
Convertible	I	N/A
Value Line Cash	M	7.0

VANGUARD

P.O. Box 2600
Valley Forge, PA 19482
(215) 648-6000
(800) 662-2739

- 1985–87 Gain = 11.5%, Risk = 0.82, Expense Ratio = 0.52
- Two switches per year.
- Phone redemptions.
- Minimum $1500, subsequent $100 non-IRA.
- Minimum $500, subsequent $100 IRA.

Name	Type	1985–87 Gain
Naess & Thomas	A	4.6
Explorer II	A	N/A
Explorer	A	1.7
Morgan WL	A	13.5
World US	G	11.7
Extended Market Portfolio	G	N/A
Quantitative	B	N/A
Index 500 Portfolio	B	17.4
Windsor II	B	N/A
Windsor	B	15.9
Star	B	N/A
Convertible Securities	I	N/A
High Yield Stock	I	14.6
Wellington	I	15.8
Wellesley	I	13.9
Money Market Prime	M	6.8

For information on funds in general, contact:

Investment Company Institute
1600 M St. NW
Washington, D.C. 20036

Appendix C
Newsletters

Fund Exchange
1200 Westlake Ave N.
Suite 507
Seattle, WA 98109-3530
ph: (206) 285-8877

written by Paul Merriman
$99/yr; has hotline

Growth Fund Guide
Growth Fund Research Building
P.O. Box 6600
Rapid City, SD 57709
ph: (605) 341-1971
    (800) 621-8322 (orders only)

written by Walter Rouleau
$85/yr; has hotline

Hulbert Financial Digest
316 Commerce St.
Alexandria, VA 22314
ph: (703) 683-5905
    (800) 443-0100; Ext. 459

written by Mark Hulbert
(For ordering information and a special
discount offer, see back page of this book.)

Investech Mutual Fund Advisor
2472 Birch Glen
Whitefish, MT 59937
ph: (406) 862-7777

written by James Stack
$150/yr; has hotline

Kinsman's Low-Risk Growth Letter
899 Northgate Drive, Third Floor
San Rafael, CA 94903
ph: (415) 479-3200

written by Robert Kinsman
$175/yr; has hotline

Lynn Elgert Report
P.O. Box 1283
Grand Island, NE 68802
ph: (308) 381-2121

written by Lynn Elgert
$190/yr; has hotline

Margo's Market Monitor
P.O. Box 642
Lexington, MA 02173
ph: (617) 861-0302

written by Margo Ballantine
$125/yr; no hotline

Mutual Fund Forecaster
3471 North Federal Highway
Ft. Lauderdale, FL 33306
ph: (800) 327-6720

written by Norman Fosback
and Glen Parker
$49/yr; has hotline

Mutual Fund Investing
7811 Montrose Road
Potomac, MD 20854
ph: (301) 340-2100

written by Jay Schabacker
$99/yr; has hotline

The Mutual Fund Strategist
P.O. Box 446
Burlington, VT 05402
ph: (802) 658-3513

written by Charles Hooper
$149/yr; has hotline

No-Load Fund-X
235 Montgomery Street
San Francisco, CA 94104
ph: (415) 986-7979

written by Burton Berry
$95/yr; no hotline

No-Load Fund Investor
P.O. Box 283
Hastings-on-Hudson, NY 10706
ph: (914) 693-7420

written by Sheldon Jacobs
$82/yr; no hotline

Peter Dag Investment Letter
65 Lakefront Drive
Akron, OH 44319
ph: (216) 644-2782

written by Peter Dag
$250/yr; no hotline

Professional Tape Reader
P.O. Box 2407
Hollywood, FL 33022
ph: not available

written by Stan Weinstein
$250/yr; has hotline

Stockmarket Cycles
2260 Cahuenga Blvd.
Suite 305
Los Angeles, CA 90068
ph: (213) 465-5543

written by Peter Eliades
$198/yr; has hotline

Switch Fund Advisory
1385 Piccard Drive
Rockville, MD 20850
ph: (301) 840-0301

written by Jay Schabacker
$140/yr; has hotline

Telephone-Switch Newsletter
P.O. Box 2538
Huntington Beach, CA 92647
ph: (714) 898-2588

written by Richard Fabian
$117/yr; has hotline

Weber's Fund Advisor
P.O. Box 92
Bellerose, NY 11426
ph: not available

written by Ken Weber
$135/yr; has hotline

Worry-Free Investing
7910 Woodmont Avenue
Suite 1200
Bethesda, MD 20814
ph: (301) 951-3800

written by Bert Dohmen Ramirez
$99/yr; no hotline

Note: For a sample of up to 20 newsletters for around $20, write to:

Select Information Exchange
2315 Broadway
New York, NY 10024

Ask them for their free 56-pp guide before you send money. Include your home and business phone numbers should they have questions.

Appendix D

Tables

- WK #s for the MMP, S&P 500 and DJUA tables correspond to WK #s and Dates in the last table in this appendix.
- Use your own WK #s if you wish. Use these tables as guides for constructing your own tables from the templates at the end of Chapter 5.

Vanguard MMP and 26-MAV
(Aug 7, 1987 to Jul 29, 1988)

WK	MMP	Sum	MAV	WK	MMP	Sum	MAV
345	6.6	158.9	6.1	371	6.8	182.1	7.0
346	6.6	159.9	6.2	372	6.8	182.3	7.0
347	6.6	160.9	6.2	373	6.7	182.4	7.0
348	6.6	161.9	6.2	374	6.7	182.5	7.0
349	6.5	162.8	6.3	375	6.6	182.6	7.0
350	6.6	163.7	6.3	376	6.6	182.6	7.0
351	6.6	164.6	6.3	377	6.5	182.5	7.0
352	6.7	165.6	6.4	378	6.5	182.3	7.0
353	6.8	166.6	6.4	379	6.5	182.0	7.0
354	6.9	167.7	6.5	380	6.5	181.6	7.0
355	7.0	168.8	6.5	381	6.5	181.1	7.0
356	7.1	170.0	6.5	382	6.5	180.5	6.9
357	7.3	171.3	6.6	383	6.5	179.7	6.9
358	7.3	172.5	6.6	384	6.5	178.9	6.9
359	7.3	173.7	6.7	385	6.5	178.1	6.8
360	7.3	174.8	6.7	386	6.6	177.4	6.8
361	7.3	175.8	6.8	387	6.7	176.8	6.8
362	7.3	176.8	6.8	388	6.7	176.2	6.8
363	7.2	177.6	6.8	389	6.8	175.8	6.8
364	7.2	178.4	6.9	390	6.9	175.5	6.7
365	7.3	179.1	6.9	391	7.0	175.2	6.7
366	7.3	179.8	6.9	392	6.9	174.8	6.7
367	7.3	180.5	6.9	393	7.1	174.6	6.7
368	7.2	181.1	7.0	394	7.1	174.5	6.7
369	7.1	181.6	7.0	395	7.2	174.6	6.7
370	6.9	181.9	7.0	396	7.3	175.0	6.7

S & P 500 and 45-MAV
(Aug 7, 1987 to Jul 29, 1988)

WK	S & P 500	Sum	MAV		WK	S & P 500	Sum	MAV
345	323.00	12481.84	277.37		371	250.96	12819.49	284.88
346	333.99	12582.12	279.60		372	257.63	12776.71	283.93
347	335.90	12682.54	281.83		373	261.61	12745.83	283.24
348	327.04	12770.74	283.79		374	262.46	12721.38	282.70
349	316.70	12849.18	285.54		375	267.30	12707.16	282.38
350	321.98	12927.18	287.27		376	264.94	12684.07	281.87
351	314.86	12996.27	288.81		377	271.12	12661.82	281.37
352	320.16	13071.93	290.49		378	258.51	12632.90	280.73
353	328.07	13154.14	292.31		379	258.89	12609.63	280.21
354	311.07	13215.99	293.69		380	269.43	12588.96	279.75
355	282.70	13247.52	294.39		381	259.77	12555.28	279.01
356	248.22	13248.39	294.41		382	260.14	12513.79	278.08
357	251.79	13250.45	294.45		383	261.33	12468.15	277.07
358	250.41	13253.94	294.53		384	257.48	12418.48	275.97
359	245.64	13253.13	294.51		385	256.78	12369.63	274.88
360	242.00	13236.40	294.14		386	253.02	12314.28	273.65
361	240.34	13210.46	293.57		387	253.42	12253.11	272.29
362	223.92	13164.28	292.54		388	266.45	12210.28	271.34
363	235.32	13125.52	291.68		389	271.26	12162.88	270.29
364	249.16	13094.64	290.99		390	270.68	12110.56	269.12
365	252.02	13066.96	290.38		391	273.78	12050.35	267.79
366	247.08	13028.56	289.52		392	271.78	11986.23	266.36
367	243.40	12987.76	288.62		393	270.02	11929.21	265.09
368	252.05	12949.15	287.76		394	272.05	11884.56	264.10
369	246.50	12905.76	286.79		395	263.50	11826.08	262.80
370	257.07	12864.66	285.88		396	272.02	11783.24	261.85

DJUA and 50-MAV
(Aug 7, 1987 to Jul 29, 1988)

WK	DJUA	Sum	MAV	WK	DJUA	Sum	MAV
345	204.54	10453.52	209.07	371	186.28	9849.78	197.00
346	213.79	10448.16	208.96	372	184.09	9814.90	196.30
347	210.59	10445.04	208.90	373	184.57	9780.39	195.61
348	205.01	10451.27	209.03	374	182.61	9746.46	194.93
349	201.52	10451.70	209.03	375	182.37	9708.71	194.17
350	199.92	10449.87	209.00	376	177.34	9668.97	193.38
351	194.17	10444.42	208.89	377	180.71	9636.36	192.73
352	195.23	10441.47	208.83	378	173.07	9605.10	192.10
353	200.75	10441.16	208.82	379	171.47	9572.45	191.45
354	196.06	10434.95	208.70	380	176.56	9549.68	190.99
355	190.14	10415.68	208.31	381	169.16	9516.74	190.33
356	183.56	10389.43	207.79	382	169.87	9481.12	189.62
357	182.55	10361.82	207.24	383	170.64	9453.06	189.06
358	188.06	10338.40	206.77	384	169.04	9427.09	188.54
359	181.96	10307.27	206.15	385	168.39	9398.62	187.97
360	180.18	10275.51	205.51	386	168.74	9368.72	187.37
361	180.18	10246.05	204.92	387	170.87	9335.82	186.72
362	173.19	10207.18	204.14	388	178.34	9308.61	186.17
363	175.73	10173.44	203.47	389	179.11	9280.50	185.61
364	178.05	10141.05	202.82	390	180.60	9255.20	185.10
365	175.79	10097.86	201.96	391	181.66	9230.50	184.61
366	175.08	10050.12	201.00	392	180.42	9205.95	184.12
367	181.72	10006.48	200.13	393	178.52	9184.56	183.69
368	178.40	9960.16	199.20	394	179.65	9162.51	183.25
369	182.25	9916.25	198.33	395	175.50	9133.47	182.67
370	190.02	9885.52	197.71	396	182.85	9102.53	182.05

WKs Used in Book
(Week 1 is January 2, 1981 / Week 396 is July 29, 1988)

WK	MO	Day	Year	WK	MO	Day	Year	WK	MO	Day	Year
5	Jan	30	1981	175	May	4		345	Aug	7	
10	Mar	6		180	Jun	8		350	Sep	11	
15	Apr	10		185	Jul	13		355	Oct	16	
20	May	15		190	Aug	17		360	Nov	20	
25	Jun	19		195	Sep	21		365	Dec	25	1988
30	Jul	24		200	Oct	26		370	Jan	29	
35	Aug	28		205	Nov	30	1985	375	Mar	4	
40	Oct	2		210	Jan	4		380	Apr	8	
45	Nov	6		215	Feb	8		385	May	13	
50	Dec	11		220	Mar	15		390	Jun	17	
55	Jan	15	1982	225	Apr	19		395	Jul	22	
60	Feb	19		230	May	24		400	Aug	26	
65	Mar	26		235	Jun	28		405	Sep	30	
70	Apr	30		240	Aug	2		410	Nov	4	
75	Jun	4		245	Sep	6		415	Dec	9	
80	Jul	9		250	Oct	11		420	Jan	13	1989
85	Aug	13		255	Nov	15		425	Feb	17	
90	Sep	17		260	Dec	20	1986	430	Mar	24	
95	Oct	22		265	Jan	24		435	Apr	28	
100	Nov	26		270	Feb	28		440	Jun	2	
105	Dec	31		275	Apr	4		445	Jul	7	
110	Feb	4	1983	280	May	9		450	Aug	11	
115	Mar	11		285	Jun	13		455	Sep	15	
120	Apr	15		290	Jul	18		460	Oct	20	
125	May	20		295	Aug	22		465	Nov	24	
130	Jun	24		300	Sep	26		470	Dec	29	
135	Jul	29		305	Oct	31	1987	475	Feb	2	1990
140	Sep	2		310	Dec	5		480	Mar	9	
145	Oct	7		315	Jan	9		485	Apr	13	
150	Nov	11		320	Feb	13		490	May	18	
155	Dec	16	1984	325	Mar	20		495	Jun	22	
160	Jan	20		330	Apr	24		500	Jul	27	
165	Feb	24		335	May	29					
170	Mar	30		340	Jul	3					

Appendix E

Bibliography

American Association of Individual Investors. Very good magazine with a lot of NLF and TA discussions. Lots of discussion on fundamentals too. $48/yr for main publication. $24/yr for PC publication.

> AAII
> 612 North Michigan Avenue
> Chicago, IL 60611

American Association of Microcomputer Investors. For PC buffs only.

> AAMI
> P.O. Box 1384
> Princeton, NJ 08542

Barron's. If data were gold, this would be the richest vein around. No better way to keep abreast of the market in general. Has a very good, extensive quarterly review of mutual funds.

> Barron's
> 200 Burnett Road
> Chicopee, MA 01020

The Dow Jones-Irwin Guide to Investment Software by Robert Schwabach. Dow Jones-Irwin. 1986. The best book on PC investment software I have seen. If you have a PC, buy it!

The Dow Jones-Irwin Guide to Mutual Funds by Donald D. Rugg and Norman B. Hale. Dow Jones-Irwin. 1983. Very good introductory book for NLF investors. Authors expound Dow Theory.

How to Forecast Interest Rates by Martin J. Pring. McGraw-Hill. 1981. Martin Pring gives a very good discussion of fundamentals.

Investment Analysis with Your Microcomputer by Leslie E. Sparks. TAB Books. 1983. An interesting book for those who can use a PC. If you have such a machine, it is worth reading. Gives good ideas on how you can use your PC without buying expensive, limited investment software. Has BASIC program listings.

Market Timing with No-Load Mutual Funds by Paul A. Merriman. Henry Holt & Co. 1987. Mr. Merriman is a trend-follower.

Microcomputer Investors Association. For PC buffs only.

Microcomputer Investors Association
902 Anderson Drive
Fredricksburg, VA 22405

The New Mutual Fund Investment Advisor by Richard C. Dorf. Probus. 1986. Springboarded Mr. Dorf to writing a newsletter.

No-Load Mutual Fund Guide by William E. Donoghue. Harper & Row. 1983. Very popular NLF author. Has a newsletter. This book will allay any fears you might have about investing in NLFs. It is a well-done pep talk and is easy to read.

Secrets of the Temple by William Greider. Simon & Schuster, 1987. This is highly recommended if you want the low-down on the Federal Reserve Board. Written by a famous (and reputable) columnist. Will open your eyes to some surprising tidbits from the world of ultra-high finance. Don't read it if you have trouble sleeping at night.

Smart Investing Using Your Personal Computer by Michael Shapiro. MacMillan. 1985. Extremely good analysis of software available for PCs. Also has good information on databases to be tapped. Author is strictly IBM-PC oriented but this is his only fault.

Stock Market Logic by Norman Fosback. Kingsport Press, TN. 1985. This is the single best book I've seen on TA. If you don't have it and are interested in TA, get it. (See Appendix C for address.)

Technical Analysis Explained by Martin J. Pring. McGraw-Hill. 1985. The Bible for chartists ("Prussian helmets," "shoulders," "necklaces," and the like). This book has little or no math-based TA, but it is quite popular. Very good discussion of fundamentals.

The Wall Street Gurus by Peter Brimelow. Random House, 1986. A very entertaining book about newsletter writers. This is an absolute must if you would enjoy a glimpse at the personalities (some of them quite colorful) who predict the stock market. I recommend it. Used to come free with a subscription to the *Hulbert Financial Digest*.

Winning on Wall Street by Dr. Martin Zweig. Warner Books. 1986. Very good book explaining Dr. Zweig's "Super Model." He is one of the best technicians and is among the all-time tops in Hulbert's rankings but gives advice only for individual stocks, options, and selling short.

Index

Index

The *Hulbert Financial Digest* (*HFD*) is the only source of objective performance comparisons of over 100 of the nation's leading investment advisory newsletters. In addition to tracking the actual performance of the 250 portfolios these newsletters recommend, the *HFD* measures advisors' track records in timing switches into and out of the stock, gold, and bond markets.

Besides these performance comparisons, each issue of the *HFD* reports on which stocks and mutual funds currently are most recommended by the newsletters in the *HFD*'s universe, as well as those that are most recommended for sale or selling short. Furthermore, the *HFD* measures sentiment in the stock, gold, and bond markets among all advisers followed by the *HFD* and also among those that have beaten the market over the past four years.

In addition to the monthly newsletter, the *HFD* produces an annual *Almanac* of all the performance data available for each newsletter, dating back as far as 1980 in some cases. This data is then grouped into a number of rankings, both on a total-return and risk-adjusted basis, as well as into detailed graphs plotting each newsletter's performance alongside the S & P 500.

The regular price of the *Digest* is $135/year (12 monthly issues). But readers of this book are entitled to an introductory discount of 50 percent, meaning that you can subscribe for just $67.50. To obtain the *Digest*, or to purchase a copy of the most recent edition of the *Almanac*, write them at 315 Commerce Street, Alexandria, VA 22314.